SCHAUM'S OUTLINE OF

THEORY AND PROBLEMS

OF

STRUCTURAL STEEL DESIGN
(Load and Resistance Factor Method)

•

ABRAHAM J. ROKACH, MSCE

Director of Building Design and Software
American Institute of Steel Construction, Inc.

SCHAUM'S OUTLINE SERIES
McGraw-Hill
New York   San Francisco   Washington, D.C.   Auckland   Bogotá
Caracas   Lisbon   London   Madrid   Mexico City   Milan
Montreal   New Delhi   San Juan   Singapore
Sydney   Tokyo   Toronto

ABRAHAM J. ROKACH is Director of Building Design and Software at the American Institute of Steel Construction, Inc. Previously, he had been a practicing structural engineer for twenty years. He holds a B.E. degree from the City University of New York and an M.S. from the Massachusetts Institute of Technology. He has lectured at the University of Illinois and elsewhere and is the author of *Guide to LRFD* and the *Reliability of Expert Systems for Computer-Aided Structural Design*. He is a Fellow of the American Society of Civil Engineers and Secretary of the AISC Committee on Specifications.

Schaum's Outline of Theory and Problems of
STRUCTURAL STEEL DESIGN (LRFD METHOD)

9 10 VFM VFM 05 04

ISBN 0-07-053563-9

Sponsoring Editor: John Aliano
Production Supervisor: Stacey Alexander
Editing Supervisors: Meg Tobin, Maureen Walker

Library of Congress Cataloging-in-Publication Data

Rokach, Abraham J.
  Schaum's outline of theory and problems of structural steel design (LRFD method)/Abraham J. Rokach.
    p. cm.—(Schaum's outline series)
  ISBN 0-07-053563-9
  1. Building, Iron and steel—Problems, exercises, etc. 2. Steel, Structural—Problems, exercises, etc. 3. Load resistance factor design—Problems, exercises, etc. I. Title. II. Title: Structural steel design (LRFD method)
TA684.R66 1991
624.1′821—dc20   89-13665
                                                       CIP

McGraw-Hill

A Division of The McGraw·Hill Companies

Preface

In 1986 a new method of structural steel design was introduced in the United States with the publication of the *Load and Resistance Factor Design Specification for Structural Steel Buildings*. Load and resistance factor design, or LRFD, has joined the old allowable stress design (ASD) method as a recognized means for the design of structural steel frameworks for buildings.

Although ASD has enjoyed a long history of successful usage and is familiar to engineers and architects, the author and most experts prefer LRFD because it is a truer representation of the actual behavior of structural steel and unlike ASD, it can provide equivalent margins of safety for all structures under all loading conditions (as explained in Chap. 1). For these reasons it is anticipated that LRFD will replace ASD as the standard method of structural steel design.

This work is the first Schaum's Outline on the subject of structural steel design. After a long and rewarding use of other titles in the Schaum's Series (first as an undergraduate and graduate engineering student, then through 20 years of professional practice, and as a university professor), the author is pleased to have been given the opportunity to write this book. Because of the newness of LRFD and the scarcity of instructional materials, this book was written for as wide an audience as possible, including students enrolled in undergraduate and graduate engineering and architectural curricula, and practicing engineers, architects, and structural steel detailers. The author believes that everyone in need of instruction and/or experience in LRFD can benefit from the Schaum's approach of learning by problem-solving. The only prerequisite for an understanding of this text is the same as for an undergraduate course in structural steel design: a basic knowledge of engineering mechanics.

The author wishes to thank Mr. John F. Carleo, Publisher; Mr. John A. Aliano, Executive Editor; Ms. Margaret A. Tobin, Editing Supervisor, of the Schaum Division at McGraw-Hill, and their staff for their valuable contributions to this work. Special thanks go to the author's wife, Pninah, for her patience and assistance with typing the manuscript. Too numerous to mention, but significant in developing his knowledge and enjoyment of the subject matter, are his mentors and professional and academic colleagues, especially the people at AISC.

ABRAHAM J. ROKACH

CONTENTS

Introduction

This book covers structural steel design for buildings using the *load and resistance factor design* (LRFD) method. The following authorities on the LRFD method are cited frequently in the text, usually in abbreviated form.

AISC: American Institute of Steel Construction, Inc., Chicago, Illinois.

AISC LRFD Specification: *Load and Resistance Factor Design Specification for Structural Steel Buildings*, published by AISC.

AISC LRFD Manual: *Load and Resistance Factor Design Manual of Steel Construction*, also published by AISC.

Equations in this text are numbered as follows. Equations taken from the AISC LRFD Specification are accompanied by their AISC numbers in parentheses, thus (   ); other equations are numbered in brackets, thus [   ].

Chapter 1

Structural Steel

NOTATION

E = modulus of elasticity of steel = 29,000 kips per square inch (ksi)

F_u = tensile strength, ksi

F_y = yield stress, yield point, or yield strength, ksi

DEFINITIONS

Structural steel, as defined by AISC (in the LRFD Specification and elsewhere), refers to the steel elements of a structural frame supporting the design loads. It includes steel beams, columns, beam-columns, hangers, and connections.

Beam—A structural member whose primary function is to carry loads transverse to its longitudinal axis. Beams are usually horizontal and support the floors in buildings. (See Fig. 1-1.)

Column—A structural member whose primary function is to carry loads in compression along its longitudinal axis. In building frames, the columns are generally the vertical members which support the beams. (See Fig. 1-1.)

Beam-column—A structural member whose function is to carry loads both transverse and parallel to its longitudinal axis. A building column subjected to horizontal forces (such as wind) is actually a beam-column.

Hanger—A structural member carrying loads in tension along its longitudinal axis.

Connection—The material used to join two or more structural members. Examples of connections are beam-to-beam and beam-to-column.

MECHANICAL PROPERTIES

The major advantage of steel is its high strength relative to the strengths of the other common structural materials: wood, masonry, and concrete. Unlike masonry and concrete, which are weak in tension, steel is strong in both tension and compression. Because of its high strength, structural steel is widely used in construction. The tallest and longest-span structures are predominantly steel.

Typical stress-strain curves for structural steel are shown in Fig. 1-2. They are based on the application of tensile forces to a test specimen. The ordinates (i.e., vertical axes) indicate *stress,* which is defined as load divided by cross-sectional area. Units for stress are kips (or kilopounds; i.e., 1000 lb) per square inch, commonly noted as ksi. The abscissas (i.e., horizontal axes) indicate *strain,* which is a measure of elongation under tension and is defined as the increase in length divided by the original length. Units for strain are inches per inch; strain is dimensionless.

The stress-strain curve in Fig. 1-2(a) is that of A36 steel, the most commonly used structural steel. Note the linear relationship between stress and strain in the "elastic range," that is, until the yield point is reached. The most important design properties of A36 steel [see Fig. 1-2(a)] are

F_y, the *yield point,* the stress at which the proportionality between stress and strain ceases. A36 steel has both an upper and a lower yield point. For design purposes, the yield point of A36 steel is taken as $F_y = 36$ ksi, the minimum lower yield point.

3

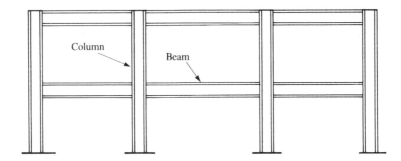

Fig. 1-1   Structural steel frame

F_u, the *tensile strength*, the maximum stress that the material is capable of sustaining. For A36 steel, $F_u = 58$ to 80 ksi.

E, the *modulus of elasticity*, which is the (constant) ratio of stress to strain in the elastic range. For A36 steel, $E = 29,000$ ksi.

The stress-strain curve in Fig. 1-2(*b*) is characteristic of several of the higher-strength steels. All structural steels have the same modulus of elasticity ($E = 29,000$ ksi). Unlike A36 steel, however, the higher-strength steels do not have a definite yield point. For these steels, F_y is the *yield strength* as determined by either of the two methods shown in Fig. 1-2(*b*): the 0.2 percent offset value or the 0.5 percent strain value.

In the AISC Specifications and Manuals, F_y is called the *yield stress* and, depending on the grade of steel, can be either the yield point or the yield strength, as defined above.

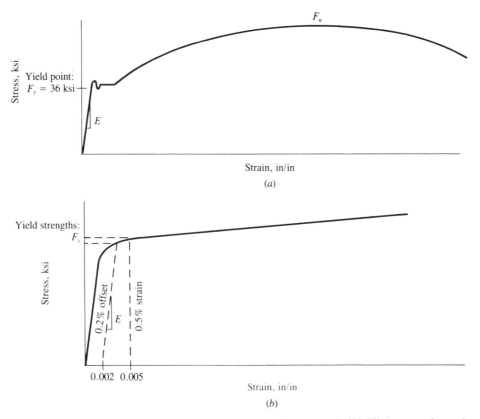

Fig. 1-2   Stress-strain curves for structural steels: (*a*) A36 steel; (*b*) High-strength steel

AVAILABILITY

Fourteen types of structural steel have been approved by the AISC LRFD Specification for use in buildings. In the LRFD Specification, Sec. A3.1, they are listed by their ASTM (American Society for Testing and Materials) specification numbers. The yield stress of these steels ranges from 36 ksi for the common A36 steel to 100 ksi for A514 steel. As can be seen from Table 1-1 (adapted from Part 1 of the AISC LRFD Manual), the yield stress of a given grade of steel is not a constant. It varies with plate thickness; very thick structural shapes and plates have reduced yield stresses.

A36 steel is by far the most commonly used type of structural steel for two reasons:

1. In many applications, the loads and stresses are moderate. Little, if any, saving would result from the use of higher-strength steels.

2. Even where stress considerations would favor the use of lighter (possibly more economical) high-strength members, other criteria may govern. Heavier members may be required to provide increased *stiffness* to prevent overall or local instability or excessive deflection. Because stiffness is a function of the geometric properties of the member and is not affected by strength, no advantage would be gained from using high-strength steel in such cases.

Table 1-1   Availability of Structural Steel

Steel Type	ASTM Designation	F_y, ksi	Plate Thickness, in
Carbon	A36	36	≤ 8
		32	> 8
	A529	42	$\leq \frac{1}{2}$
High-strength low-alloy	A441	50	$\leq 1\frac{1}{2}$
		46	$\frac{3}{4} - 1\frac{1}{2}$
		42	$1\frac{1}{2} - 4$
		40	$4 - 8$
	A572—Grade 65	65	$\leq 1\frac{1}{4}$
	—Grade 60	60	$\leq 1\frac{1}{4}$
	—Grade 50	50	≤ 4
	—Grade 42	42	≤ 6
Corrosion-resistant high-strength low-alloy	A242	50	$\leq \frac{3}{4}$
		46	$\frac{3}{4} - 1\frac{1}{2}$
		42	$1\frac{1}{2} - 4$
	A588	50	≤ 4
		46	$4 - 5$
		42	$5 - 8$
Quenched and tempered alloy	A514	100	$\leq 2\frac{1}{2}$
		90	$2\frac{1}{2} - 6$

STRUCTURAL SHAPES

A structural member can be a *rolled shape* or can be *built up* from two or more rolled shapes or plates, connected by welds or bolts. The more economical rolled shapes are utilized whenever possible. However, special conditions (such as the need for heavier members or particular cross-sectional geometries) may dictate the use of built-up members.

Available rolled shapes are catalogued in Part 1 of the AISC Manual. Those most commonly used in building construction include wide flange (or W), angle (or L), channel (or C), and tee (or WT). They are shown in Table 1-2 with examples of their nomenclature. Examples of common built-up shapes are given in Fig. 1-3.

Table 1-2   Rolled Structural Steel Shapes and Their Designations

Type of Shape	Cross Section	Example of Designation	Explanation of Designation
W (wide flange)		W14×90*	Nominal depth, 14 in; weight, 90 lb/ft
C (channel)		C12×30	Depth, 12 in; weight, 30 lb/ft
L (angle)		L4×3×$\frac{1}{4}$	Long leg, 4 in; short leg, 3 in; thickness, $\frac{1}{4}$ in
WT (structural tee cut from W shape)		WT7×45*	Nominal depth, 7 in, weight, 45 lb/ft

* Cutting a W14×90 in half longitudinally results in two WT7×45.

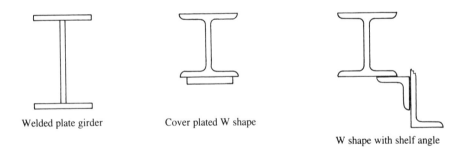

Welded plate girder   Cover plated W shape

W shape with shelf angle

Fig. 1-3   Common built-up structural shapes

DESIGN METHODS

Two methods for selecting structural steel members are recognized in current engineering practice in the United States. The *allowable stress design* (ASD) method has been codified by AISC, from 1923 to the present, in nine successive editions of their *Specification for the Design, Fabrication and Erection of Structural Steel for Buildings* (also known as the *AISC Specification*). This document has been incorporated by reference in virtually every building code in the United States. Containing the AISC Specification as well as numerous design aids for the ASD method has been the AISC *Manual of Steel Construction* (also known as the *AISC Manual*). The new *load and resistance factor design* (LRFD) method was introduced officially by AISC in 1986 with their publication of the *Load and Resistance Factor Design Specification for Structural Steel Buildings* (also known as the *AISC LRFD Specification*) and the *Load and Resistance Factor Design Manual of Steel Construction* (also known as the *AISC LRFD Manual*). The LRFD Manual contains the LRFD Specification and many tables and charts to assist users of the LRFD method.

This book, devoted exclusively to the LRFD method of structural steel design, is based on the AISC LRFD Specification. At the date of publication of this text, almost all U.S. jurisdictions have approved the use of the AISC LRFD Specification. It is anticipated that LRFD will soon be universally accepted in this country and will eventually become the standard method of structural steel design.

ASD VERSUS LRFD

(This section, which compares the two methods of structural steel design, is not essential for an understanding of the LRFD method or the remainder of this book. Hence, it may be skipped by students and others. It should, however, be of interest to those readers who have used ASD or are otherwise familiar with it.)

The ASD method is characterized by the use of one judgmental factor of safety. A limiting stress (usually F_y) is divided by a factor of safety (FS, determined by the authors of the Specification) to arrive at an allowable stress

$$\text{Allowable stress} = \frac{F_y}{\text{FS}}$$

Actual stresses in a steel member are calculated by dividing forces or moments by the appropriate section property (e.g., area or section modulus). The actual stresses are then compared with the allowable stresses to ascertain that

$$\text{Actual stress} \leq \text{allowable stress}$$

No distinction is made among the various kinds of loads. Because of the greater variability and uncertainty of the live load and other loads in comparison with the dead load, a uniform reliability for all structures is not possible.

The LRFD method is explained in detail in Chap. 2 and the succeeding chapters. Briefly, LRFD uses a different factor for each type of load and another factor for the strength or resistance. Each factor is the result of a statistical study of the variability of the subject quantity. Because the different factors reflect the degrees of uncertainty in the various loads and the resistance, a uniform reliability is possible.

Chapter 2

Introduction to LRFD

NOTATION

D = dead load

E = earthquake load

L = live load

L_r = roof live load

M = margin of safety

Q = load

R = rain load

R = resistance

R_n = nominal resistance

S = snow load

W = wind load

$\mathcal{B}$ = reliability index

γ = load factor

ϕ = resistance factor

σ = standard deviation

BASIC CONCEPTS

Load and resistance factor design (LRFD) is a method for designing structures so that no applicable limit state is exceeded when the strucure is subjected to all appropriate combinations of factored loads. *Limit state* is a condition in which a structure or a structural component becomes unfit. A structural member can have several limit states. *Strength* limit states concern safety and relate to maximum load-carrying capacity (e.g., plastic hinge and buckling). *Serviceability* limit states relate to performance under normal service conditions (e.g., excessive deformation and vibration).

The LRFD method, as applied to each limit state, may be summarized by the formula

$$\Sigma\gamma_i Q_i \leq \phi R_n \qquad\qquad [2.1]$$

In the terminology of the AISC LRFD Specification, the left side of the inequality is the *required strength* and the right side is the *design strength*. The left side represents the load combinations; that is, the summation (denoted by Σ) of the various loads (or load effects) Q_i, multiplied by their respective load factors γ_i. The left side is material-independent; the loads are taken from the governing building code and the LRFD load factors were derived from statistical building load studies. Loads and load combinations are covered later in this chapter. On the right side of the inequality, the design strength for the given limit state is the product of the nominal strength or resistance R_n and its resistance factor ϕ. Succeeding chapters of this text cover the limit states applicable to columns, beams, and other structural elements, together with the corresponding resistances and resistance factors.

Associated with each limit state are values for R_n and ϕ, where R_n (as calculated from the equations given in the subsequent chapters) defines the boundary of structural usefulness; ϕ (always less than or equal to one) depends on the variability of R_n. Test data were analyzed to determine the uncertainty in each resistance. The greater the scatter in the test data for a given resistance, the lower its ϕ factor.

PROBABILITY THEORY

The following is a brief, simplified explanation of the basis of LRFD in probability theory.

The load effect Q and the resistance R are assumed to be statistically independent random variables with probability distributions as shown in Fig. 2-1(a). Let the margin of safety

$$M = R - Q \qquad [2.2]$$

As long as M is positive (i.e., $R > Q$), a margin of safety exists. However, because Q and R are random variables, there will always be some probability of failure ($M < 0$). This unacceptable probability is shown shaded in Fig. 2-1(a) and (b). The latter figure is a probability distribution for M, which is also a random variable.

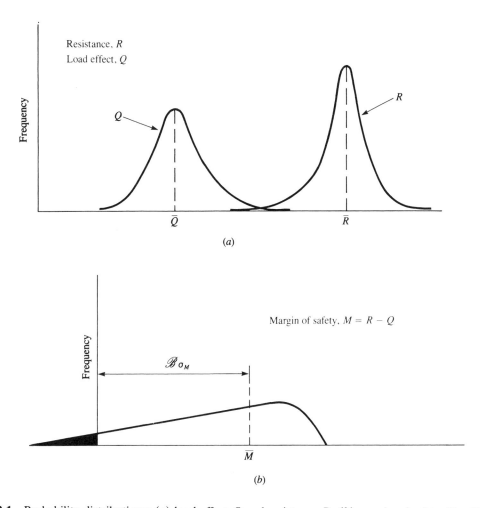

Fig. 2-1 Probability distributions: (a) load effect Q and resistance R; (b) margin of safety $M = R - Q$

Referring to Fig. 2-1(b), the probability of failure can be set to a predetermined small quantity (say, 1 in 100,000) by specifying that the mean value of M be $\mathscr{B}$ standard deviations above zero; i.e.

$$\bar{M} = \mathscr{B}\sigma_M \qquad [2.3]$$

where $\bar{M}$ = mean value of M

σ_M = standard deviation of M

$\mathscr{B}$ = reliability index

In Eq. [2.1], the one parameter left to the discretion of the authors of the LRFD Specification is ϕ; the load factors γ_i have been derived independently by others from load statistics. The resistance factor ϕ depends on $\mathscr{B}$ as well as on the uncertainty in the resistance R_n. The selection of a reliability index $\mathscr{B}$ determines the value of ϕ for each limit state. In general, to reduce the probability of failure, $\mathscr{B}$ would be increased, resulting in a lower value for ϕ.

LOADS

Structural loads are classified as follows.

Dead load (*D*)—The weight of the structure and all other permanently installed features in the building, including built-in partitions.

Live load (*L*)—The gravity load due to the intended usage and occupancy; includes the weight of people, furniture, and movable equipment and partitions. In LRFD, the notation L refers to floor live loads and L_r, to roof live loads.

Rain load (*R*)—Load due to the initial rainwater or ice, excluding the contribution of ponding.

Snow load (*S*).

Wind load (*W*).

Earthquake load (*E*).

In design, the dead load is calculated from the actual weights of the various structural and nonstructural elements. All the other design loads are specified by the governing building code. When beams support large floor areas or columns support several floors, building codes generally allow a live-load reduction. The reduced live load is used in LRFD.

LOAD COMBINATIONS

The *required strength* is defined in the AISC LRFD Specification as the maximum (absolute value) force obtained from the following load combinations.

$$1.4D \tag{A4-1}$$

$$1.2D + 1.6L + 0.5 \ (L_r \text{ or } S \text{ or } R) \tag{A4-2}$$

$$1.2D + 1.6 \ (L_r \text{ or } S \text{ or } R) + (0.5L \text{ or } 0.8W) \tag{A4-3}$$

$$1.2D + 1.3W + 0.5L + 0.5 \ (L_r \text{ or } S \text{ or } R) \tag{A4-4}$$

$$1.2D + 1.5E + (0.5L \text{ or } 0.2S) \tag{A4-5}$$

$$0.9D - (1.3W \text{ or } 1.5E) \tag{A4-6}$$

[*Exception*: The load factor on L in combinations (A4-3), (A4-4), and (A4-5) shall equal 1.0 for garages, areas occupied as places of public assembly, and all areas where the live load is greater than $100 \, \text{lb/ft}^2$.]

Loads D, L, L_r, S, R, W, and E represent either the loads themselves or the load effects (i.e., the forces or moments caused by the loads). In the preceding expressions, only one load assumes its maximum lifetime value at a time, while the others are at their "arbitrary point-in-time" values. Each combination models the design loading condition when a different load is at its maximum.

Load Combination	Load at Its Lifetime Maximum
(A4-1)	D (during construction; other loads not present)
(A4-2)	L
(A4-3)	L_r or S or R (a roof load)
(A4-4)	W (acting in the direction of D)
(A4-5)	E (acting in the direction of D)
(A4-6)	W or E (opposing D)

Load combinations (A4-1) to (A4-6) are for computing strength limit states. In determining serviceability limit states (e.g., deflections) the unfactored (service) loads are used.

Solved Problems

2.1. The moments acting on a floor beam are a dead-load moment of 50 kip-ft and a live-load moment of 35 kip-ft. Determine the required strength.

Because dead load and floor live load are the only loads acting on the member, $L_r = S = R = W = E = 0$. By inspection of formulas (A4-1) to (A4-6), it is obvious that one of the first two formulas must govern, as follows.

$$1.4D = 1.4 \times 50 \text{ kip-ft} = 70 \text{ kip-ft} \qquad (A4\text{-}1)$$
$$1.2D + 1.6L = 1.2 \times 50 \text{ kip-ft} + 1.6 \times 35 \text{ kip-ft} = 116 \text{ kip-ft} \qquad (A4\text{-}2)$$

Because it produces the maximum required strength, the second load combination governs. The required strength is 116 kip-ft.

2.2. Floor beams W21×50, spaced 10 ft 0 in center-to-center, support a superimposed dead load of 65 lb/ft² and a live load of 40 lb/ft². Determine the governing load combination and the corresponding factored load.

$$\text{Total dead load } D = 50 \text{ lb/ft} + 65 \text{ lb/ft}^2 \times 10.0 \text{ ft} = 700 \text{ lb/ft}$$
$$\text{Total live load } L = 40 \text{ lb/ft}^2 \times 10.0 \text{ ft} = 400 \text{ lb/ft}$$

As in Prob. 2.1, $L_r = S = R = W = E = 0$.
The two relevant load combinations are

$$1.4D = 1.4 \times 700 \text{ lb/ft} = 980 \text{ lb/ft} \qquad (A4\text{-}1)$$
$$1.2D + 1.6L = 1.2 \times 700 \text{ lb/ft} + 1.6 \times 400 \text{ lb/ft} = 1480 \text{ lb/ft} \qquad (A4\text{-}2)$$

The second load combination, which gives the maximum factored load, 1480 lb/ft (or 1.48 kips/ft), governs.

2.3. Roof design loads include a dead load of 35 lb/ft², a live (or snow) load of 25 lb/ft², and a wind pressure of 15 lb/ft² (upward or downward). Determine the governing loading.

The six load combinations are

Load Combination	Factored Load, lb/ft^2	
(A4-1)	1.4×35	= 49
(A4-2)	$1.2 \times 35 + 0 + 0.5 \times 25$	= 55
(A4-3)	$1.2 \times 35 + 1.6 \times 25 + 0.8 \times 15$	= 94
(A4-4)	$1.2 \times 35 + 1.3 \times 15 + 0 + 0.5 \times 25$	= 74
(A4-5)	$1.2 \times 35 + 0 + 0.2 \times 25$	= 47
(A4-6)	$0.9 \times 35 - 1.3 \times 15$	= 12

The third load combination governs; it has a total factored load of 94 lb/ft^2.

2.4. The axial forces on a building column from the code-specified loads have been calculated as 200 kips of dead load, 150 kips (reduced) floor live load, 25 kips from the roof (L_r or S or R), 100 kips from wind, and 40 kips from earthquake. Determine the required strength of the column.

Load Combination	Factored Axial Force, kips	
(A4-1)	1.4×200	= 280
(A4-2)	$1.2 \times 200 + 1.6 \times 150 + 0.5 \times 25$	= 493
(A4-3a)	$1.2 \times 200 + 1.6 \times 25 + 0.5 \times 150$	= 355
(A4-3b)	$1.2 \times 200 + 1.6 \times 25 + 0.8 \times 100$	= 360
(A4-4)	$1.2 \times 200 + 1.3 \times 100 + 0.5 \times 150 + 0.5 \times 25$	= 458
(A4-5a)	$1.2 \times 200 + 1.5 \times 40 + 0.5 \times 150$	= 375
(A4-5b)	$1.2 \times 200 + 1.5 \times 40 + 0.2 \times 25$	= 305
(A4-6a)	$0.9 \times 200 - 1.3 \times 100$	= 50
(A4-6b)	$0.9 \times 200 - 1.5 \times 40$	= 120

The required strength for the column is 493 kips, based on the second load combination.

2.5. Repeat Prob. 2.4 for a garage column.

According to the AISC LRFD Specification, load combinations (A4-3) to (A4-5) are modified for garages, areas of public assembly, and areas with live load exceeding 100 lb/ft^2, as follows.

$$1.2D + 1.6 \ (L_r \text{ or } S \text{ or } R) + (1.0L \text{ or } 0.8W) \qquad (A4\text{-}3')$$

$$1.2D + 1.3W + 1.0L + 0.5 \ (L_r \text{ or } S \text{ or } R) \qquad (A4\text{-}4')$$

$$1.2D + 1.5E + (1.0L \text{ or } 0.2S) \qquad (A4\text{-}5')$$

The solution to Prob. 2.4 is still valid for garages except for load combinations (A4-3a), (A4-4), and (A4-5A), which become

Load Combination	Factored Axial Force, kips	
(A4-3a')	$1.2 \times 200 + 1.6 \times 25 + 1.0 \times 150$	= 430
(A4-4')	$1.2 \times 200 + 1.3 \times 100 + 1.0 \times 150 + 0.5 \times 25$	= 533
(A4-5a')	$1.2 \times 200 + 1.5 \times 40 + 1.0 \times 150$	= 450

Because 533 kips is greater than 493 kips, the required strength for the garage column is 533 kips, which is obtained from modified load combination (*A4-4*).

Supplementary Problems

2.6. A beam-column is subjected to the following forces by the service loads indicated. Axial compression, $P = 60$ kips (dead load), 5 kips (live load). Bending, $M = 10$ kip-ft (dead load), 3 kip-ft (live load). Determine the governing load combination and the required axial compressive and bending strengths.

Ans. Load combination (*A4-1*) governs for axial compression; the required strengths are $P_u = 84$ kips, $M_u = 14$ kip-ft. Load combination (*A4-2*) governs for bending moment; the required strengths are $P_u = 80$ kips, $M_u = 17$ kip-ft. Both of the preceding P_u-M_u pairs should be checked in the design of the beam-column.

2.7. A member is subjected to the following axial forces: 35 kips (axial compression from dead load) and 30 kips (axial compression or tension from wind). Determine the governing load combinations and the required strengths.

Ans. Axial compression: $P_u = 81$ kips; load combination (*A4-4*). Axial tension: $P_u = 8$ kips; load combination (*A4-6*).

2.8. The axial forces on a building column are as follows: 50 kips dead load, 40 kips floor live load, 10 kips roof live load, and 55 kips wind. Determine the required strength.

Ans. Axial compression: $P_u = 157$ kips; load combination (*A4-4*). Axial tension: $P_u = 27$ kips; load combination (*A4-6*).

Chapter 3

Tension Members

NOTATION

A_e = effective net cross-sectional area of member, in^2

A_g = gross cross-sectional area of member, in^2

A_n = net cross-sectional area of member, in^2

E = modulus of elasticity of steel = 29,000 ksi

F_u = specified minimum tensile strength, ksi

F_y = specified minimum yield stress, ksi

g = gage (i.e., the transverse center-to-center spacing between fastener gage lines), in

l = member length, in

P = (unfactored) axial force in member, kips

P_n = nominal axial strength of member, kips

s = pitch (i.e., the longitudinal center-to-center spacing of any two consecutive holes), in

U = reduction coefficient

Δ = axial elongation of member, in

$\phi_t P_n$ = design strength of tension member, in

ϕ_t = resistance factor for tension = 0.90 or 0.75

INTRODUCTION

This chapter covers members subjected to pure tension, such as hangers and truss members. When a tensile force is applied through the centroidal axis of a member, the result is a uniform tension stress at each cross section. Tensile forces not acting through the centroid cause bending in addition to tension; lateral forces also cause bending. Members with combined bending and tension are discussed in Chap. 7.

CROSS-SECTIONAL AREAS

The design tensile strength of a structural steel member depends on the appropriate cross-sectional area. The three cross-sectional areas of interest are the gross area A_g, the net area A_n, and the effective net area A_e.

The *gross area* of a member at any point is the total area of the cross section, with no deductions for holes.

The *net area* is the gross area minus the area of the holes. In computing the net area for tension, the width of a hole is taken as $\frac{1}{16}$ in greater than its specified dimension. Since tolerances require that a bolt hole be $\frac{1}{16}$ in greater than the diameter of the bolt, the width of a hole is assumed for design purposes to be twice $\frac{1}{16}$ in, or $\frac{1}{8}$ in, greater than the diameter of the bolt.

The net area of an element is its net width multiplied by its thickness. For one hole, or two or more holes running perpendicular to the axis of the member, the net width is the gross width minus the sum of the widths of the holes. However, if a chain of holes extends across a part in a diagonal or zigzag fashion, the net width is the gross width minus the sum of the hole dimensions plus the

14

quantity $s^2/4g$ for each gage space in the chain, where

s = pitch (i.e., the longitudinal center-to-center spacing of any two consecutive holes), in

g = gage (i.e., the transverse center-to-center spacing between fastener gage lines), in (See Fig. 3-1.)

It may be necessary to examine several chains to determine which chain has the least net width.

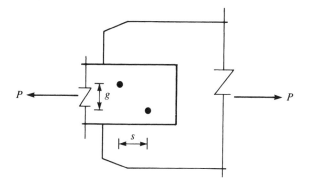

Fig. 3-1   Definitions of s and g

The concept of *effective net area* accounts for shear lag in the vicinity of connections. When the member end connection transmits tension directly to all cross-sectional elements of the member, A_e equals A_n. But if the end connection transmits tension through some, but not all, of the cross-sectional elements, a reduced effective net area is used instead. For bolted and riveted members

$$A_e = UA_n \qquad\qquad (B3\text{-}1)$$

For welded members

$$A_e = UA_g \qquad\qquad (B3\text{-}2)$$

Design values for U and A_e are given in Sec. B3 of the AISC LRFD Specification. For W, M, or S shapes and structural tees cut from these shapes:

If the tensile force is transmitted by transverse welds, A_e equals the area of the directly connected elements.

If the force is transmitted by bolts, the value of U depends on the criteria listed in Table 3-1.

Table 3-1   Values of U for Bolted W, M, S, WT, MT, and ST Shapes

Criteria	U
(*a*) Flange width $\geq \frac{2}{3} \times$ depth; connection is to the flanges; minimum of three fasteners per line in the direction of stress	0.90
(*b*) Minimum of three fasteners per line in the direction of stress otherwise not meeting criteria (*a*)	0.85
(*c*) Two fasteners per line in the direction of stress	0.75

DESIGN TENSILE STRENGTH

Two criteria limit the design tensile strength $\phi_t P_n$.

a.   For yielding of the gross cross section

$$\phi_t = 0.90$$
$$P_n = F_y A_g$$

(D1-1)

b.   For fracture in the net cross section

$$\phi_t = 0.75$$
$$P_n = F_u A_e$$

(D1-2)

where ϕ_t = resistance factor for tension
P_n = nominal axial strength, kips
F_y = specified minimum yield stress, ksi
F_u = specified minimum tensile strength, ksi

Limitation *a* is intended to prevent excessive elongation of the member. Since the fraction of the total member length occupied by fastener holes is usually small, the effect of early yielding of the reduced cross sections on the total elongation of the member is negligible. Hence the gross section is used. Limit state *b* deals with fracture at the cross section with the minimum A_e.

DISPLACEMENT

The increase in the length of a member due to axial tension under service loads is

$$\Delta = \frac{Pl}{EA_g}$$

[3.1]

where Δ = axial elongation of the member, in
P = (unfactored) axial tensile force in the member, kips
l = length of the member, in
E = modulus of elasticity of steel = 29,000 ksi

Solved Problems

3.1.   Determine the gross and net cross-sectional areas of a plate 12 in × 2 in with a 1-in-diameter hole. (See Fig. 3-2.)

Gross area = gross width × thickness

$$A_g = 12 \text{ in} \times 2 \text{ in} = 24 \text{ in}^2$$

Net area = net width × thickness
Net width = gross width − hole diameter
For design, hole diameter = 1 in + $\frac{1}{16}$ in = 1.06 in
Net width = 12 in − 1.06 in = 10.94 in

$$A_n = 10.94 \text{ in} \times 2 \text{ in} = 21.88 \text{ in}^2$$

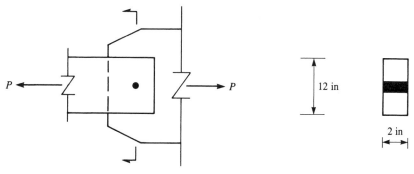

Fig. 3-2

3.2.   Use the same information as in Prob. 3.1, except with two 1-in-diameter holes positioned as shown in Fig. 3-3.

$$\text{Gross width of plate} = 12 \text{ in} \qquad A_g = 24 \text{ in}^2 \qquad \text{as above}$$

Chain *ACE* or *BDF* (one hole):

$$\text{Net width} = 12 \text{ in} - 1.06 \text{ in} = 10.94 \text{ in}$$

Chain *ACDF* (two holes, one space):

$$\text{Net width} = \text{gross width} - \Sigma \text{ hole diameters} + \Sigma \frac{s^2}{4g}$$

$$= 12 \text{ in} - 2 \times 1.06 \text{ in} + \frac{(4 \text{ in})^2}{4 \times 6 \text{ in}}$$

$$= 10.54 \text{ in}$$

Because 10.54 in < 10.94 in, chain *ACDF* is critical in this case.

$$A_n = \text{net width} \times \text{thickness}$$

$$= 10.54 \text{ in} \times 2 \text{ in} = 21.08 \text{ in}^2$$

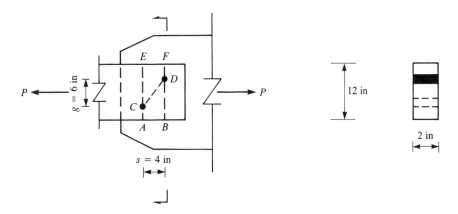

Fig. 3-3

3.3.   Use the same information as in Prob. 3.1, except with three 1-in-diameter holes positioned as shown in Fig. 3-4.

$$A_g = 24 \text{ in}^2$$

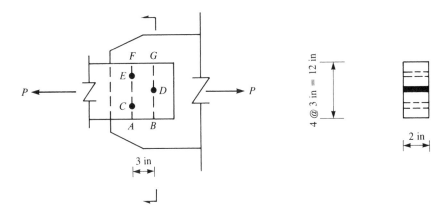

Fig. 3-4

Regarding net width, by inspection, chains BDG (one hole), $ACDG$ (two holes, one space), and $BDEF$ (two holes, one space) are not critical. (The reader can verify this by calculation.) For the other chains

Chain	Net Width (in) = Gross Width $- \Sigma$ Hole Diameters $+ \Sigma \dfrac{s^2}{4g}$	
$ACEF$	$12 - 2 \times 1.06$	$= 9.88$ in
$ACDEF$	$12 - 3 \times 1.06 + 2 \times \dfrac{3^2}{4 \times 3}$	$= 10.31$ in

Chain $ACEF$ with the minimum net width, 9.88 in, is critical.

$$A_n = 9.88 \text{ in} \times 2 \text{ in} = 19.75 \text{ in}^2$$

3.4. Holes have been punched in the flanges of the W10×49 in Fig. 3-5 for four 1-in-diameter bolts. The holes lie in the same cross-sectional plane; $A_g = 14.4 \text{ in}^2$. Determine the net area.

For design, hole diameter $= 1 \text{ in} + \frac{1}{8} \text{ in} = 1.13 \text{ in}$.

$$A_n = A_g - 4 \times \text{hole diameter} \times \text{flange thickness}$$
$$= 14.4 \text{ in}^2 - 4 \times 1.13 \text{ in} \times 0.560 \text{ in}$$
$$A_n = 11.88 \text{ in}^2$$

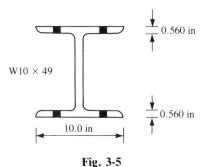

Fig. 3-5

In Probs. 3.5 to 3.8, determine the design tensile strength of a W10×49 in A36 steel, with the conditions stated.

3.5.   No holes; the two flanges and the web are all welded to the supporting member.

Here, $A_e = A_g = 14.4\,\text{in}^2$. For A36 steel, $F_y = 36$ ksi and $F_u = 58$ ksi.
   Design strength $\phi_t P_n = $ minimum of

$$0.90 F_y A_g = 0.90 \times 36\,\text{ksi} \times 14.4\,\text{in}^2 = 467\,\text{kips}$$
$$0.75 F_u A_e = 0.75 \times 58\,\text{ksi} \times 14.4\,\text{in}^2 = 626\,\text{kips}$$

$\phi_t P_n = 467$ kips, based on yielding of the gross section.

3.6.   No holes; only the flanges of the W10×49 are welded to the support.

$$A_g = 14.4\,\text{in}^2$$

For welded connections, effective net area

$$A_e = \text{area of directly connected elements}$$
$$= \text{area of the two flanges}$$
$$= 2(10.0\,\text{in} \times 0.560\,\text{in}) = 11.20\,\text{in}^2$$

Design strength $\phi_t P_n = $ minimum of

$$0.90 F_y A_g = 0.90 \times 36\,\text{ksi} \times 14.4\,\text{in}^2 = 467\,\text{kips}$$
$$0.75 F_u A_e = 0.75 \times 58\,\text{ksi} \times 11.20\,\text{in}^2 = 487\,\text{kips}$$

Again $\phi_t P_n = 467$ kips, based on yielding of the gross section.

3.7.   The hole pattern of Fig. 3-5, but not at the end support; the flanges of the W10×49 are welded to the support.

$$A_g = 14.4\,\text{in}^2$$

At the support, $A_e = $ flange area $= 11.20\,\text{in}^2$, as in Prob. 3.6. At the holes (away from the member end), $A_e = A_n = 11.88\,\text{in}^2$, as in Prob. 3.4.
   The design strength $\phi_t P_n = $ the minimum of

$$0.90 F_y A_g = 0.90 \times 36\,\text{ksi} \times 14.4\,\text{in}^2 = 467\,\text{kips}$$
$$0.75 F_u A_e = 0.75 \times 58\,\text{ksi} \times 11.2\,\text{in}^2 = 487\,\text{kips}$$
$$0.75 F_u A_e = 0.75 \times 58\,\text{ksi} \times 11.88\,\text{in}^2 = 517\,\text{kips}$$

The design strength for tension is 467 kips.

3.8.   The connection of the W10×49 to its support is by bolting as in Fig. 3-5, two bolts per line along the member length direction (i.e., a total of eight holes).

Reduction coefficient $U = 0.75$. For bolted connections, $A_e = U A_n = 0.75 \times 11.88\,\text{in}^2 = 8.91\,\text{in}^2$.
   Design strength $\phi_t P_n = $ minimum of

$$0.90 F_y A_g = 0.90 \times 36\,\text{ksi} \times 14.4\,\text{in}^2 = 467\,\text{kips}$$
$$0.75 F_u A_e = 0.75 \times 58\,\text{ksi} \times 8.91\,\text{in}^2 = 388\,\text{kips}$$

$\phi_t P_n = 388$ kips, based on fracture of the net section.

3.9.   How much service dead load can be carried by the W10×49 in Probs. 3.5 to 3.8?

Assuming that dead load is the only load, the governing load combination in Chap. 2 is the first: $1.4D$.

$$1.4D \leq \phi_t P_n$$

Maximum service dead load $D = \phi_t P_n / 1.4$.

In Probs. 3.5 to 3.7, $\phi_t P_n = 467$ kips. Maximum service dead load $= 467$ kips$/1.4 = 333$ kips.
In Prob. 3.8, $\phi_t P_n = 388$ kips. Maximum service dead load $= 388$ kips$/1.4 = 277$ kips.

3.10. A W10×49 tension hanger, 5 ft long, carries a service load of 250 kips. Calculate its axial elongation.

$$\text{Elongation } \Delta = \frac{Pl}{EA_g} = \frac{250 \text{ kips} \times (5.0 \text{ ft} \times 12 \text{ in/ft})}{29{,}000 \text{ ksi} \times 14.4 \text{ in}^2} = 0.036 \text{ in}$$

Supplementary Problems

In Probs. 3.11 to 3.13, determine the net cross-sectional area and critical chain of holes.

3.11. A 10 in × 1.5 in plate with two $\frac{15}{16}$-in holes, as in Fig. 3-6.

Ans. $A_n = 12.0$ in^2; critical chain is $ABCD$.

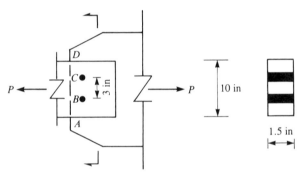

Fig. 3-6

3.12. A 10 in × 1.5 in plate with four $\frac{15}{16}$-in holes, as in Fig. 3-7.

Ans. $A_n = 12.0$ in^2; critical chain is $ACEG$.

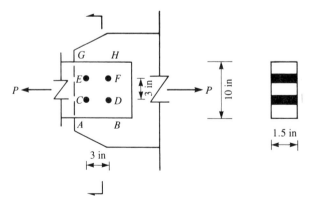

Fig. 3-7

3.13. A 10 in × 1.5 in plate with five $\frac{15}{16}$-in holes, as in Fig. 3-8.

    Ans. $A_n = 11.50\ \text{in}^2$; critical chain is *ACEFH*.

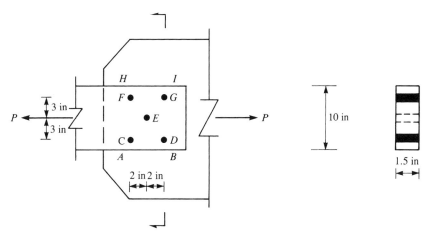

Fig. 3-8

In Probs. 3.14 to 3.16, determine the design tensile strength of the double-channel configuration (2 C6×10.5) in Fig. 3-9. Steel is A36. The cross-sectional area of each channel is 3.09 in^2.

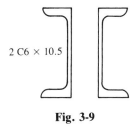

Fig. 3-9

3.14. All elements of the channels are welded to the support. At certain sections away from the end connection, a single $\frac{3}{4}$-in-diameter bolt joins the channels, as in Fig. 3.10, to form a built-up section.

    Ans. $\phi_t P_n = 200$ kips.

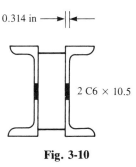

Fig. 3-10

3.15. Only the webs of the channels are welded to the support. Away from the support, some sections have a $\frac{3}{4}$-in-diameter bolt, as in Fig. 3-9, to form a built-up section.   *Ans.* $\phi_t P_n = 164$ kips.

3.16. The connection of the channels to their support is as shown in Fig. 3-10 with three $\frac{3}{4}$-in-diameter bolts in the direction of stress.   *Ans.* $\phi_t P_n = 200$ kips.

3.17. Calculate the increase in length of the 3-ft-long tension hanger in Fig. 3-9 (2 C6×10.5) under an axial service load of 100 kips.   *Ans.* $\Delta = 0.020$ in.

Chapter 4

Columns and Other Compression Members

NOTATION

A_g = gross cross-sectional area of member, in^2

b = width, in

b_f = width of flange, in

d = depth, in

E = modulus of elasticity of steel = 29,000 ksi

F_{cr} = critical comprehensive stress, ksi

F_r = compressive residual stress in flange, ksi

F_y = specified minimum yield stress, ksi

G = alignment chart parameter defined in Eq. [4.2]

G' = alignment chart parameter defined in Eq. [4.1]

h_c, h_w = web dimensions defined in Fig. 4-1 in

I = moment of inertia, in^4

K = effective length factor

KL = effective length, ft

Kl = effective length, in

L = length of member, ft

l = length of member, in

P = (unfactored) axial force in member, kips

P_n = nominal axial strength of member, kips

P_u = required axial strength, kips

r = radius of gyration of the cross section, in

t = thickness, in

t_w = thickness of web, in

Δ = axial shortening of member, in

λ_c = column slenderness parameter

λ_p = limiting width-thickness ratio for compact section

λ_r = limiting width-thickness ratio for column design

$\phi_c P_n$ = design strength of compression member, kips

ϕ_c = resistance factor for compression = 0.85

INTRODUCTION

This chapter covers members subjected to pure compression such as columns and truss members. When a compressive force is applied through the centroidal axis of a member, a uniform compression stress develops at each cross section. Bending is caused by compressive forces not acting through the centroid or by lateral forces. Bending combined with compression is discussed in Chap. 8.

The strength of compression members is limited by instability. The instability can be either local buckling or overall (column) buckling.

LOCAL BUCKLING

The cross sections of structural steel members are classified as either compact, noncompact, or slender-element sections, depending on the width-thickness ratios of their elements.

A section is *compact* if the flanges are continuously connected to the web, and the width-thickness ratios of all its compression elements are equal to or less than λ_p.

A section is *noncompact* if the width-thickness ratio of at least one element is greater than λ_p, provided the width-thickness ratios of all compression elements are equal to or less than λ_r.

If the width-thickness ratio of a compression element is greater than λ_r, that element is a slender compression element; the cross section is called a *slender-element* section.

Steel members with compact sections can develop their full compressive strength without local instability. Noncompact shapes can be stressed to initial yielding before local buckling occurs. In members with slender elements, elastic local buckling is the limitation on strength.

Columns with compact and noncompact sections are designed by the method described herein (and in Chap. E of the AISC LRFD Specification). Nearly all building columns are in this category. For the occasional case of a slender-element column, the special design procedures listed in App. B5.3 of the AISC LRFD Specification are required, to account for local buckling. Because of the penalties imposed by App. B5.3, it is generally more economical to avoid slender elements by increasing thicknesses.

To summarize: if, for all elements of the cross section, the width-thickness ratios (b/t, d/t_w, or h_c/t_w) are equal to or less than λ_r, column design should be by the method of this chapter. Otherwise, the method given in App. B5.3 of the LRFD Specification must be used. The width-thickness ratios for columns and the corresponding values of λ_r are defined in Table 4-1 and Fig. 4-1, which are based on Sec. B5 of the AISC LRFD Specification.

Table 4-1 Limiting Width-Thickness Ratios for Columns

Column Element	Width-Thickness Ratio	Limiting Width-Thickness Ratio, λ_r	
		General	A36 Steel
Flanges of W and other I shapes and channels; outstanding legs of pairs of angles in continuous contact	b/t	$95/\sqrt{F_y}$	15.8
Flanges of square and rectangular box sections; flange cover plates and diaphragm plates between lines of fasteners or welds	b/t	$238/\sqrt{F_y - F_r}^*$	46.7 (rolled) 53.9 (welded)
Legs of single angle struts and double angle struts with separators; unstiffened elements (i.e., supported along one edge)	b/t	$76/\sqrt{F_y}$	12.7
Stems of tees	d/t	$127/\sqrt{F_y}$	21.2
All other stiffened elements (i.e., supported along two edges)	b/t h_c/t_w	$253/\sqrt{F_y}$	42.2

$^*F_r$ = compressive residual stress in flange: 10 ksi for rolled shapes, 16.5 ksi for welded sections.

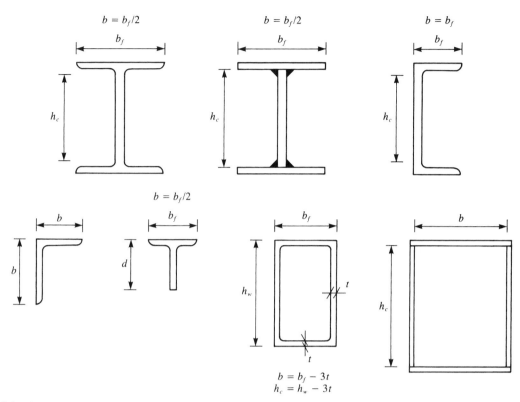

Fig. 4-1 Definitions of widths (b, d, and h_c) and thickness (flange or leg thickness t and web thickness t_w) for use in Table 4-1

COLUMN BUCKLING

The most significant parameter affecting column stability is the *slenderness ratio Kl/r,* where l is the actual unbraced length of the column, in; Kl is the effective length of the column, in; and r is the radius of gyration of the column cross section, in. Column strength equations are normally written for ideal "pin-ended" columns. To make the strength equations applicable to all columns, an *effective length factor K* is used to account for the influence of end conditions on column stability.

Two methods for determining K for a column are presented in Sec. C2 of the Commentary on the AISC LRFD Specification: a *judgmental* method and an approximate *analytical* method. A discussion of the two methods follows.

EFFECTIVE LENGTH FACTOR: JUDGMENTAL METHOD

Six cases are shown in Table 4-2 for individual columns, with their corresponding K values, both theoretical and recommended. The more conservative recommendations (from the Structural Stability Research Council) reflect the fact that perfect fixity cannot be achieved in real structures.

The LRFD Specification distinguishes between columns in braced and unbraced frames. In braced frames, sidesway is inhibited by diagonal bracing or shear walls. In Table 4-2, case *d* (the classical pin-ended column, $K = 1.0$) as well as cases *a* and *b* represent columns in braced frames; $K \le 1.0$. AISC recommends that K for compression members in braced frames "shall be taken as unity, unless structural analysis shows that a smaller value may be used." It is common practice to assume $K = 1.0$ for columns in braced frames.

Table 4-2 Effective Length Factors *K* for Columns

	(a)	(b)	(c)	(d)	(e)	(f)
Buckled Shape of Column Shown by Dashed Line						
Theoretical *K* value	0.5	0.7	1.0	1.0	2.0	2.0
Recommended design values when ideal conditions are approximated	0.65	0.80	1.2	1.0	2.10	2.0
End condition code		Rotation fixed and translation fixed				
		Rotation free and translation fixed				
		Rotation fixed and translation free				
		Rotation free and translation free				
Reproduced with permission from the AISC LRFD Manual.						

Cases *c*, *e*, and *f* in Table 4-2 cover columns in unbraced frames (sidesway uninhibited); $K \geq 1.0$. The *K* values recommended therein may be used in column design.

EFFECTIVE LENGTH FACTOR: ANALYTICAL METHOD

If beams are rigidly connected to a column, nomographs are available for approximating *K* for that column. Two such "alignment charts" have been developed: one for "sidesway inhibited" (i.e., braced frames, $K \leq 1.0$); the other, for "sidesway uninhibited" (i.e., unbraced frames, $K \geq 1.0$). Again, for columns in braced frames, it is customary to conservatively let $K = 1.0$. For columns in unbraced frames, the alignment chart in Fig. 4-2 may be used to determine *K*. Because the alignment charts were developed with the assumption of purely elastic action, the stiffness reduction factors (SRF) in Table 4-3 are available to account for inelastic column behavior. (Figure 4-2 has been reproduced with permission from the Commentary on the AISC LRFD Specification. Table 4-3 is a corrected version of Table A in the AISC LRFD Manual, Part 2.)

The procedure for obtaining *K* from Fig. 4-2 is as follows.

1. At each of the two joints (*A* and *B*) at the ends of the column, determine *I* (the moment of inertia, in⁴) and *l* (the unbraced length, in) of each column *ci* and each beam *gi* rigidly connected to that joint and lying in the plane in which buckling of the column is being considered.

2. At each end of the column, *A* and *B*

$$G' = \frac{(I/l)_{c1} + (I/l)_{c2}}{(I/l)_{g1} + (I/l)_{g2}} \qquad [4.1]$$

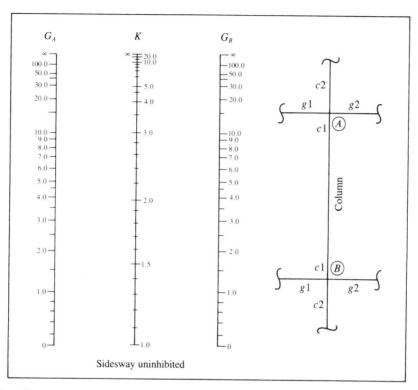

Fig. 4-2   Alignment chart for effective length of columns in unbraced frames having rigid joints

**Table 4-3   Stiffness Reduction Factors for A36 Steel for Use
with Fig. 4-2**

P_u*/A_g, ksi	SRF	P_u/A_g, ksi	SRF
30	0.05	20	0.76
29	0.14	19	0.81
28	0.22	18	0.85
27	0.30	17	0.89
26	0.38	16	0.92
25	0.45	15	0.95
24	0.52	14	0.97
23	0.58	13	0.99
22	0.65	12	1.00
21	0.70		
* P_u is the required strength and A_g is the gross cross-sectional area of the subject column.			

3.   Adjust for inelastic column action

$$G_A = G'_A \times \text{SRF}$$
$$G_B = G'_B \times \text{SRF}$$

[4.2]

where SRF is the stiffness reduction factor for the column obtained from Table 4-3.

4.   For a column end attached to a foundation, $G = 10$ for a "pin" support and $G = 1$ for a rigid support are recommended.

5.   Determine K by drawing a straight line from G_A to G_B on the alignment chart in Fig. 4-2.

DESIGN COMPRESSIVE STRENGTH

Column buckling can be either elastic or inelastic. For design purposes, $\lambda_c = 1.5$ is taken as the boundary between elastic and inelastic column buckling.

$$\lambda_c = \frac{Kl}{r\pi} \sqrt{\frac{F_y}{E}} \tag{E2-4}$$

For columns with cross-sectional elements having width-thickness ratios equal to or less than λ_r, the design compressive strength is $\phi_c P_n$, where

$$\phi_c = 0.85$$
$$P_n = A_g F_{cr} \tag{E2-1}$$

If $\lambda_c \leq 1.5$, column buckling is inelastic.

$$F_{cr} = (0.658^{\lambda_c^2}) F_y \tag{E2-2}$$

or in the alternate form given in the Commentary on the AISC LRFD Specification

$$F_{cr} = [\exp(-0.419\lambda_c^2)] F_y \tag{C-E2-1}$$

where $\exp(x) = e^x$.

If $\lambda_c > 1.5$, column buckling is elastic.

$$F_{cr} = \left[\frac{0.877}{\lambda_c^2}\right] F_y \tag{E2-3}$$

The terms in these equations include

λ_c = slenderness parameter

F_y = specified minimum yield stress, ksi

E = modulus of elasticity of steel = 29,000 ksi

ϕ_c = resistance factor for compression

P_n = nominal compressive strength, kips

A_g = gross cross-sectional area, in^2

F_{cr} = critical compressive stress, ksi

Equation ($E2$-3) is the Euler equation for column instability multiplied by 0.877 to account for the initial out-of-straightness of actual columns. Equation ($E2$-2) and (its equivalent) Eq. (C-$E2$-1) are empirical equations for inelastic column buckling, providing a transition from $F_{cr} = F_y$ at $\lambda_c = 0$ (i.e., $Kl/r = 0$) to the modified Euler equation [Eq. ($E2$-3)] for elastic buckling at $\lambda_c > 1.5$. For A36 steel $\lambda_c = 1.5$ corresponds to a slenderness ratio Kl/r of 133.7.

COLUMN DESIGN

According to Sec. B7 of the AISC LRFD Specification, for compression members Kl/r "preferably should not exceed 200."

In design, selection of an appropriate column can be facilitated by referral to tables in one of two ways. The design compressive strengths $\phi_c P_n$ of W and other rolled shapes are tabulated in the AISC LRFD Manual, Part 2. Column shapes can be selected directly from those tables. For built-up sections and rolled shapes not tabulated, Table 4-4 for A36 steel (and similar tables for other grades of steel in the AISC LRFD Specification) can be used in iterative design. In both cases, reference to tables replaces the need to solve the column strength equations [Eqs. ($E2$-1) to ($E2$-4)].

Table 4-4 Design Compressive Stresses for A36 Steel

Design Stress for Compression Members of 36 ksi Specified Yield-Stress Steel, $\phi_c = 0.85$*

$\dfrac{Kl}{r}$	$\phi_c F_{cr}$, ksi	$\dfrac{Kl}{r}$	$\phi_c F_{cr}$, ksi	$\dfrac{Kl}{r}$	$\phi_c F_{cr}$, ksi	$\dfrac{Kl}{r}$	$\phi_c F_{cr}$, ksi	$\dfrac{Kl}{r}$	$\phi_c F_{cr}$, ksi
1	30.60	41	28.01	81	21.66	121	14.16	161	8.23
2	30.59	42	27.89	82	21.48	122	13.98	162	8.13
3	30.59	43	27.76	83	21.29	123	13.80	163	8.03
4	30.57	44	27.64	84	21.11	124	13.62	164	7.93
5	30.56	45	27.51	85	20.92	125	13.44	165	7.84
6	30.54	46	27.37	86	20.73	126	13.27	166	7.74
7	30.52	47	27.24	87	20.54	127	13.09	167	7.65
8	30.50	48	27.11	88	20.36	128	12.92	168	7.56
9	30.47	49	26.97	89	20.17	129	12.74	169	7.47
10	30.44	50	26.83	90	19.98	130	12.57	170	7.38
11	30.41	51	26.68	91	19.79	131	12.40	171	7.30
12	30.37	52	26.54	92	19.60	132	12.23	172	7.21
13	30.33	53	26.39	93	19.41	133	12.06	173	7.13
14	30.29	54	26.25	94	19.22	134	11.88	174	7.05
15	30.24	55	26.10	95	19.03	135	11.71	175	6.97
16	30.19	56	25.94	96	18.84	136	11.54	176	6.89
17	30.14	57	25.79	97	18.65	137	11.37	177	6.81
18	30.08	58	25.63	98	18.46	138	11.20	178	6.73
19	30.02	59	25.48	99	18.27	139	11.04	179	6.66
20	29.96	60	25.32	100	18.08	140	10.89	180	6.59
21	29.90	61	25.16	101	17.89	141	10.73	181	6.51
22	29.83	62	24.99	102	17.70	142	10.58	182	6.44
23	29.76	63	24.83	103	17.51	143	10.43	183	6.37
24	29.69	64	24.67	104	17.32	144	10.29	184	6.30
25	29.61	65	24.50	105	17.13	145	10.15	185	6.23
26	29.53	66	24.33	106	16.94	146	10.01	186	6.17
27	29.45	67	24.16	107	16.75	147	9.87	187	6.10
28	29.36	68	23.99	108	16.56	148	9.74	188	6.04
29	29.28	69	23.82	109	16.37	149	9.61	189	5.97
30	29.18	70	23.64	110	16.19	150	9.48	190	5.91
31	29.09	71	23.47	111	16.00	151	9.36	191	5.85
32	28.99	72	23.29	112	15.81	152	9.23	192	5.79
33	28.90	73	23.12	113	15.63	153	9.11	193	5.73
34	28.79	74	22.94	114	15.44	154	9.00	194	5.67
35	28.69	75	22.76	115	15.26	155	8.88	195	5.61
36	28.58	76	22.58	116	15.07	156	8.77	196	5.55
37	28.47	77	22.40	117	14.89	157	8.66	197	5.50
38	28.36	78	22.22	118	14.70	158	8.55	198	5.44
39	28.25	79	22.03	119	14.52	159	8.44	199	5.39
40	28.13	80	21.85	120	14.34	160	8.33	200	5.33

* When element width-thickness ratio exceeds λ_r, see App. B5.3, LRFD Specification.
Reproduced with permission from the AISC LRFD Manual.

Building columns are most commonly W shapes, in the W14–W4 series. The W14 and W12 series are well suited to carrying heavy loads in multistory buildings. The W16 to W40 series are seldom used for columns because of their inefficiency due to their relatively low values of r_y (the radius of gyration about the weak y axis). The most efficient column sections are structural shapes with $r_x = r_y$ (i.e., equal radii of gyration about both principal axes). Included in this category are pipe and tube shapes, which are often used in lightly loaded single-story applications. Because they are rolled only with relatively small cross sections, structural pipes and tubes are not available for carrying heavy column loads.

DISPLACEMENT

The decrease in the length of a member due to axial compression under service loads is

$$\Delta = \frac{Pl}{EA_g} \qquad\qquad [4.3]$$

where Δ = axial shortening of the member, in

P = (unfactored) axial compressive force in the member, kips

l = length of the member, in

Solved Problems

In Probs. 4.1 to 4.3, determine whether the given column shape is a slender-element section:

(a)   In A36 steel ($F_y = 36$ ksi)

(b)   If $F_y = 50$ ksi

4.1.   W14×34.

If the width-thickness ratio of an element is greater than λ_r, it is a slender element.
Referring to Table 4-1 and Fig. 4-1, for the flanges of a W shape

$$\lambda_r = \frac{95}{\sqrt{F_y}} = \begin{cases} \dfrac{95}{\sqrt{36}} = 15.8 & \text{if} \quad F_y = 36 \text{ ksi} \\[2ex] \dfrac{95}{\sqrt{50}} = 13.4 & \text{if} \quad F_y = 50 \text{ ksi} \end{cases}$$

for the web of a W shape

$$\lambda_r = \frac{253}{\sqrt{F_y}} = \begin{cases} \dfrac{253}{\sqrt{36}} = 42.2 & \text{if} \quad F_y = 35 \text{ ksi} \\[2ex] \dfrac{253}{\sqrt{50}} = 35.8 & \text{if} \quad F_y = 50 \text{ ksi} \end{cases}$$

From the Properties Tables for W Shapes, in Part 1 of the AISC LRFD Manual (Compact Section Criteria), for a W14×34, flange $b/t = b_f/2t_f = 7.4$, web $h_c/t_w = 43.1$.
Since web ($h_c/t_w = 43.1$) > ($\lambda_r = 42.2$), the web of a W14×34 is a slender element in A36 steel. A W14×34 is a slender-element section if $F_y = 36$ or 50 ksi.

4.2.   W14×43.

From the Properties Tables for W Shapes, for a W14×43, flange $b/t = b_f/2t_f = 7.5$, web $h_c/t_w = 37.4$.
(a)   In A36 steel, flange $\lambda_r = 15.8$, web $\lambda_r = 42.2$. (See Prob. 4.1.) Since flange ($b/t = 7.5$) < ($\lambda_r = 15.8$) and web ($h_c/t_w = 37.4$) < ($\lambda_r = 42.2$), a W14×43 column is not a slender-element section in A36 steel.

(b)   However, if $F_y = 50$ ksi, flange $\lambda_r = 13.4$, web $\lambda_r = 35.8$. (See Prob. 4.1.) Because web ($h_c/t_w = 37.4) > (\lambda_r = 35.8$), a W14×43 column is a slender-element section if $F_y = 50$ ksi.

4.3.   The welded section in Fig. 4-3.

Referring to Table 4-1 and Fig. 4-1, for the flanges of a welded box section

$$\lambda_r = \frac{238}{\sqrt{F_y - F_r}} = \begin{cases} \dfrac{238}{\sqrt{36 - 16.5}} = 53.9 & \text{if} \quad F_y = 36 \text{ ksi} \\[3mm] \dfrac{238}{\sqrt{50 - 16.5}} = 41.1 & \text{if} \quad F_y = 50 \text{ ksi} \end{cases}$$

for the web

$$\lambda_r = \frac{253}{\sqrt{F_y}} = \begin{cases} \dfrac{253}{\sqrt{36}} = 42.2 & \text{if} \quad F_y = 36 \text{ ksi} \\[3mm] \dfrac{253}{\sqrt{50}} = 35.8 & \text{if} \quad F_y = 50 \text{ ksi} \end{cases}$$

For the 18 in × 18 in box section in Fig. 4-3,

$$b = h_c = 18 \text{ in} - 2 \times \tfrac{1}{2} \text{ in} = 17 \text{ in}$$

$$t_f = t_w = t = \tfrac{1}{2} \text{ in}$$

$$\frac{b}{c} = \frac{h_c}{t_w} = \frac{17 \text{ in}}{\tfrac{1}{2} \text{ in}} = 34$$

(a)   In A36 steel, b/t and $h_c/t_w < \lambda_r$ in all cases; there are no slender elements.

(b)   If $F_y = 50$ ksi, there are also no slender elements, because b/t and $h_c/t_w < \lambda_r$ in all cases.

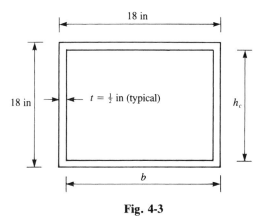

Fig. 4-3

In Probs. 4.4 to 4.7, determine the effective length factor K, from Table 4-2, for the given columns.

4.4.   A building column free to rotate at each end, in a braced frame.

As a result of the bracing, lateral translation of the ends of the column is inhibited. "Rotation free and translation fixed" at both ends is case d in Table 4-2; $K = 1.0$.

4.5.   A building column in a braced frame; deep beams rigidly connected to the column restrict rotation of its ends.

This corresponds to case a, "rotation fixed and translation fixed" at each end. Although $K = 0.65$ is indicated for this case in Table 4-2, it is customary to let $K = 1.0$ as a conservative minimum.

4.6. A building column in a rigid frame (not braced); end rotation is inhibited by deep beams.

"Rotation fixed and translation free" is case c; $K = 1.2$ is recommended.

4.7. The same as in Prob. 4.6, except that the base of the column is "pin-connected" to a footing.

"Rotation fixed and translation free" at the top and "rotation free and translation fixed" at the bottom is case f; $K = 2.0$.

In Probs. 4.8 to 4.10, use the alignment chart to determine K. All steel is A36.

4.8. The column shown in Fig. 4-4.

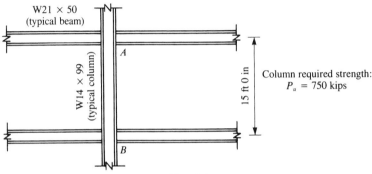

Fig. 4-4

All columns are W14×99, 15 ft 0 in long; all beams are W21×50, 30 ft 0 in long. The webs of all members are in the same plane, as shown.

For the typical column, W14×99: $I_x = 1110 \text{ in}^4$

$$l = 15.0 \text{ ft} \times 12 \text{ in/ft} = 180 \text{ in}$$

$$\frac{I_c}{l_c} = \frac{1110 \text{ in}^4}{180 \text{ in}} = 6.17 \text{ in}^3$$

For the typical beam, W21×50: $I_x = 948 \text{ in}^4$

$$l = 30.0 \text{ ft} \times 12 \text{ in/ft} = 360 \text{ in}$$

$$\frac{I_g}{l_g} = \frac{984 \text{ in}^4}{360 \text{ in}} = 2.73 \text{ in}^3$$

According to Eq. [4.1], the alignment chart parameter

$$G' = \frac{(I/l)_{c1} + (I/l)_{c2}}{(I/l)_{g1} + (I/l)_{g2}}$$

At both the upper (A) and lower (B) joints

$$G_A = G_B = \frac{2 \times 6.17 \text{ in}^3}{2 \times 2.73 \text{ in}^3} = 2.26$$

From Eq. [4.2], $G = G' \times \text{SRF}$.
Determining SRF (the stiffness reduction factor):

$$\frac{P_u}{A_g} = \frac{750 \text{ kips}}{29.1 \text{ in}^2} = 25.8 \text{ ksi}$$

Interpolating in Table 4-3, SRF = 0.39. At joints A and B, $G_A = G_B = G' \times \text{SRF} = 2.26 \times 0.39 = 0.88$. In Fig. 4-2, a straight line drawn from $G_A = 0.88$ to $G_B = 0.88$ intersects with $K = 1.3$.

4.9. Repeat Prob. 4.8, with the W14×99 columns (in Fig. 4-4) turned 90°.

For the typical column, W14×99: $I_y = 402$ in^4

$$l = 180 \text{ in} \qquad I_c/l_c = \frac{402 \text{ in}^4}{180 \text{ in}} = 2.23 \text{ in}^3$$

Typical beam $I_g/l_g = 2.73$, as in Prob. 4.8.
At joints A and B

$$G' = \frac{2 \times 2.23 \text{ in}^3}{2 \times 2.73 \text{ in}^3} = 0.82$$

The stiffness reduction factor, SRF = 0.39, as above. At joints A and B, $G_A = G_B = G' \times \text{SRF} = 0.82 \times 0.39 = 0.32$.
In Fig. 4-2, a straight line extended from $G_A = 0.32$ to $G_B = 0.32$ indicates that $K = 1.1$.

4.10. The column shown in Fig. 4-5. Column connection to the footing is (a) rigid, (b) pinned.

The W10×33 column is 12 ft 0 in high; the W16×26 beam is 30 ft 0 in long. The webs of the column and the beam are in the plane of the frame.

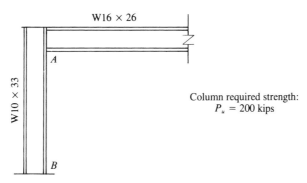

Column required strength:
$P_u = 200$ kips

Fig. 4-5

For the W10×33 column: $I_x = 170$ in^4

$$l = 12.0 \text{ ft} \times 12 \text{ in/ft} = 144 \text{ in}$$

$$\frac{I_c}{l_c} = \frac{170 \text{ in}^4}{144 \text{ in}} = 1.18 \text{ in}^3$$

For the W16×26 beam: $I_x = 301$ in^4

$$l = 30.0 \text{ ft} \times 12 \text{ in/ft} = 360 \text{ in}$$

$$\frac{I_c}{l_c} = \frac{301 \text{ in}^4}{360 \text{ in}} = 0.84 \text{ in}^3$$

From Eq. [4.1], $G'_A = 1.18/0.84 = 1.41$

$$\frac{P_u}{A_g} = \frac{200 \text{ kips}}{9.71 \text{ in}^2} = 20.6 \text{ ksi}$$

From Table 4-3, by interpolation, SRF = 0.72. At joint A, $G_A = G'_A \times \text{SRF} = 1.41 \times 0.72 = 1.02$.

(a) For rigid attachment to the foundation, $G_B = 1.0$. $K = 1.3$ in Fig. 4-2.

(b) For pin connection to the foundation, $G_B = 10$. Drawing a line in Fig. 4-2 from $G_A = 1.02$ to $G_B = 10$ indicates that $K = 1.9$.

4.11. In A36 steel, select a 6-in pipe (see Table 4-5) for a required axial compressive strength of 200 kips; $KL = 10.0$ ft

Table 4-5   6-in Pipe Sections

	A, in^2	r, in
Standard weight	5.58	2.25
Extrastrong	8.40	2.19
Double extrastrong	15.60	2.06

Try a 6-in standard weight pipe:

$$\frac{Kl}{r} = \frac{10.0 \text{ ft} \times 12 \text{ in/ft}}{2.25 \text{ in}} = 53.3$$

From Table 4-4 by interpolation, $\phi_c F_{cr} = 26.34$ ksi.

The design strength for this pipe, $\phi_c P_n = \phi_c F_{cr} = A_g = 26.34 \text{ kips} \times 5.58 \text{ in}^2 = 147 \text{ kips} < 200$ kips required.

Try a 6-in extrastrong pipe:

$$\frac{Kl}{r} = \frac{10.0 \text{ ft} \times 12 \text{ in/ft}}{2.19 \text{ in}} = 54.8$$

Interpolating in Table 4-4, $\phi_c F_{cr} = 26.13$ ksi. The design strength, $\phi_c P_n = \phi_c F_{cr} A_g = 26.13 \text{ kips/in}^2 \times 8.40 \text{ in}^2 = 219 \text{ kips} > 200$ kips required. This is okay.

4.12. Determine the design strength of a W8×40 column (A36 steel).

$$K_x L_x = K_y L_y = 15.0 \text{ ft}$$

For a W8×40 section, $A = 11.7$ in^2, $r_x = 3.53$ in, $r_y = 2.04$ in. Since $r_y < r_x$, $K_y l_y / r_y$ governs.

$$\frac{K_y l_y}{r_y} = \frac{15.0 \text{ ft} \times 12 \text{ in/ft}}{2.04 \text{ in}} = 88.2$$

From Table 4-4, $\phi_c F_{cr} = 20.32$ ksi.

The design strength of the column

$$\phi_c P_n = \delta_c F_{cr} A_g = 20.32 \text{ kips/in}^2 \times 11.7 \text{ in}^2 = 238 \text{ kips}$$

4.13. From the Column Tables in the AISC LRFD Manual, select a W10 column (A36 steel) for a required strength of 360 kips; $K_x L_x = K_y L_y = 12.0$ ft.

From Table 4-6 (reproduced with permission from the AISC LRFD Manual), it can be seen that in A36 steel, for $K_y L_y = 12.0$ ft, the design axial strength of a W10×49 column, $\phi_c P_n = 372$ kips. Since the 372 kips > 360 kips required strength, use a W10×49 column.

4.14. Select the most economical W10 column for the case shown in Fig. 4-6. Given: A36 steel; $K = 1.0$; required strength = 360 kips.

From Fig. 4-6: $K_x L_x = 1.0 \times 24.0 \text{ ft} = 24.0$ ft, $K_y L_y = 1.0 \times 12.0 \text{ ft} = 12.0$ ft. Assume y-axis buckling governs. From Table 4-6, for $K_y L_y = 12.0$ ft, select a W10×49 ($\phi_c P_n = 372$ kips > 360 kips required). Check x-axis buckling.

Table 4-6

$F_y = 36$ ksi												

$F_y = 50$ ksi	COLUMNS W shapes Design axial strength in kips ($\phi = 0.85$)											

Designation	W10											
Wt./ft	60		54		49		45		39		33	
F_y	36	50	36	50	36	50	36	50	36	50	36	50
0	539	748	483	672	441	612	407	565	352	489	297	413
6	517	706	464	634	422	577	380	515	328	444	276	373
7	509	692	457	621	416	565	371	497	320	428	269	360
8	500	675	449	606	409	551	361	478	311	412	261	345
9	491	657	440	590	401	536	350	458	301	393	252	329
10	480	638	431	572	392	520	337	436	290	374	243	312
11	469	617	420	553	382	502	324	412	278	353	233	294
12	457	595	409	533	372	484	311	388	266	332	222	276
13	444	571	398	512	361	465	296	364	254	310	211	257
14	430	547	385	490	350	444	282	339	241	289	200	239
15	416	523	373	468	338	424	267	315	228	267	189	220
16	401	497	360	445	326	403	252	290	215	246	177	202
17	387	472	346	422	314	382	237	266	201	225	166	184
18	371	446	332	399	301	361	222	243	188	205	155	167
19	356	421	318	376	288	340	207	221	175	185	144	150
20	340	395	304	353	275	319	192	199	162	167	133	135
22	309	346	276	309	250	278	164	164	138	138	112	112
24	278	299	248	266	224	239	138	138	116	116	94	94
26	248	255	221	227	199	204	118	118	99	99	80	80
28	219	220	195	196	175	176	102	102	85	85	69	69
30	191	191	170	170	153	153	88	88	74	74	60	60
32	168	168	150	150	134	134	78	78	65	65	53	53
33	158	158	141	141	126	126	73	73	61	61		
34	149	149	133	133	119	119						
36	133	133	118	118	106	106						

Effective length (in feet) KL with respect to least radius of gyration r_y

Properties												
U	1.38	1.52	1.38	1.53	1.39	1.54	1.75	1.93	1.77	1.96	1.81	2.00
P_{wo} (kips)	99	138	83	116	73	101	79	109	64	89	55	77
P_{wi} (ksi)	15	21	13	19	12	17	13	18	11	16	10	15
P_{wo} (kips)	209	246	143	168	111	131	121	142	88	104	69	81
P_{ro} (kips)	94	130	77	106	64	88	78	108	57	79	38	53
L_o (ft)	10.7	9.1	10.7	9.1	10.6	9.0	8.4	7.1	8.3	7.0	8.1	6.9
L_r (ft)	48.1	32.6	43.9	30.2	40.7	28.3	35.1	24.1	31.2	21.8	27.4	19.7
A (in^2)	17.6		15.8		14.4		13.3		11.5		9.71	
l_x (in^4)	341		303		272		248		209		170	
l_y (in^4)	116		103		93.4		53.4		45		36.6	
r_y (in)	2.57		2.56		2.54		2.01		1.98		1.94	
Ratio r_x/r_y	1.71		1.71		1.71		2.15		2.16		2.16	

Note: Heavy line indicates $Kl\,r$ of 200.
Reproduced with permission from the AISC LRFD Manual.

35

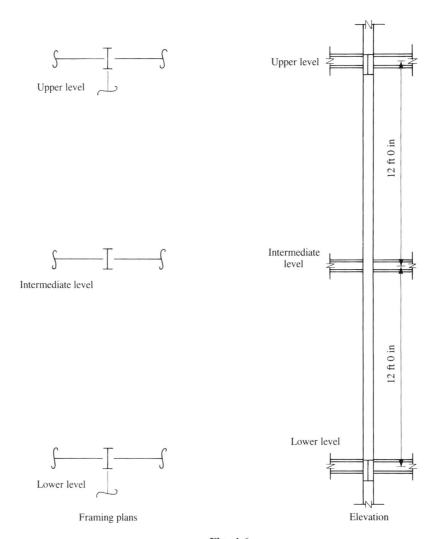

Fig. 4-6

For a W10×49, the ratio $r_x/r_y = 1.71$. (See bottom line in Table 4-6.) The equivalent $K_y L_y$ for use in the Column Tables:

$$(K_y L_y)_{\text{equiv}} = \frac{K_x L_x}{r_x/r_y} = \frac{24.0\,\text{ft}}{1.71} = 14.0\,\text{ft}$$

In Table 4-6, for $KL = 14.0$ ft, the W10×49 with a design strength $\phi_c P_n = 350$ kips is not adequate.

Use a W10×54 column with a design strength $\phi_c P_n = 385$ kips $(KL = 14.0\,\text{ft}) > 360$ kips required. Since $r_x/r_y = 1.71$ for the W10×54, as originally assumed, recomputation of $(K_y L_y)_{\text{equiv}}$ is not necessary.

4.15. A W10×49 column, 10 ft long, carries a service load of 250 kips. Calculate its axial shortening.

$$\text{Shortening, } \Delta = \frac{Pl}{EA_g} = \frac{250\,\text{kips} \times (10.0\,\text{ft} \times 12\,\text{in/ft})}{29{,}000\,\text{kips/in}^2 \times 14.4\,\text{in}^2}$$

$$= 0.072\,\text{in}$$

4.16. The section shown in Fig. 4-3 is used for a 40-ft column; $K_x = K_y = 1.0$. Determine the design compressive strength if the steel is A36.

The design compressive strength

$$\phi_c P_n = \phi_c F_{cr} A_g \qquad (E2\text{-}1)$$

The value of $\phi_c F_{cr}$ can be obtained from Table 4-4, if Kl/r is known. In this problem

$$Kl = 1.0 \times 40.0 \text{ ft} \times 12 \text{ in/ft} = 480 \text{ in}$$

$$r = \sqrt{\frac{I}{A}}$$

$$A = (18 \text{ in})^2 - (17 \text{ in})^2 = 35.0 \text{ in}^2$$

$$I_x = I_y = I = \frac{(18 \text{ in})^4 - (17 \text{ in})^4}{12} = 1788 \text{ in}^4$$

$$r = \sqrt{\frac{1788 \text{ in}^4}{35.0 \text{ in}^2}} = 7.15 \text{ in}$$

$$\frac{Kl}{r} = \frac{480 \text{ in}}{7.15 \text{ in}} = 67.2$$

By interpolation in Table 4-4, for $Kl/r = 67.2$, $\phi_c F_{cr} = 24.13$ ksi, the design compressive strength

$$\phi_c P_n = 24.13 \text{ kips/in}^2 \times 35.0 \text{ in}^2 = 845 \text{ kips}$$

Supplementary Problems

Are the following columns slender-element sections if

(*a*) $F_y = 36$ ksi?

(*b*) $F_y = 50$ ksi?

4.17. W12×26.   *Ans.*   (*a*) Yes. (*b*) Yes.

4.18. W12×35.   *Ans.*   (*a*) No. (*b*) Yes.

4.19. From Table 4-2, determine the effective length factor K for a column totally fixed at the bottom and totally free at the top.   *Ans.* $K = 2.1$; case *e*.

4.20. Use the alignment chart to calculate K for the column in Fig. 4-7 (A36 steel). All columns are W12×45, 15 ft 0 in long; all beams are W16×31, 20 ft 0 in long. The webs of all members are in the same plane.   *Ans.* $K = 1.3$.

4.21. Complete the design of the column in Prob. 4.8. Assume $K_y = 1.4$, $L_y = 15.0$ ft, for buckling perpendicular to the frame in Fig. 4-4. Select the most economical W14.   *Ans.*   W14×109.

4.22. Complete the design of the column in Prob. 4.9. Assume $K_x = 1.4$, $L_x = 15.0$ ft. Select the most economical W14.   *Ans.*   W14×99.

4.23. Repeat Prob. 4.14 for a required strength of 300 kips.   *Ans.*   W10×45.

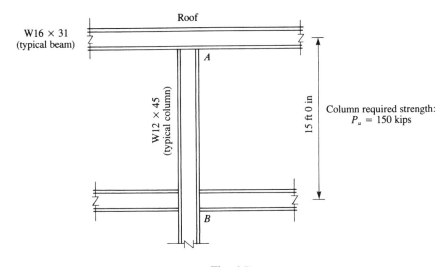

Fig. 4-7

4.24. Calculate the decrease in length of the 24-ft column in Prob. 4.22 under an axial load of 200 kips.

Ans. $\Delta = 0.15$ in.

Chapter 5

Compact Beams and Other Flexural Members

NOTATION

A = cross-sectional area of member, in^2

A_w = area of the web, in^2

b = width, in

b_f = width of flange, in

C_b = bending coefficient, defined in Eq. [5.10]

C_w = warping constant, in^6

c = distance from the centroid to the extreme fiber, in

d = overall depth, in

E = modulus of elasticity of steel = 29,000 ksi

F_r = compressive residual stress in flange, ksi

F_y = specified minimum yield stress, ksi

f_b = maximum normal stress due to bending, ksi

G = shear modulus of elasticity of steel = 11,200 ksi

h = web dimension defined in Fig. 5-7, in

h_c, h_w = web dimensions defined in Fig. 5-2, in

I = moment of inertia, in^4

J = torsional constant, in^4

L_b = unbraced length, ft

L_m = limiting unbraced length for full plastic bending capacity ($C_b > 1.0$), ft

L_p = limiting unbraced length for full plastic bending capacity ($C_b = 1.0$), ft

L_r = unbraced length which is the boundary between elastic and inelastic lateral-torsional buckling, ft

l = length of member, in

M = bending moment, kip-in

M_{cr} = elastic buckling moment, kip-in

M_n = nominal flexural strength of member, kip-in

M_p = plastic moment, kip-in

M_r = buckling moment at $L_b = L_r$ and $C_b = 1.0$, kip-in

M_1 = smaller end moment in an unbraced length of beam, kip-in

M_2 = larger end moment in an unbraced length of beam, kip-in

P = concentrated load on member, kips

r = radius of gyration, in

S = elastic section modulus, in^3

t = thickness, in

t_w = thickness of web, in

V = shear force, kips

V_n = nominal shear strength, kips

w = unit load, kips per linear ft

X_1 = parameter defined in Eq. $(F1\text{-}8)$

X_2 = parameter defined in Eq. $(F1\text{-}9)$

x = subscript relating symbol to the major principal centroidal axis

y = subscript relating symbol to the minor principal centroidal axis

Z = plastic section modulus, in^3

Δ = deflection of beam, in

λ_p = limiting width-thickness ratio for compact section

$\phi_b M_n$ = design flexural strength, kip-in

ϕ_b = resistance factor for flexure = 0.90

$\phi_v V_n$ = design shear strength, kips

ϕ_v = resistance factor for shear = 0.90

INTRODUCTION

This chapter covers compact flexural members not subjected to torsion or axial force. Compactness criteria as they relate to beams are described in the next section; noncompact flexural members are covered in Chap. 6. Axial tension combined with bending is the subject of Chap. 7; axial compression combined with bending is discussed in Chap. 8. Torsion and the combination of torsion with flexure are covered in Chap. 9.

The strength of flexural members is limited by *local buckling* of a cross-sectional element (e.g., the web or a flange), *lateral-torsional buckling* of the entire member, or the development of a *plastic hinge* at a particular cross section.

The equations given in this chapter (and in Chap. F of the AISC LRFD Specification) are valid for flexural members with the following kinds of compact cross sections and loadings: *doubly*

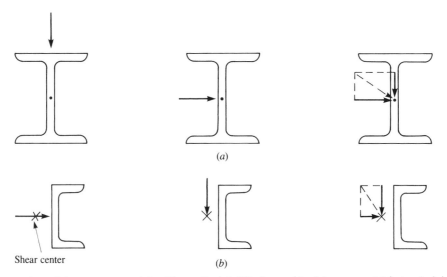

Fig. 5-1 Examples of beams covered in Chap. 5: (*a*) W shape (doubly symmetric) loaded in a plane of symmetry; (*b*) channel shape (singly symmetric) loaded through shear center in plane of symmetry or parallel to web

symmetric (e.g., W, box, and solid rectangular shapes), loaded in a plane of symmetry [as in Fig. 5-1(a)] and *singly symmetric* (e.g., channel shapes), loaded in the plane of symmetry or through the shear center parallel to the web [as in Fig. 5-1(b)].

The *shear center* is defined and its significance is explained in Chap. 9. Shear center locations for channels are given in the Properties Tables in Part 1 of the AISC LRFD Manual.

Loads not applied as shown in Fig. 5-1(a) and (b) will cause torsion, or twisting of the member. However, if restraint against torsion is provided at the load points and points of support, the equations of this chapter are still valid.

COMPACTNESS

The concept of compactness relates to local buckling. As described in more detail in Chap. 4, cross sections are classified as compact, noncompact, or slender-element sections. A section is compact if the flanges are continuously connected to the web, and the width-thickness ratios of all its compression elements are equal to or less than λ_p. Structural steel members with compact sections can develop their full strength without local instability. In design, the limit state of local buckling need not be considered for compact members.

Compactness criteria for beams (as stated in Sec. B5 of the AISC LRFD Specification) are given in Table 5-1 and Fig. 5-2. If the width-thickness ratios of the web and flange in flexural compression are equal to or less than λ_p, beam design is by the standard method described in this chapter. Otherwise the special provisions of Chap. 6 (taken from the appendixes of the AISC LRFD Specification) are required.

Table 5-1 Limiting Width-Thickness Ratios for Beams

Beam Element	Width-Thickness Ratio	Limiting Width-Thickness Ratio, λ_p	
		General	A36 Steel
Flanges of W and other I shapes and channels	b/t	$65/\sqrt{F_y}$	10.8
Flanges of square and rectangular box sections; flange cover plates and diaphragm plates between lines of fasteners or welds	b/t	$190/\sqrt{F_y}$	31.7
Webs in flexural compression	h_c/t_w	$640/\sqrt{F_y}$	106.7

FLEXURAL BEHAVIOR

The distribution of internal normal strains and stresses on the cross section of a beam is shown in Fig. 5-3. It is based on the idealized stress-strain diagram for structural steel in Fig. 5-4, which is a simplified version of the actual stress-strain curves in Fig. 1-2.

As shown in Fig. 5-3, the normal strain distribution is always linear. The magnitude of strain is proportional to the distance from the neutral (or centroidal) axis. On one side of the neutral axis, the fibers of the flexural member are in tension (or elongation); on the other side, in compression (or shortening). The distribution of normal stresses depends on the magnitude of the load. Under working loads and until initial yielding, stresses (which are proportional to strains in Fig. 5-4) are also linearly distributed on the cross section. Beyond initial yielding, the strain will increase under additional load. The maximum stress, however, is the yield stress F_y. Yielding will proceed inward, from the outer fibers to the neutral axis, as the load is increased, until a *plastic hinge* is formed.

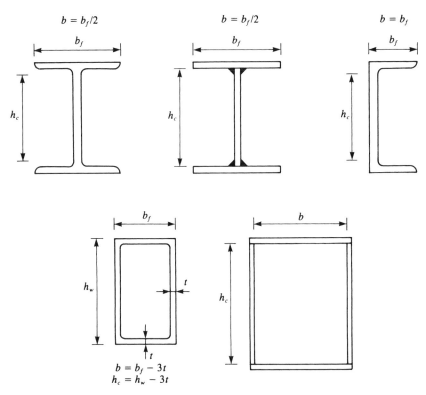

Fig. 5-2 Definitions of widths (b and h_c) and thickness (flange thickness t and web thickness t_w) for use in Table 5-1

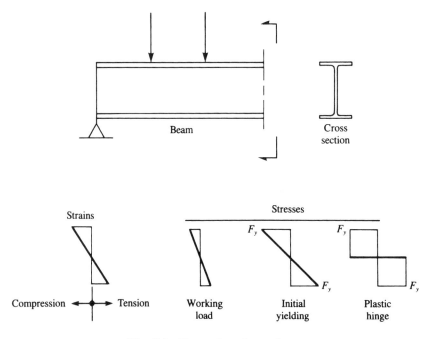

Fig. 5-3 Flexural strains and stresses

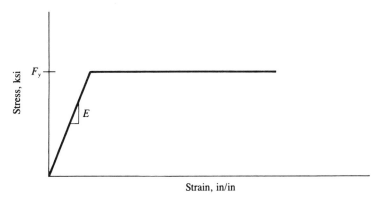

Fig. 5-4   Idealized stress-strain diagram for structural steel

The plastic hinge condition (under which the entire cross section has yielded) represents the absolute limit of usefulness of the cross section. Only beams which are compact (i.e., not susceptible to local buckling) and adequately braced (to prevent lateral-torsional buckling) can attain this upper limit of flexural strength.

The relationships between moment and maximum (extreme fiber) bending stresses, tension or compression, at a given cross section have been derived in a number of engineering mechanics textbooks. At the various stages of loading, they are as follows:

Until initial yielding

$$M = Sf_b \qquad\qquad [5.1]$$

At initial yielding

$$M_r = SF_y \qquad\qquad [5.2]$$

At full plastification (i.e., plastic hinge)

$$M_p = ZF_y \qquad\qquad [5.3]$$

Because of the presence of residual stresses F_r (prior to loading, as a result of uneven cooling after rolling of the steel member), yielding actually begins at an applied stress of $F_y - F_r$. Equation [5.2] should be modified to

$$M_r = S(F_y - F_r) \qquad\qquad [5.4]$$

Equation [5.3] is still valid, however. The plastic moment is not affected by residual stresses. (Because of their existence in a zero-moment condition before the application of loads, the tensile and compressive residual stresses must be in equilibrium.)

The terms in Eqs. [5.1] to [5.4] are defined as

M = bending moment due to the applied loads, kip-in

M_r = bending moment at initial yielding, kip-in

M_p = plastic moment, kip-in

S = elastic section modulus, in^3

Z = plastic section modulus, in^3

f_b = maximum normal stress due to bending, ksi

F_y = specified minimum yield stress, ksi

F_r = the maximum compressive residual stress in either flange; 10 ksi for rolled shapes; 16.5 ksi for welded shapes

$$\text{Elastic section modulus } S = \frac{I}{c} \qquad\qquad [5.5]$$

where I is the moment of inertia of the cross section about its centroidal axis, in^4; and c is the distance from the centroid to the extreme fiber, in. The Properties Tables in Part 1 of the AISC LRFD Manual include the values of I, S, and Z for all the rolled shapes listed.

ELASTIC VERSUS PLASTIC ANALYSIS

Design by either elastic or plastic analysis is permitted by the AISC LRFD Specification (Sec. A5.1). The more popular elastic analysis has been adopted throughout this text. When an elastic analysis procedure (such as moment distribution or a typical frame analysis computer program) is used, the factored moments are obtained assuming linear elastic behavior. Although this assumption is incorrect at the strength limit states, the fact that elastic analysis is less complex and is valid under normal service loads has led to its widespread use.

Several restrictions have been placed on plastic design. They are stated in the AISC LRFD Specification in Secs. A5.1, B5.2, C2.2, E1.2, F1.1, H1.2, and I1.

DESIGN FLEXURAL STRENGTH: $C_b = 1.0$, $L_b \leq L_r$

The design strength of flexural members is $\phi_b M_n$, where $\phi_b = 0.90$. For compact sections, the design bending strength is governed by the limit state of lateral-torsional buckling.

As the name implies, lateral-torsional buckling is an overall instability condition of a beam involving the simultaneous twisting of the member and lateral buckling of the compression flange. To prevent lateral-torsional buckling, a beam must be braced at certain intervals against either twisting of the cross section or lateral displacement of the compression flange. Unlike the bracing of columns (which requires another structural member framing into the column), the bracing of beams to prevent lateral-torsional buckling can be minimal. Even the intermittent welding of a metal (floor or roof) deck to the beam may be sufficient bracing for this purpose.

The equations for the nominal flexural strength M_n follow from the preceding discussion of flexural behavior. Length L_b is defined as the distance between points of bracing. Compact shapes bending about their minor (or y) axes will not buckle before developing a plastic hinge.

$$M_{ny} = M_{py} = Z_y F_y \qquad [5.6]$$

for bending about the minor axis regardless of L_b.

Compact sections bending about their major (or x) axes will also develop their full plastic moment capacity without buckling, if $L_b \leq L_p$.

$$M_{nx} = M_{px} = Z_x F_y \qquad [5.7]$$

for bending about the major axis if $L_b \leq L_p$.

If $L_b = L_r$, lateral-torsional buckling occurs at initial yielding. From Eq. [5.4],

$$M_{nx} = M_{rx} = S_x(F_y - F_r) \qquad [5.8]$$

for bending about the major axis if $L_b = L_r$.

If $L_p < L_b < L_r$, M_n for bending about the major axis is determined by linear interpolation between Eqs. [5.7] and [5.8]:

$$M_{nx} = M_{px} - (M_{px} - M_r)\left(\frac{L_b - L_p}{L_r - L_p}\right) \qquad [5.9]$$

In the foregoing

Z_y = plastic section modulus with respect to the minor centroidal (or y) axis, in^3

Z_x = plastic section modulus with respect to the major centroidal (or x) axis, in^3

S_x = elastic section modulus with respect to the major centroidal (or x) axis, in^3

Lengths L_p and L_r are defined in Sec. F1.2 of the AISC LRFD Specification as follows.

For I-shaped sections and channels bending about their major axis

$$L_p = \frac{300 r_y}{\sqrt{F_y}} \qquad (F1\text{-}4)$$

For solid rectangular bars and box beams

$$L_p = \frac{3750 r_y}{M_p} \sqrt{JA} \qquad (F1\text{-}5)$$

where r_y = the radius of gyration with respect to the minor centroidal (or y) axis, in

A = cross-sectional area, in^2

J = torsional constant, in^4

The limiting laterally unbraced length L_r and the corresponding buckling moment M_r are determined as follows.

For I-shaped sections, doubly symmetric and singly symmetric with the compression flange larger than or equal to the tension flange, and channels loaded in the plane of the web

$$L_r = \frac{r_y X_1}{F_y - F_r} \sqrt{1 + \sqrt{1 + X_2 (F_y - F_r)^2}} \qquad (F1\text{-}6)$$

$$M_r = (F_y - F_r) S_x \qquad (F1\text{-}7)$$

where

$$X_1 = \frac{\pi}{S_x} \sqrt{\frac{EGJA}{2}} \qquad (F1\text{-}8)$$

$$X_2 = 4 \frac{C_w}{I_y} \left(\frac{S_x}{GJ} \right)^2 \qquad (F1\text{-}9)$$

where E = modulus of elasticity of steel = 29,000 ksi

G = shear modulus of elasticity of steel = 11,200 ksi

I_y = moment of inertia about the minor centroidal (or y) axis, in^4

C_w = warping constant, in^6

For symmetric box sections bending about the major axis and loaded in the plane of symmetry, M_r and L_r shall be determined from formulas ($F1\text{-}7$) and ($F1\text{-}10$), respectively.

For solid rectangular bars bending about the major axis

$$L_r = \frac{57,000 r_y \sqrt{JA}}{M_r} \qquad (F1\text{-}10)$$

$$M_r = F_y S_x \qquad (F1\text{-}11)$$

Values of J and C_w for many structural shapes are listed in Torsion Properties Tables in Part 1 of the AISC LRFD Manual.

The practical design of steel beams ($C_b = 1.0$) can best be done graphically by (1) reference to the beam graphs in the section entitled Design Moments in Beams, in Part 3 of the AISC LRFD Manual, where $\phi_b M_n$ is plotted versus L_b for $F_y = 36$ and 50 ksi or (2) constructing a graph similar to Fig. 5-5 from data in the Load Factor Design Selection Table, also in Part 3 of the AISC LRFD Manual.

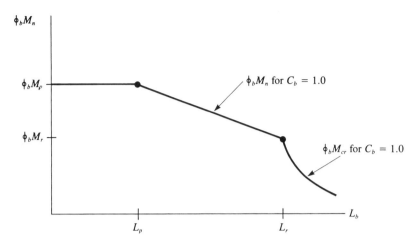

Fig. 5-5   Determination of design flexural strength $\phi_b M_p$ ($C_b = 1.0$)

BENDING COEFFICIENT C_b

The bending coefficient is defined as

$$C_b = \left[1.75 + 1.05\frac{M_1}{M_2} + 0.3\left(\frac{M_1}{M_2}\right)^2 \right] \le 2.3 \qquad [5.10]$$

where M_1 is the smaller and M_2 is the larger end moment for the unbraced segment of the beam under consideration. If the rotations due to end moments M_1 and M_2 are in opposite directions, then M_1/M_2 is negative; otherwise, M_1/M_2 is positive. Coefficient $C_b = 1.0$ for unbraced cantilevers and for members where the moment within part of the unbraced segment is greater than or equal to the larger segment end moment (e.g., simply supported beams, where $M_1 = M_2 = 0$).

Coefficient C_b accounts for the effect of moment gradient on lateral-torsional buckling. The LRFD moment capacity equations were derived for a beam with a constant moment braced only at the supports, failing in lateral-torsional buckling; $C_b = 1.0$. If the moment diagram between two successive braced points is not constant, the described region is less susceptible to lateral-torsional buckling; in general, $1.0 \le C_b \le 2.3$.

DESIGN FLEXURAL STRENGTH: $C_b \ge 1.0$, $L_b \le L_r$

Incorporating C_b requires modification of Eqs. [5.8] and [5.9]. Equation [5.7] does not change.

$$M_{nx} = M_{px} = Z_x F_y \qquad [5.7]$$

for bending about the major axis if $L_b \le L_m$. However,

$$M_{nx} = C_b M_r = C_b S_x (F_y - F_r) \le M_{px} \qquad [5.11]$$

for bending about the major axis if $L_b = L_r$, and the linear interpolation equation, Eq. [5.9], becomes

$$M_n = C_b \left[M_p - (M_p - M_r)\left(\frac{L_b - L_p}{L_r - L_p}\right) \right] \le M_p \qquad (F1\text{-}3)$$

for $L_m < L_b < L_r$. All the terms in the equations are as defined above. The relationships are shown graphically in Fig. 5-6, where it can be seen that L_m is the unbraced length at which Eqs. [5.7] and (F1-3) intersect.

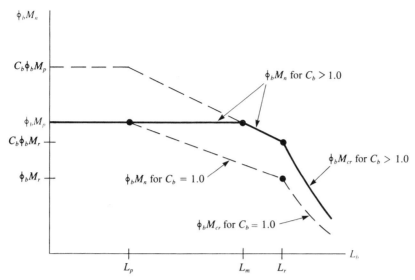

Fig. 5-6   Determination of design flexural strength $\phi_b M_n$ $(C_b > 1.0)$

The design of steel beams $(1.0 < C_b \leq 2.3)$ should be done graphically by developing a plot similar to that in Fig. 5-6. After determining C_b with Eq. [5.10], one can find the other required parameters $(L_p,\ \phi_b M_p,\ L_r,\ \text{and } \phi_b M_r)$ in the Load Factor Design Selection Table in Part 3 of the AISC LRFD Manual.

When $C_b > 1.0$, there is a twofold advantage in including $C_b > 1.0$ in Eqs. [5.11] and (F1-3), and not conservatively letting $C_b = 1.0$ (as in the graphs in Part 3 of the AISC LRFD Manual): (1) the unbraced length for which $M_n = M_p$ is extended from L_p to L_m, and (2) for $L_b > L_m$, the moment capacity M_n is multiplied by C_b. The reader can find these facts depicted in Fig. 5-6.

DESIGN FLEXURAL STRENGTH: $L_b > L_r$

If the unbraced length $L_b > L_r$ and $C_b = 1.0$, elastic lateral-torsional buckling occurs. There is a significant reduction in the flexural design strength $\phi_b M_n$ as L_b increases beyond L_r. Intermediate bracing should be provided, if possible, to avoid such uneconomical designs. However, if $L_b > L_r$

$$M_n = M_{cr} \leq M_p \qquad (F1\text{-}12)$$

for bending of a compact section about its major axis.

The critical elastic moment M_{cr} is defined as follows. For doubly symmetric I-shaped members and channels loaded in the plane of the web

$$M_{cr} = C_b \frac{\pi}{L_b} \sqrt{EI_y GJ + \left(\frac{\pi E}{L_b}\right)^2 I_y C_w}$$

$$= \frac{C_b S_x X_1 \sqrt{2}}{L_b / r_y} \sqrt{1 + \frac{X_1^2 X_2}{2(L_b / r_y)^2}} \qquad (F1\text{-}13)$$

For solid rectangular bars and symmetric box sections

$$M_{cr} = \frac{57{,}000 C_b \sqrt{JA}}{L_b / r_y} \qquad (F1\text{-}14)$$

GROSS AND NET CROSS SECTIONS

Flexural members are usually designed on the basis of their gross sections. According to Sec. B1 of the AISC LRFD Specification, the rules for beams with holes in the flanges are as follows:

(1) No deducation is made for holes in a given flange if the area of the holes is equal to or less than 15 percent of the gross area of the flange.

(2) For holes exceeding this limit, only the area of holes in excess of 15 percent is deducted.

DESIGN SHEAR STRENGTH

The shear strength of beams should be checked. Although flexural strength usually controls the selection of rolled beams, shear strength may occasionally govern, particularly for short-span members or those supporting concentrated loads. In built-up members, the thickness of the web plate is often determined by shear.

For rolled shapes and built-up members without web stiffeners, the equations in Sec. F2 of the AISC LRFD Specification can be somewhat simplified, as follows. The design shear strength is $\phi_v V_n$, where $\phi_v = 0.90$.

For $\dfrac{h}{t_w} \leq \dfrac{418}{\sqrt{F_y}}$

$$V_n = 0.6F_y A_w \qquad [5.12]$$

For $\dfrac{418}{\sqrt{F_y}} < \dfrac{h}{t_w} \leq \dfrac{523}{\sqrt{F_y}}$

$$V_n = 0.6F_y A_w \frac{418/\sqrt{F_y}}{h/t_w} \qquad [5.13]$$

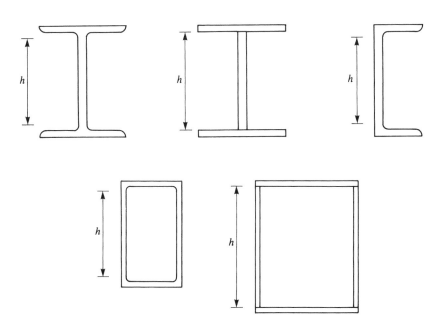

Fig. 5-7 Definition of h for various shapes

For $\dfrac{h}{t_w} > \dfrac{523}{\sqrt{F_y}}$

$$V_n = A_w \frac{132{,}000}{(h/t_w)^2} \qquad\qquad [5.14]$$

where V_n = nominal shear strength, kips

A_w = area of the web, $\text{in}^2 = d t_w$

d = overall depth, in

t_w = thickness of web, in

h = the following web dimensions, in: clear distance between fillets, for rolled shapes; clear distance between flanges for welded sections (See Fig. 5-7.)

The limit states for shear strength are yielding of the web in Eq. [5.12], inelastic buckling of the web in Eq. [5.13], and elastic buckling of the web in Eq. [5.14].

DISPLACEMENT AND VIBRATION

The two primary serviceability considerations for beams are displacement and vibration. Traditionally, the maximum deflections of floor beams have been limited to $\frac{1}{360}$ of the span under the service live load specified in the governing building code. Depending on the use of the member and its span, other deflection criteria (stated in inches or in fractions of the span) may be more appropriate. Formulas for maximum beam deflections under various loading conditions are given in many textbooks on engineering mechanics and in the AISC LRFD Manual, Part 3, under the heading Beam Diagrams and Formulas. The most common beam loadings are shown here in Table 5-2, together with the resulting maximum shears, moments, and deflections.

Table 5-2   Beam Formulas

Loading Condition	Maximum Value	Location
Simple beam—uniform load 	$M = \dfrac{wl^2}{8}$	Midspan
	$V = \dfrac{wl}{2}$	Ends
	$\Delta = \dfrac{5wl^4}{384EI}$	Midspan
Simple beam—concentrated load at center 	$M = \dfrac{Pl}{4}$	Midspan
	$V = \dfrac{P}{2}$	Ends
	$\Delta = \dfrac{Pl^3}{48EI}$	Midspan

Table 5-2—contd.

Loading Condition	Maximum Value	Location
Simple beam—concentrated load at any point 	$M = \dfrac{Pab}{l}$ $V = \dfrac{Pa}{l}$ $\Delta = \dfrac{Pab(a+2b)\sqrt{3a(a+2b)}}{27EIl}$	Point of load Right end $x = \sqrt{\dfrac{a(a+2b)}{3}}$
Cantilever beam—uniform load 	$M = \dfrac{wl^2}{2}$ $V = wl$ $\Delta = \dfrac{wl^4}{8EI}$	Fixed end Fixed end Free end
Cantilever beam—concentrated load at free end 	$M = Pl$ $V = P$ $\Delta = \dfrac{Pl^3}{3EI}$	Fixed end Fixed end Free end

Beams that are otherwise satisfactory have occasionally been the cause of annoying floor vibrations. Particularly sensitive are large open floor areas with long-span beams, free of partitions and other significant sources of damping, or energy release. To prevent excessive vibration it has been customary to specify the minimum depth of floor beams as a fraction (e.g., $\frac{1}{20}$) of their span. Another approach is to perform a simplified dynamic analysis. The subject of structural dynamics is beyond the scope of this text. Information on beam vibrations is available in several published journal papers, including:

T. M. Murray, "Acceptability Criterion for Occupant-Induced Floor Vibrations," *AISC Engineering Journal*, 2d Quarter, 1981.

T. M. Murray, "Design to Prevent Floor Vibrations," *AISC Engineering Journal*, 3d Quarter, 1975.

Solved Problems

In Probs. 5.1 to 5.3, determine whether the given beam is compact: (a) in A36 steel ($F_y = 36$ ksi), (b) if $F_y = 50$ ksi.

5.1. W6×15.

If the width-thickness ratio of an element is greater than λ_p, the section is noncompact.
Referring to Table 5-1 and Fig. 5-2, for the flanges of a W shape

$$\lambda_p = \frac{65}{\sqrt{F_y}} = \begin{cases} \dfrac{65}{\sqrt{36}} = 10.8 & \text{if} \quad F_y = 36\,\text{ksi} \\[2mm] \dfrac{65}{\sqrt{50}} = 9.2 & \text{if} \quad F_y = 50\,\text{ksi} \end{cases}$$

for the web of a W shape

$$\lambda_p = \frac{640}{\sqrt{F_y}} = \begin{cases} \dfrac{640}{\sqrt{36}} = 106.7 & \text{if} \quad F_y = 36\,\text{ksi} \\[2mm] \dfrac{640}{\sqrt{50}} = 90.5 & \text{if} \quad F_y = 50\,\text{ksi} \end{cases}$$

From the Properties Tables for W Shapes, in Part 1 of the AISC LRFD Manual (Compact Section Criteria): for a W6×15

$$\text{flange } \frac{b}{t} = \frac{b_f}{2t_f} = 11.5$$

$$\text{web } \frac{h_c}{t_w} = 21.6$$

Since flange ($b/t = 11.5$) > ($\lambda_p = 10.8$), the W6×15 beam is noncompact in A36 steel. Likewise, it is noncompact if $F_y = 50$ ksi.

5.2. W12×65.

From the Properties Tables for W Shapes, for a W12×65

$$\text{flange } \frac{b}{t} = \frac{b_f}{2t_f} = 9.9$$

$$\text{web } \frac{h_c}{t_w} = 24.9$$

(a) In A36 steel

$$\text{flange } \lambda_p = 10.8$$
$$\text{web } \lambda_p = 106.7 \qquad (\text{See Prob. 5.1.})$$

Since flange ($b/t = 9.9$) < ($\lambda_p = 10.8$), and web ($h_c/t_w = 24.9$) < ($\lambda_p = 106.7$), a W12×65 beam is compact in A36 steel.

(b) However, if $F_y = 50$ ksi

$$\text{flange } \lambda_p = 9.2$$
$$\text{web } \lambda_p = 90.5 \qquad (\text{See Prob. 5.1.})$$

Because flange ($b/t = 9.9$) > ($\lambda_p = 9.2$), a W12×65 beam is noncompact if $F_y = 50$ ksi.

5.3. The built-up beam section in Fig. 5-8.

Referring to Fig. 5-2:

$$\text{flange} \frac{b}{t} = \frac{b_f}{2t_f} = \frac{18 \text{ in}}{2 \times 1 \text{ in}} = 9.0$$

$$\text{web} \frac{h_c}{t_w} = \frac{40 \text{ in}}{0.5 \text{ in}} = 80.0$$

(a) The beam is compact in A36 steel because flange $(b/t = 9.0) < (\lambda_p = 10.8)$ and web $(h_c/t_w = 80.0) < (\lambda_p = 106.7)$.

(b) The beam is also compact if $F_y = 50$ ksi because flange $(b/t = 9.0) < (\lambda_p = 9.2)$ and web $(h_c/t_w = 80.0) < (\lambda_p = 90.5)$.

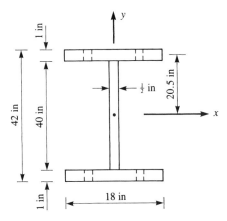

Fig. 5-8

5.4. For the cross section in Fig. 5-8, with four $1\frac{1}{16}$-in-diameter holes for bolts (two holes per flange, as shown), determine the design values of

(a) S_x, the elastic section modulus for major axis bending.

(b) Z_x, the plastic section modulus for major-axis bending.

For design purposes, the width of each bolt hole is taken as $\frac{1}{16}$ in greater than the nominal dimension of the hole. The "15 percent rule" is then applied to determine whether the gross section may be used in flexural design. For each flange

$$\text{Hole area} = 2 \times (1\tfrac{1}{16} + \tfrac{1}{16}) \text{ in} \times 1 \text{ in} = 2.25 \text{ in}^2$$

$$\text{Gross area} = 18 \text{ in} \times 1 \text{ in} = 18 \text{ in}^2$$

$$\frac{\text{Hole area}}{\text{Gross area}} = \frac{2.25 \text{ in}^2}{18 \text{ in}^2} = 13\%$$

Since the area of the holes is less than 15 percent of the flange area, the holes may be disregarded; the gross cross section is used in flexural design.

(a) $S_x = I_x/c$, where x is the major *centroidal* axis. For the symmetric section in Fig. 5-7, the centroid can be located by inspection. (Otherwise, calculation would be required.) Also

$$c = \frac{d}{2} = \frac{42 \text{ in}}{2} = 21 \text{ in}$$

The contributions of the two flanges and the web to the moment of inertia I_x are

Elements	$\dfrac{BT^3}{12} + AD^2$
2 Flanges	$\left[\dfrac{18 \text{ in} \times (1 \text{ in})^3}{12} + (18 \text{ in} \times 1 \text{ in})(20.5 \text{ in})^2\right] \times 2 = 15{,}132 \text{ in}^4$
Web	$\dfrac{0.5 \text{ in} \times (40 \text{ in})^3}{12} + 0. = 2{,}667 \text{ in}^4$
I_x	$17{,}799 \text{ in}^4$

$$S_x = \frac{17{,}799 \text{ in}^4}{21 \text{ in}} = 848 \text{ in}^3$$

(b) $Z_x = \Sigma AD$, where A is the cross-sectional area of each element and D represents its distance from the centroidal axis. In calculating Z_x, the upper half of the web (in flexural compression) and the lower half (in flexural tension) are taken separately.

Elements	AD
2 Flanges	$[(18 \text{ in} \times 1 \text{ in}) \times 20.5 \text{ in}] \times 2 = 738 \text{ in}^3$
2 half-Webs	$[(20 \text{ in} \times 0.5 \text{ in}) \times 10 \text{ in} \times 2 = 200 \text{ in}^3$
Z_x	938 in^3

$$Z_x = 938 \text{ in}^3$$

5.5. Repeat Prob. 5.4 for four $1\frac{9}{16}$-in-diameter holes.

For each flange, gross area $= 18 \text{ in}^2$ (as in Prob. 5.4), 15 percent of gross area $= 0.15 \times 18 \text{ in}^2 = 2.70 \text{ in}^2$, hole area $= 2 \times (1\frac{9}{16} + \frac{1}{16}) \text{in} \times 1 \text{ in} = 3.25 \text{ in}^2$.

In flexural design, only the hole area in excess of 15 percent of the flange area is deducted. Design hole area $= 3.25 \text{ in}^2 - 2.70 \text{ in}^2 = 0.55 \text{ in}^2$ for each flange.

(a) Adjusting I_x in Prob. 5.4:

$$\text{Hole } I_x = \Sigma AD^2 = [0.55 \text{ in}^2 \times (20.5 \text{ in})^2] \times 2 = 462 \text{ in}^4$$
$$\text{Net section } I_x = \text{gross section } I_x - \text{hole } I_x$$
$$= 17{,}799 \text{ in}^4 - 462 \text{ in}^4$$
$$= 17{,}337 \text{ in}^4$$
$$\text{Net section } S_x = \frac{I_x}{c} = \frac{17{,}337 \text{ in}^2}{21 \text{ in}} = 826 \text{ in}^3$$

(b) Adjusting Z_x in Prob. 5.4:

$$\text{Hole } Z_x = \Sigma AD = (0.55 \text{ in}^2 \times 20.5 \text{ in}) \times 2 = 23 \text{ in}^3$$
$$\text{Net section } Z_x = \text{gross section } Z_x - \text{hole } Z_x$$
$$= 938 \text{ in}^3 - 23 \text{ in}^3$$
$$= 915 \text{ in}^3$$

5.6. For a simply supported W24×76 beam, laterally braced only at the supports, determine the flexural design strength for (a) minor-axis bending and (b) major-axis bending. Use the Load Factor Design Selection Table for Beams in Part 3 of the AISC LRFD Manual, an excerpt from which appears herein (with permission) as Table 5-3. Steel is A36.

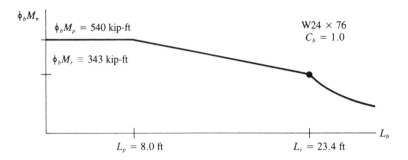

Fig. 5-9

The W24×76 is a compact section. This can be verified by noting that in the Properties Tables in Part 1 of the AISC LRFD Manual, both $b_f/2t_f$ and h_c/t_w for a W24×76 beam are less than the respective flange and web values of λ_p for $F_y = 36$ ksi (Table 5-1).

(a) For minor- (or y-) axis bending, $M_{ny} = M_{py} = Z_y F_y$ regardless of unbraced length (Eq. [5.6]). The flexural design strength for minor-axis bending of a W24×76 is always equal to $\phi_b M_{ny} = \phi_b Z_y F_y = 0.90 \times 28.6$ in$^3 \times 36$ ksi = 927 kip-in = 77 kip-ft.

(b) The flexural design strength for major-axis bending depends on C_b and L_b. For a simply supported member, the end moments $M_1 = M_2 = 0$; $C_b = 1.0$.

Figure 5-9 can be plotted from the information in Table 5-3:

$$\text{For } 0 < L_b < (L_p = 8.0 \text{ ft}), \quad \phi_b M_n = \phi_b M_p = 540 \text{ kip-ft}$$

At $L_b = L_r = 23.4$ ft, $\phi_b M_{nx} = \phi_b M_r = 343$ kip-ft. Linear interpolation is required for $L_p < L_b < L_r$. For $L_b > L_r$, refer to the beam graphs in Part 3 of the AISC LRFD Manual.

Table 5-3   Excerpt from Load Factor Design Selection Table (AISC LRFD Manual, Part 3)

Z_x, in^3	Shape	For $F_y = 36$ ksi			
		$\phi_b M_p$, kip-ft	$\phi_b M_r$, kip-ft	L_p ft	L_r ft
224	**W24×84**	**605**	**382**	**8.1**	**24.5**
221	W21×93	597	374	7.7	26.6
212	W14×120	572	371	15.6	67.9
211	W18×97	570	367	11.0	38.1
200	**W24×76**	**540**	**343**	**8.0**	**23.4**
198	W16×100	535	341	10.5	42.1
196	W21×83	529	333	7.6	24.9
192	W14×109	518	337	15.5	62.7
186	W18×86	502	324	11.0	35.5
186	W12×120	502	318	13.0	75.5
177	**W24×68**	**478**	**300**	**7.8**	**22.4**
175	W16×89	473	302	10.4	38.6

Note: Flexural design strength $\phi_b M_n = \phi_b M_p$ as tabulated is valid for $L_b \leq L_m$. If $C_b = 1.0$, $L_m = L_p$; otherwise, $L_m > L_p$. Here $\phi_b = 0.90$.

5.7. For the same W24×76 beam in major-axis bending, laterally braced at its centerline, with either a uniform load or a concentrated load at the center, determine the flexural design strength.

According to Eq. [5-10]

$$C_b = \left[1.75 + 1.05\frac{M_1}{M_2} + 0.3\left(\frac{M_1}{M_2}\right)^2\right] \le 2.3$$

Refer to Table 5-2. For either unbraced half of the beam under either loading indicated, $M_1 = 0$ and $M_2 > 0$; $M_1/M_2 = 0$. In Eq. [5-10], $C_b = (1.75 + 1.05 \times 0 + 0.3 \times 0) = 1.75$.

   Figure 5-10 can be derived from Fig. 5-9 as follows. For all L_b, the design flexural strength for $C_b = 1.75$, $\phi_b M_{nx}(C_b = 1.75) = 1.75 \times \phi_b M_{nx}(C_b = 1.0) \le \phi_b M_{px}$. The previous $(C_b = 1.0)$ design flexural strengths are multiplied by $(C_b = 1.75)$; however, the plastic moment strength $(\phi_b M_{px} = 540 \text{ kip-ft})$ cannot be exceeded.

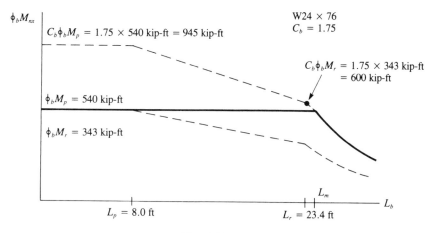

Fig. 5-10

5.8. Select the most economical rolled shape for a 27-ft simply supported floor beam. The upper (compression) flange of the beam is adequately welded to the floor deck at 1 ft 0-in intervals. Dead load supported by the beam (including its own weight) is 1.3 kips per linear foot; live load is 2.6 kips per linear foot. Steel is A36. Assume:

(*a*)   There is no member depth limitation.

(*b*)   The deepest (architecturally allowable) member is a W21.

(*c*)   The deepest desired member is a W18.

For the case of dead load and floor live load only, the critical load combination in Chap. 2 is formula (*A4-2*):

$$1.2D + 1.6L + 0.5(L_r \text{ or } S \text{ or } R) = 1.2 \times 1.3 \text{ kips/ft} + 1.6 \times 2.6 \text{ kips/ft} + 0 = 5.7 \text{ kips/ft}$$

For uniformly distributed loads, maximum $M = wl^2/8$ and $V = wl/2$. (See Table 5-2.)

$$\text{Required } M_u = \frac{5.7 \text{ kips/ft} \times (27 \text{ ft})^2}{8} = 521 \text{ kip-ft}$$

$$\text{Required } V_u = 5.7 \frac{\text{kips}}{\text{ft}} \times \frac{27 \text{ ft}}{2} = 77 \text{ kips}$$

Here, $L_b = 1.0 < L_p$ (all rolled shapes).

(a) In Table 5-3, as in the beam Selection Table in the LRFD Manual, the most economical beams appear in boldface print. Of those beams, the one of least weight for which $\phi_b M_n = \phi_b M_p \geq$ 521 kip-ft is a W24×76.

Checking shear strength with Eq. [5.12], for $h/t_w \leq (418/\sqrt{F_y} = 418/\sqrt{36} =)69.7$

$$V_n = 0.6 F_y A_w = 0.6 \times 36 \text{ ksi} \times dt_w$$
$$\phi_v V_n = 0.90 \times 0.6 \times 36 \text{ ksi } dt_w = 19.4 \text{ ksi} \times dt_w$$

For a W24×76, $h/t_w = 49.0 < 69.7$. (See Properties Tables for W Shapes in the AISC LRFD Manual, Part 1.) Then $\phi_v V_n = 19.4 \text{ ksi} \times 23.92 \text{ in} \times 0.440 \text{ in} = 205 \text{ kips} > 77$ kips required. Use a W24×76.

(b) By inspection of Table 5-3, the least-weight W21 for which $\phi_b M_{nx} = \phi_b M_{px} \geq 521$ kip/ft is a W21×83. Checking shear: $\phi_v V_n = 19.4 \text{ ksi} \times dt_w$. For a W21×83, $\phi_v V_n = 19.4 \text{ ksi} \times 21.43 \text{ in} \times 0.515 \text{ in} = 214 \text{ kips} > 77$ kips required. Use a W21×83.

(c) By inspection of Table 5-3, the least-weight W18 for which $\phi_b M_{nx} = \phi_b M_{px} \geq 521$ kip-ft is a W18×97. Checking shear: $\phi_v V_n = 19.4 \text{ ksi} \times dt_w$. For a W18×97, $\phi_v V_n = 19.4 \text{ ksi} \times 18.59 \text{ in} \times 0.535 \text{ in} = 193 \text{ kips} > 77$ kips required. Use a W18×97.

(Note: In lieu of calculations, the design shear strengths $\phi_v V_n$ for W shapes can be found tabulated in the section Uniform Load Constants in Part 3 of the AISC LRFD Manual.)

5.9. Repeat Prob. 5.8 assuming that the floor deck is not present and the beam is laterally braced only at midspan and the supports.

$$L_b = \frac{27 \text{ ft}}{2} = 13.5 \text{ ft}$$

For this case, $C_b = 1.75$, as in Prob. 5.7. From Fig. 5-10, it is evident that $L_b = 13.5 \text{ ft} < L_m$ for a W24×76. Similar plots will show the same values for the other beam sections in Table 5-3. For these shapes, the design flexural strength $\phi_b M_{nx} = \phi_p M_{px}$, as for the fully braced case. Accordingly, the results of Prob. 5.8 are still valid.

5.10. Repeat Prob. 5.8 for a beam braced only at its end supports.

Here, $C_b = 1.0$. For some of the W shapes in question, $L_b > L_r$. The beam graphs in Part 3 of the AISC LRFD Manual (for $C_b = 1.0$, $F_y = 36$ ksi) are helpful in this case. In the graphs, the solid lines denote the most economical W shape; the dashed lines indicate alternates. One page of the AISC beam graphs is reproduced (with permission) as Fig. 5-11, where it can be seen that at $L_b = 27$ ft, among the members with $\phi_b M_n \geq 521$ kip-ft, a W21×101 (solid line) is most economical; a W18×119 (dashed line) can be used if beam depth is limited to 18 in.

5.11. Determine C_b for the span of the continuous beam shown in Fig. 5-12.

(a) Lateral braces are provided only at the supports.

(b) Lateral braces are provided at midspan and the supports.

(a) In Eq. [5.10], $M_1/M_2 = -(500 \text{ kip-ft}/500 \text{ kip-ft}) = -1.0$ where M_1/M_2 is negative because the end moments M_1 and M_2 cause rotations in opposite directions.

$$C_b = 1.75 + 1.05 \frac{M_1}{M_2} + 0.3 \left(\frac{M_1}{M_2}\right)^2 \leq 2.3$$
$$= 1.75 + 1.05(-1.0) + 0.3(-1.0)^2$$
$$= 1.75 - 1.05 + 0.3$$
$$= 1.0$$

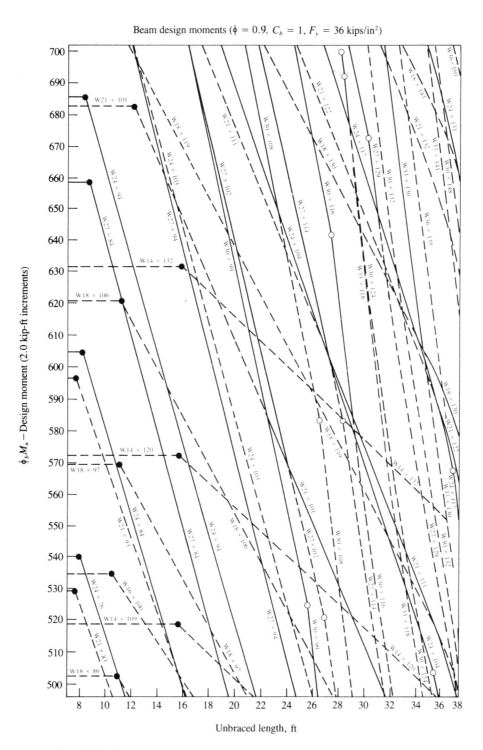

Beam design moments ($\phi = 0.9$, $C_b = 1$, $F_y = 36$ kips/in²)

Fig. 5-11   (*Reproduced with permission from the AISC LRFD Manual.*)

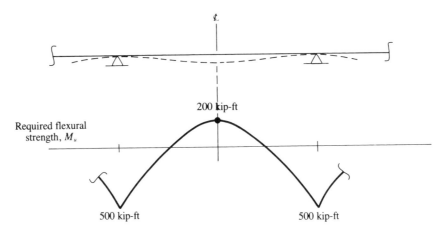

Fig. 5-12

(b)   In Eq. [5.10], $M_1/M_2 = +(200 \text{ kip-ft}/500 \text{ kip-ft}) = +0.4$ for both halves of the span. Here, M_1/M_2 is positive because the moments M_1 and M_2 cause rotations in the same direction.

$$C_b = 1.75 + 1.05(+0.4) + 0.3(+0.4)^2$$
$$= 1.75 + 0.42 + 0.05$$
$$= 2.22$$

5.12. Determine C_b for the span of the continuous beam shown in Fig. 5.13. Lateral bracing is provided only at the supports.

In Eq. [5.10], $M_1/M_2 = +(400 \text{ kip-ft}/400 \text{ kip-ft}) = +1.0$, where M_1/M_2 is positive because the end moments M_1 and M_2 cause rotations in the same direction.

$$C_b = 1.75 + 1.05\frac{M_1}{M_2} + 0.3\left(\frac{M_1}{M_2}\right)^2 \le 2.3$$
$$= 1.75 + 1.05(+1.0) + 0.3(+1.0)^2 \le 2.3$$
$$= 1.75 + 1.05 + 0.3 \le 2.3$$
$$= 3.10 \le 2.3$$
$$= 2.3$$

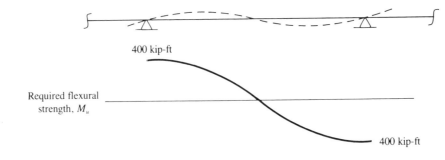

Fig. 5-13

5.13. Determine the following parameters for the built-up section in Fig. 5-8: $\phi_b M_{px}$, $\phi_b M_r$, L_p, and L_r (strong axis bending). Assume A36 steel.

According to Eq. [5.7], $M_{px} = Z_x F_y$. As determined in Prob. 5.4, $Z_x = 938$ in^3.

$$\phi_b M_{px} = \phi_b Z_x F_y = 0.90 \times 938 \text{ in}^3 \times 36 \text{ ksi}$$
$$= 30{,}391 \text{ kip-in} = 2533 \text{ kip-ft}$$

According to Eq. [5-8], $M_r = S_x(F_y - F_r)$. The residual stress $F_r = 16.5$ kips for welded shapes. As determined in Prob. 5.4, $S_x = 848$ in^3.

$$\phi_b M_r = \phi_b S_x(F_y - F_r) = 0.90 \times 848 \text{ in}^3 \times (36 - 16.5)\text{ksi}$$
$$= 14{,}882 \text{ kip-in} = 1240 \text{ kip-ft}$$

According to Eq. (F1-4), for I-shaped members

$$L_p = \frac{300 r_y}{\sqrt{F_y}}$$

The radius of gyration

$$r_y = \sqrt{\frac{I_y}{A}}$$

The contributions of the two flanges and the web to the moment of inertia I_y are

Elements	$\dfrac{BT^3}{12} + AD^2$
2 Flanges	$\left[\dfrac{1 \text{ in} \times (18 \text{ in})^3}{12} + 0\right] \times 2 = 972 \text{ in}^4$
Web	$\dfrac{40 \text{ in} \times (0.5 \text{ in})^3}{12} + 0 = 0.4 \text{ in}^4$
I_y	972 in^4

Cross-sectional area $A = (18 \text{ in} \times 1 \text{ in}) \times 2 + 40 \text{ in} \times 0.5 \text{ in} = 56 \text{ in}^2$ and

$$r_y = \sqrt{\frac{972 \text{ in}^2}{56 \text{ in}^2}} = 4.17 \text{ in}$$

$$L_p = \frac{300 \times 4.17 \text{ in}}{\sqrt{36}} = 208 \text{ in} = 17.4 \text{ ft}$$

According to Eq. (F1-6), for I-shaped members

$$L_r = \frac{r_y X_1}{F_y - F_r} \sqrt{1 + \sqrt{1 + X_2(F_y - F_r)^2}}$$

where

$$X_1 = \frac{\pi}{S_x} \sqrt{\frac{EGJA}{2}}$$

$$X_2 = 4 \frac{C_w}{I_y} \left(\frac{S_x}{GJ}\right)^2$$

Here, $r_y = 4.17$ in, $F_y - F_r = (36 - 16.5)$ ksi $= 19.5$ ksi, $S_x = 848$ in^3, $A = 56$ in^2, $E = 29{,}000$ ksi, $G = 11{,}200$ ksi, and

$$J \cong \frac{\Sigma bt^3}{3} = \tfrac{1}{3}\{[18 \text{ in} \times (1 \text{ in})^3]2 + [40 \text{ in} \times (0.5 \text{ in})^3]\}$$

$$= 13.67 \text{ in}^4$$

For I-shaped members, $C_w = (I_y/4)(d - t_f)^2$. Then

$$X_2 = \frac{4[(I_y/4)(d - t_f)^2]}{I_y} \left(\frac{S_x}{GJ}\right)^2 = \left[\frac{S_x(d - t_f)}{GJ}\right]^2$$

$$= \left[\frac{848 \text{ in}^3 \times (42 - 1) \text{ in}}{11{,}200 \text{ ksi} \times 13.67 \text{ in}^4}\right]^2 = 0.05$$

$$X_1 = \frac{\pi}{848 \text{ in}^3} \sqrt{\frac{29{,}000 \text{ ksi} \times 11{,}200 \text{ ksi} \times 13.67 \text{ in}^4 \times 56 \text{ in}^2}{2}} = 1306$$

$$L_r = \frac{4.17 \text{ in} \times 1306}{19.5 \text{ ksi}} \sqrt{1 + \sqrt{1 + 0.05(19.5 \text{ ksi})^2}}$$

$$= 658 \text{ in} = 55 \text{ ft}$$

5.14. Simply supported 30-ft-long floor beams, W18×35, are spaced 10 ft 0 in center-to-center. What is their maximum deflection under a live load of 50 lb/ft²?

$$w = 50 \frac{\text{lb}}{\text{ft}^2} \times 10.0 \text{ ft} = 500 \frac{\text{lb}}{\text{ft}} = 0.5 \frac{\text{kips}}{\text{ft}}$$

For a W18×35 beam, $I_x = 510$ in. From Table 5-2, for a uniformly loaded simply supported beam, the maximum deflection

$$\Delta = \frac{5wl^4}{384EI}$$

$$= \frac{5 \times 0.5 \dfrac{\text{kips}}{\text{ft}} \times (30 \text{ ft})^4}{384 \times 29{,}000 \dfrac{\text{kips}}{\text{in}^2} \times 510 \text{ in}^4} \times (12 \text{ in/ft})^3$$

$$= 0.62 \text{ in}$$

Since live load deflection

$$\Delta = 0.62 \text{ in} < \frac{L}{360} = \frac{30 \text{ ft} \times 12 \text{ in/ft}}{360} = 1.0 \text{ in}$$

it should generally be acceptable.

5.15. Determine the maximum deflections of the same W18×35 beams under concentrated loads of 7.5 kips at midspan.

From Table 5-2, for a concentrated load on a simply supported beam at midspan; the maximum deflection

$$\Delta = \frac{Pl^3}{48EI} = \frac{7.5 \text{ kips} \times (30 \text{ ft})^3 \times (12 \text{ in/ft})^3}{48 \times 29{,}000 \dfrac{\text{kips}}{\text{in}^2} \times 510 \text{ in}^4}$$

$$= 0.49 \text{ in}$$

Supplementary Problems

Are the beams in Probs. 5.16 and 5.17 compact

(a)   In A36 steel?

(b)   If $F_y = 50$ ksi?

5.16. W14×90.

   Ans. (*a*) Yes. (*b*) No.

5.17. W21×68.

   Ans. (*a*) Yes. (*b*) Yes.

5.18. For the W10×49 in Prob. 3.4 (Chap. 3), determine the appropriate design cross section for bending.

   Ans. The gross section.

5.19. The simply supported beam in Fig. 5-14 is subjected to a concentrated factored force of 50 kips. Steel is A36. Assume continuous lateral bracing.

   (*a*) Determine the required flexural strength.

   (*b*) Select the most economical W shape.

   (*c*) Select the most economical W21.

   (*d*) Select the most economical W16.

   Ans. (*a*) $M_u = 400$ kip-ft. (*b*) W24×62. (*c*) W21×68. (*d*) W16×77.

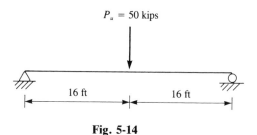

$P_u = 50$ kips

16 ft   16 ft

Fig. 5-14

5.20. The beam in Fig. 5-14 is braced at the supports and quarter points only. Determine C_b for each unbraced length.

   Ans. (See Fig. 5-15.)

$C_b =$ 1.75   1.30   1.30   1.75

Fig. 5-15

5.21. Select the most economical W section for the beam in Fig. 5-14, braced at the (*a*) supports and quarter points only; (*b*) supports and midspan only; (*c*) supports only.

   Ans. (*a*) W24×62. (*b*) W24×62. (*c*) W18×97.

5.22. The unfactored concentrated live load for the W24×62 beam in Fig. 5-14 is 20 kips. Determine the maximum live-load deflection.

   Ans. $\Delta = 0.61$ in.

Chapter 6

Noncompact Beams and Plate Girders

NOTATION

A = cross-sectional area of member, in^2

A_{st} = cross-sectional area of stiffener or pair of stiffeners, in^2

A_w = web area, in^2 = dt_w

a = clear distance between transverse stiffeners, in

a_r = ratio of web area to compression flange area

b = width, in

b_f = width of flange, in

C_b = bending coefficient, defined in Eq. [5.10]

C_v = shear parameter defined in Eqs. (A-G3-5) and (A-G3-6)

D = coefficient for use in Eq. (A-G4-2)

d = overall depth, in

F_{cr} = critical plate girder compression flange stress, ksi

F_r = compressive minimum yield stress, ksi

$F_{y,st}$ = specified minimum yield stress of the stiffener material, ksi

h, h_c = web dimensions defined in Fig. 6-2, in

I = moment of inertia, in^4

I_{st} = moment of inertia of stiffener or pair of stiffeners, in^4

J = torsional constant, in^4

j = coefficient defined in Eq. (A-G4-1)

k = coefficient defined in Eq. (A-G3-4)

L_b = unbraced length, ft

M_n = nominal flexural strength of member, kip-in

M_p = plastic moment, kip-in

M_r = limiting buckling moment when $\lambda = \lambda_r$, kip-in

M_u = required flexural strength, kip-in

R_{PG} = plate girder flexural coefficient, defined in Eq. (A-G2-3)

r = radius of gyration, in

r_T = radius of gyration of the compression flange plus one-third of the compression portion of the web taken about an axis in the plane of the web, in

S = elastic section modulus, in^3

S_{xc} = elastic section modulus referred to the compression flange, in^3

S_{xt} = elastic section modulus referred to the tension flange, in^3

t = thickness, in

t_f = thickness of flange, in

t_w = thickness of web, in

V_n = nominal shear strength, kips

V_u = required shear strength, kips

x = subscript relating symbol to the major principal centroidal axis

y = subscript relating symbol to the minor principal centroidal axis

Z = plastic section modulus, in³

λ = slenderness parameter (e.g., width-thickness ratio)

λ_p = largest value of λ for which $M_n = M_p$

λ_r = largest value of λ for which buckling is inelastic

$\phi_b M_n$ = design flexural strength, kip-in

ϕ_b = resistance factor for flexure = 0.90

$\phi_v V_n$ = design shear strength, kips

ϕ_v = resistance factor for shear = 0.90

INTRODUCTION

This chapter covers flexure of noncompact members, that is, beams with a width-thickness ratio (for flange or web) $> \lambda_p$. The subject of the next section is noncompact beams with a width-thickness ratio (λ): $\lambda_p < \lambda \le \lambda_r$. Plate girders with slender webs ($\lambda > \lambda_r$), usually stiffened, are covered in the following section.

NONCOMPACT BEAMS

The flexural design strength is $\phi_b M_n$, where $\phi_b = 0.90$. For noncompact beams, the nominal flexural strength M_n is the lowest value determined from the limit states of

lateral-torsional buckling (LTB)

flange local buckling (FLB)

web local buckling (WLB).

For $\lambda_p < \lambda \le \lambda_r$, M_n in each limit state is obtained by linear interpolation between M_p and M_r, as follows.

For the limit state of lateral-torsional buckling,

$$M_n = C_b\left[M_p - (M_p - M_r)\left(\frac{\lambda - \lambda_p}{\lambda_r - \lambda_p}\right) \right] \le M_p \qquad (A\text{-}F1\text{-}2)$$

For the limit states of flange and web buckling

$$M_n = M_p - (M_p - M_r)\left(\frac{\lambda - \lambda_p}{\lambda_r - \lambda_p}\right) \qquad (A\text{-}F1\text{-}3)$$

For all limit states, if $\lambda \le \lambda_p$, $M_n = M_p$. Expressions for M_p, as well as for M_r, λ, λ_p, and λ_r in each limit state, are given in Table 6-1 (which is an abridged version of Table A-F1.1 in App. F of the AISC LRFD Specification).

As shown schematically in Fig. 6-1, the flexural design of noncompact beams can be accomplished by

Looking up in Table 6-1 values for M_p and M_r, λ_p, and λ_r for each of the relevant limit states.

Graphically interpolating in each case to obtain an M_n for the given λ.

Selecting the minimum M_n as the nominal flexural strength.

Table 6-1 Flexural Strength Parameters

Cross Sections	M_p	Limit State	M_r	λ	λ_p	λ_r
Channels and doubly and singly symmetric I-shaped beams bending about major axis	$F_y Z_x$	LTB: doubly symmetric members and channels	$(F_y - F_r)S_x$	$\dfrac{L_b}{r_y}$	$\dfrac{300}{\sqrt{F_y}}$	See Eqs. (*F1-6*), (*F1-8*), and (*F1-9*) in Chap. 5
		LTB: singly symmetric members	$(F_y - F_r)S_{xc}$ $\le F_y S_{xt}$	$\dfrac{L_b}{r_y}$	$\dfrac{300}{\sqrt{F_y}}$	Value of λ for which $M_{cr} = M_r$, with $C_b = 1$
		FLB	$(F_y - F_r)S_x$	$\dfrac{b}{t}$	$\dfrac{65}{\sqrt{F_y}}$	$\dfrac{141}{\sqrt{F_y - 10}}$ for rolled shapes $\dfrac{106}{\sqrt{F_y - 16.5}}$ for welded shapes
		WLB	$F_y S_x$	$\dfrac{h_c}{t_w}$	$\dfrac{640}{\sqrt{F_y}}$	$\dfrac{970}{\sqrt{F_y}}$
Channels and doubly symmetric I-shaped members bending about minor axis	$F_y Z_y$	FLB	$F_y S_y$	Same as for major-axis bending		
Solid rectangular bars bending about major axis	$F_y Z_x$	LTB	$F_y S_x$	$\dfrac{L_b}{r_y}$	$\dfrac{3570\sqrt{JA}}{M_p}$	$\dfrac{57{,}000\sqrt{JA}}{M_r}$
Symmetric box sections loaded in a plane of symmetry	$F_y Z$	LTB	$(F_y - F_r)S_x$	$\dfrac{L_b}{r_y}$	$\dfrac{3570\sqrt{JA}}{M_p}$	$\dfrac{57{,}000\sqrt{JA}}{M_r}$
		FLB	$F_y S_x$	$\dfrac{b}{t}$	$\dfrac{190}{\sqrt{F_y}}$	$\dfrac{238}{\sqrt{F_y - F_r}}$
		WLB	$F_y S_x$	$\dfrac{h_c}{t_w}$	$\dfrac{640}{\sqrt{F_y}}$	$\dfrac{970}{\sqrt{F_y}}$

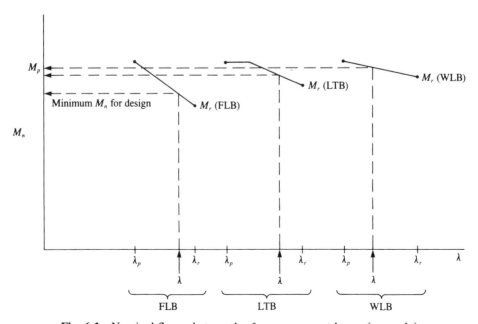

Fig. 6-1 Nominal flexural strength of a noncompact beam (example)

Shear capacity should also be checked, as indicated in Chap. 5. The design shear strength is $\phi_v V_n$, where $\phi_v = 0.90$ and V_n, the nominal shear strength, is determined from Eq. [5.12], [5.13], or [5.14].

The definitions of the terms used above are

> λ = slenderness parameter = minor axis slenderness ratio L_b/r_y for LTB = flange width-thickness ratio b/t, defined in Fig. 5-2, for FLB = web depth-thickness ratio h_c/t_w, defined in Fig. 5-2, for WLB
>
> λ_p = the largest value of λ for which $M_n = M_p$
>
> λ_r = largest value of λ for which buckling is inelastic
>
> M_n = nominal flexural strength, kip-in
>
> M_p = plastic moment, kip-in
>
> M_r = buckling moment at $\lambda = \lambda_r$, kip-in
>
> C_b = bending factor, as defined in Eq. [5.10]
>
> V_n = nominal shear strength, kips

Additional terms used in Table 6-1 are

> F_y = specified minimum yield stress, ksi
>
> Z_x = plastic section modulus about the major axis, in^3
>
> Z_y = plastic section modulus about the minor axis, in^3
>
> S_x = elastic section modulus about the major axis, in^3
>
> $S_{xc} = S_x$ with respect to the outside fiber of the compression flange, in^3
>
> $S_{xt} = S_x$ with respect to the outside fiber of the tension flange, in^3
>
> S_y = elastic section modulus about the minor axis, in^3
>
> L_b = laterally unbraced length, in
>
> r_y = radius of gyration about the minor axis, in
>
> b, t, h_c, t_w = dimensions of cross section, defined in Fig. 5-2, in
>
> A = cross-sectional area, in^2
>
> J = torsional constant, in^4
>
> F_r = compressive residual stress in the flange = 10 ksi for rolled shapes = 16.5 ksi for welded shapes

PLATE GIRDERS

In the AISC LRFD Specification, two terms are used for flexural members: *beam* and *plate girder*. The differences between them are as follows.

Beam	Plate Girder
Rolled or welded shape	Welded shape
No web stiffeners and web $h_c/t_w \leq 970/\sqrt{F_y}$	Web stiffeners or web $h_c/t_w > 970/\sqrt{F_y}$, or both

Stiffeners are discussed later in this chapter. Web stiffeners are not required if web $h_c/t_w < 260$ and adequate shear strength is provided by the web in accordance with Eqs. [5.12] to [5.14].

(*Please note*: Two different parameters in the AISC LRFD Specification refer to the clear height of the web: h and h_c. In Sec. B5 of the LRFD Specification they are thus defined:

For webs of rolled or formed sections, h is the clear distance between flanges less the fillet or corner radius at each flange; h_c is twice the distance from the neutral axis to the inside face of the compression flange less the fillet or corner radius.

For webs of built-up sections, h is the distance between adjacent lines of fasteners or the clear distance between flanges when welds are used and h_c is twice the distance from the neutral axis to the nearest line of fasteners at the compression flange or the inside face of the compression flange when welds are used.

The distinction between h and h_c is shown in Fig. 6-2, where it can be seen that for doubly symmetric cross sections, $h = h_c$.)

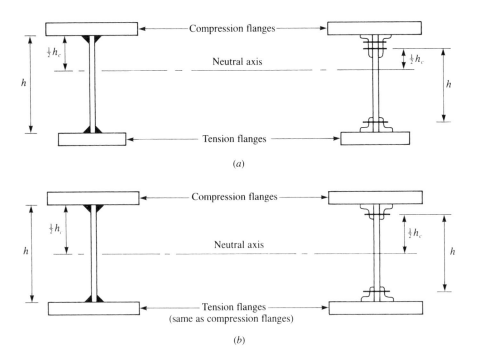

Fig. 6-2   Definitions of h and h_c: (a) singly symmetric built-up sections; (b) doubly symmetric built-up sections

For plate girders, the maximum permissible web slenderness h/t_w depends on the spacing of the stiffeners.

If

$$\frac{a}{h} \leq 1.5, \qquad \frac{h}{t_w} \leq \frac{2000}{\sqrt{F_y}} \qquad\qquad (A\text{-}G1\text{-}1)$$

If

$$\frac{a}{h} > 1.5, \qquad \frac{h}{t_w} \leq \frac{14,000}{\sqrt{F_y(F_y + F_r)}} \qquad\qquad (A\text{-}G1\text{-}2)$$

where a = clear distance between transverse stiffeners, in

t_w = web thickness, in

F_y = specified minimum yield stress of steel, ksi

F_r = compressive residual stress in flange = 16.5 ksi for plate girders

Plate girders are covered in App. G of the AISC LRFD Specification. The stiffening of slender plate girder webs enables them to exhibit significant postbuckling strength through "tension field action." After the web buckles, a girder acts like a Pratt truss: the stiffeners become vertical compression members, and the intermediate web panels act as diagonal tension members.

DESIGN FLEXURAL STRENGTH OF PLATE GIRDERS

The design flexural strength is $\phi_b M_n$, where $\phi_b = 0.90$. To determine the nominal flexural strength M_n: if $h_c/t_w \leq 970\sqrt{F_y}$, see Chap. 5 for compact shapes, and see the previous section of Chap. 6 for noncompact shapes.

If $h_c/t_w > 970/\sqrt{F_y}$ (i.e., the web is slender), M_n is governed by the limit states of tension flange yielding and compression flange buckling, as follows.

For yielding of the tension flange

$$M_{nx} = S_{xt}R_{PG}F_y \qquad (A\text{-}G2\text{-}1)$$

For buckling of the compression flange

$$M_{nx} = S_{xc}R_{PG}F_{cr} \qquad (A\text{-}G2\text{-}2)$$

The nominal flexural strength M_n is the lower value obtained from these equations, where

$$R_{PG} = 1 - 0.0005\, a_r\left(\frac{h_c}{t_w} - \frac{970}{\sqrt{F_{cr}}}\right) \leq 1.0 \qquad (A\text{-}G2\text{-}3)$$

where a_r = ratio of web area to compression flange area

F_{cr} = critical compression flange stress, ksi

F_y = minimum specified yield stress, ksi

S_{xc} = elastic section modulus referred to compression flange, in^3

S_{xt} = elastic section modulus referred to tension flange, in^3

The critical stress F_{cr} in Eq. (A-$G2$-2) depends on the slenderness parameters λ, λ_p, λ_r, and C_{PG}.

For $\lambda \leq \lambda_p$

$$F_{cr} = F_y \qquad (A\text{-}G2\text{-}4)$$

For $\lambda_p < \lambda \leq \lambda_r$

$$F_{cr} = C_b F_y\left[1 - \frac{1}{2}\left(\frac{\lambda - \lambda_p}{\lambda_r - \lambda_p}\right)\right] \leq F_y \qquad (A\text{-}G2\text{-}5)$$

For $\lambda > \lambda_r$

$$F_{cr} = \frac{C_{PG}}{\lambda^2} \qquad (A\text{-}G2\text{-}6)$$

The slenderness parameters are determined for both the limit state of lateral-torsional buckling and the limit state of flange local buckling; the lower value of F_{cr} governs.

For the limit state of lateral-torsional buckling

$$\lambda = \frac{L_b}{r_T} \qquad (A\text{-}G2\text{-}7)$$

$$\lambda_p = \frac{300}{\sqrt{F_y}} \qquad (A\text{-}G2\text{-}8)$$

$$\lambda_r = \frac{756}{\sqrt{F_y}} \qquad (A\text{-}G2\text{-}9)$$

$$C_{PG} = 286{,}000C_b \qquad (A\text{-}G2\text{-}10)$$

where C_b is determined from Eq. [5.10] and r_T is the radius of gyration of compression flange plus one-third of the compression portion of the web taken about an axis in the plane of the web, in. For the limit state of flange local buckling

$$\lambda = \frac{b_f}{2t_f} \qquad (A\text{-}G2\text{-}11)$$

$$\lambda_p = \frac{65}{\sqrt{F_y}} \qquad (A\text{-}G2\text{-}12)$$

$$\lambda_r = \frac{150}{\sqrt{F_y}} \qquad (A\text{-}G2\text{-}13)$$

$$C_{PG} = 11,200 \qquad (A\text{-}G2\text{-}14)$$

$$C_b = 1$$

The limit state of web local buckling is not applicable.

DESIGN SHEAR STRENGTH OF PLATE GIRDERS

The design shear strength is $\phi_v V_n$, where $\phi_v = 0.90$.
For $h/t_w \le 187\sqrt{k/F_y}$

$$V_n = 0.6A_w F_y \qquad (A\text{-}G3\text{-}1)$$

For $h/t_w > 187\sqrt{k/F_y}$

$$V_n = 0.6A_w F_y \left(C_v + \frac{1 - C_v}{1.15\sqrt{1 + (a/h)^2}} \right) \qquad (A\text{-}G3\text{-}2)$$

except for end panels and where

$$\frac{a}{h} > \begin{cases} 3.0 \\ \text{or} \\ \dfrac{260}{(h/t_w)^2} \end{cases} \qquad [6.1]$$

In such cases tension field action does not occur and

$$V_n = 0.6A_w F_y C_v \qquad (A\text{-}G3\text{-}3)$$

In the preceding equations

$$k = 5 + \frac{5}{(a/h)^2} \qquad (A\text{-}G3\text{-}4)$$

except that $k = 5.0$ if Expression [6.1] is true or if no stiffeners are present; A_w is the area of the web, $\text{in}^2 = dt_w$; and d is the overall depth, in.

If

$$187\sqrt{\frac{k}{F_y}} \le \frac{h}{t_w} \le 234\sqrt{\frac{k}{F_y}}, \qquad C_v = \frac{187\sqrt{k/F_y}}{h/t_w} \qquad (A\text{-}G3\text{-}5)$$

If

$$\frac{h}{t_w} > 234\sqrt{\frac{k}{F_y}}, \qquad C_v = \frac{44,000\,k}{(h/t_w)^2 F_y} \qquad (A\text{-}G3\text{-}6)$$

WEB STIFFENERS

Transverse stiffeners are required if web $h/t_w \geq 260$ or web shear strength, as determined from Chap. 5 (for unstiffened beams), is inadequate. The stiffeners should be spaced to provide sufficient shear strength in accordance with the preceding provisions for plate girders.

Additional requirements for stiffeners are

$$I_{st} \geq at_w^3 j \qquad [6.2]$$

whenever stiffeners are required

and

$$A_{st} \geq \frac{F_y}{F_{y,st}} \left[0.15 Dh t_w (1 - C_v) \frac{V_u}{\phi_v V_n} - 18 t_w^2 \right] \geq 0 \qquad (A\text{-}G4\text{-}2)$$

for tension field action

where

$$j = \frac{2.5}{(a/h)^2} - 2 \geq 0.5 \qquad (A\text{-}G4\text{-}1)$$

and I_{st} = moment of inertia of a transverse web stiffener about an axis in the web center for stiffener pairs or about the face in contact with the web plate for single stiffeners, in^4

A_{st} = cross-sectional area of a transverse web stiffeners, in^2

F_y = specified minimum yield stress of the girder steel, ksi

$F_{y,st}$ = specified minimum yield stress of the stiffener material, ksi

D = 1.0 for stiffeners in pairs
1.8 for single angle stiffeners
2.4 for single plate stiffeners

V_u = required shear strength at the location of the stiffener, ksi

and C_v and V_n are as defined above.

Plate girders with webs that depend on tension field action [i.e., their shear strength is governed by Eq. $(A\text{-}G3\text{-}2)$], must satisfy an additional criterion, flexure-shear interaction.

If

$$0.6 \frac{V_n}{M_n} \leq \frac{V_u}{M_u} \leq 1.33 \frac{V_n}{M_n}$$

then

$$\frac{M_u}{M_n} + 0.625 \frac{V_u}{V_n} \leq 1.24 \qquad (A\text{-}G5\text{-}1)$$

must be true. Here, V_u and M_u are the required shear and moment strengths at a cross section calculated from the factored loads; V_n and M_n are the nominal shear and moment strengths ($V_u \leq \phi V_n$ and $M_u \leq \phi M_n$; $\phi = 0.9$).

STIFFENER DETAILS

Special requirements apply to stiffeners at concentrated loads or reactions; see Chap. 12.

The web stiffeners provided in accordance with the provisions cited in this chapter may be one-sided or two-sided. If a pair of stiffeners is used, they can be welded to the web only. Single stiffeners are also welded to the compression flange, as are stiffeners attached to lateral bracing. The welds connecting stiffeners to girder webs are stopped short of the flange four to six web thicknesses from the near toe of the web-to-flange weld.

ROLLED VERSUS BUILT-UP BEAMS

Because they are more economical than their welded equivalents, rolled beams are used whenever possible. Rolled W shapes (the most popular beams) are available in depths of 4 to 40 in (W4 to W40). Welded girders are used when (1) the depth must exceed 40 in or (2) the rolled shapes available for the specified depth do not provide sufficient bending strength (a function of Z_x) or stiffness (a function of I_x). Regardless of whether rolled or welded shapes are utilized, beams are normally oriented to take advantage of the superior major-axis properties ($Z_x > Z_y$ and $I_x > I_y$).

Solved Problems

6.1. For the welded section in Fig. 6-3 (selected from the table of Built-Up Wide-Flange Sections in Part 3 of the AISC LRFD Manual), determine the design moment and shear strengths. Bending is about the major axis; $C_b = 1.0$. The (upper) compression flange is continuously braced by the floor deck. Steel is A36.

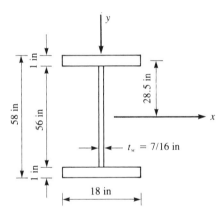

Fig. 6-3

First, compactness should be checked. Working with Table 6-1 (for a doubly symmetric I shape bending about its major axis):

Flange

$$\lambda = \frac{b}{t} = \frac{b_f}{2t_f} = \frac{18\text{ in}}{2 \times 1\text{ in}} = 9.0$$

(For the definition of b for a welded I shape, see Fig. 5-2.)

Flange

$$\lambda_p = \frac{65}{\sqrt{F_y}} = \frac{65}{\sqrt{36}} = 10.8$$

For the flange $\lambda < \lambda_p$. Therefore, the flange is compact, and $M_{nx} = M_{px}$ for the limit state of flange local buckling (FLB).

Web

$$\lambda = \frac{h_c}{t_w} = \frac{56\text{ in}}{\frac{7}{16}\text{ in}} = 128.0 \qquad \text{(See Fig. 6-2.)}$$

Web

$$\lambda_p = \frac{640}{\sqrt{F_y}} = \frac{640}{\sqrt{36}} = 106.7$$

Web

$$\lambda_r = \frac{970}{\sqrt{F_y}} = \frac{970}{\sqrt{36}} = 161.7$$

For the web, $(\lambda_p = 106.7) < (\lambda = 128.0) < (\lambda_r = 161.7)$. The web is noncompact; $M_{rx} < M_{nx} < M_{px}$ for the limit state of web local buckling (WLB); M_{nx} is determined from Eq. (A-F1-3).

Next, a check is made of lateral bracing, relating to the limit state of lateral-torsional buckling (LTB). For this continuously braced member, $L_b = 0$; $M_{nx} = M_{px}$ for LTB.

Summarizing:

Limit State	M_{nx}
LTB	M_{px}
FLB	M_{px}
WLB	$M_{rx} < M_{nx} < M_{px}$

The limit state of WLB (with minimum M_{nx}) governs. To determine M_{px}, M_{rx}, and M_{nx} for a doubly symmetric I-shaped member bending about the major axis, refer again to Table 6-1.

There $M_{px} = F_y Z_x$, $M_{rx} = F_y S_x$ for WLB and from Eq. (A-F1-3) (for WLB):

$$M_{nx} = M_{px} - (M_{px} - M_{rx})\left(\frac{\lambda - \lambda_p}{\lambda_r - \lambda_p}\right)$$

The properties S_x and Z_x of the cross section in Fig. 6-3 must now be calculated.

$$S_x = \frac{I_x}{c}, \quad \text{where} \quad c = \frac{d}{2} = \frac{58 \text{ in}}{2} = 29 \text{ in}$$

The contributions of the two flanges and the web to the moment of inertia I_x are

Elements	$\dfrac{BT^3}{12} + AD^2$	
2 Flanges	$\left[\dfrac{18 \text{ in} \times (1 \text{ in})^3}{12} + (18 \text{ in} \times 1 \text{ in})(28.5 \text{ in})^2\right]2$	$= 29{,}244 \text{ in}^4$
Web	$\dfrac{0.44 \text{ in} \times (56 \text{ in})^3}{12} + 0 =$	$6{,}403 \text{ in}^4$
I_x		$35{,}647 \text{ in}^4$

$$S_x = \frac{35{,}647 \text{ in}^4}{29 \text{ in}} = 1230 \text{ in}^3$$

To determine Z_x, we calculate ΣAD, where A is the cross-sectional area of each element and D represents its distance from the centroidal x axis.

In calculating Z_x, the upper and lower halves of the web are taken separately.

Elements	AD
Flanges	$[(18 \text{ in} \times 1 \text{ in}) \times 28.5 \text{ in}]2 = 1026 \text{ in}^3$
$2\frac{1}{2}$ Webs	$[(28 \text{ in} \times 0.44 \text{ in}) \times 14 \text{ in}]2 =$ 343 in^3
Z_x	1369 in^3

$$Z_x = 1369 \text{ in}^3$$

Determining flexural strengths, we obtain

$$M_{px} = F_y Z_x = \frac{36 \text{ kips/in}^2 \times 1369 \text{ in}^3}{12 \text{ in/ft}} = 4107 \text{ kip-ft}$$

$$M_{rx} = F_y S_x = \frac{36 \text{ kips/in}^2 \times 1230 \text{ in}^3}{12 \text{ in/ft}} = 3690 \text{ kip-ft}$$

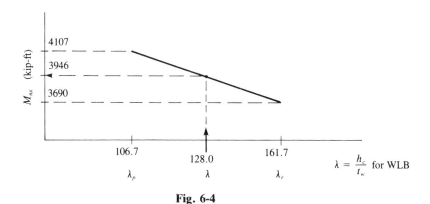

Fig. 6-4

The value of M_n can be obtained by linear interpolation using Fig. 6-4 or Eq. (A-F1-3): $M_{nx} = $ 3946 kip-ft.

The design flexural strength $\phi_b M_{nx} = 0.90 \times 3946$ kip-ft $= 3551$ kip-ft.

Shear strength for an unstiffened web is governed by Eq. [5.12], [5.13], or [5.14], depending on h/t_w.

Here, $h/t_w = 56$ in/0.44 in $= 128.0$.

$$128 > \frac{523}{\sqrt{F_y}} = \frac{523}{\sqrt{36}} = 87.2$$

Equation [5.14] governs:

$$V_n = A_w \frac{132,000}{(h/t_w)^2} = \frac{(58 \text{ in} \times 0.44 \text{ in}) \times 132,000}{(128.0)^2}$$

$$= 204.4 \text{ kips}$$

The design shear strength $\phi_v V_n = 0.90 \times 204.4$ kips $= 184.0$ kips.

6.2. The welded beam in Prob. 6.1 frames into a column as shown in Fig. 6-5. Design web stiffeners to double the shear strength of the web at the end panel.

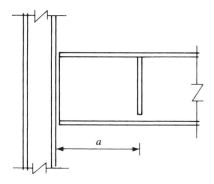

Fig. 6-5

At end panels there is no tension field action. The nominal shear strength for a stiffened web is determined from Eq. (A-G3-3): $V_n = 0.6A_w F_y C_v$. Assuming

$$\frac{h}{t_w} > 234 \sqrt{\frac{k}{F_y}}, \qquad C_v = \frac{44,000 \, k}{(h/t_w)^2 F_y} \qquad\qquad (A\text{-}G3\text{-}6)$$

Substituting for C_v in Eq. $(A\text{-}G3\text{-}3)$, we obtain

$$V_n = 0.6 A_w F_y \times \frac{44,000\, k}{(h/t_w)^2 F_y} = A_w \frac{26,400\, k}{(h/t_w)^2}$$

As indicated in the text of this chapter, the case of no stiffeners corresponds to $k = 5$. (This can be verified by comparing the just-derived expression for V_n with Eq. [5.14].)
    To double the shear strength, let $k = 2 \times 5 = 10$. In Eq. $(A\text{-}G3\text{-}4)$

$$k = 5 + \frac{5}{(a/h)^2} = 10$$

This implies $a/h = 1.0$ or $a = h$; thus, the clear distance between transverse web stiffeners $a = h = 56$ in.
    Checking the original assumption, we obtain

$$\left(\frac{h}{t_w} = \frac{56\ \text{in}}{0.44\ \text{in}} = 128.0 \right) > \left(234\sqrt{\frac{k}{F_y}} = 234\sqrt{\frac{10}{36}} = 123.3 \right) \qquad \text{o.k.}$$

Stiffener design can be determined as follows. Because tension field action is not utilized, Eqs. $(A\text{-}G4\text{-}2)$ and $(A\text{-}G5\text{-}1)$ can be ignored. However, Formula [6.2] must be satisfied: $I_{st} \geq a t_w^3 j$

where

$$j = \frac{2.5}{(a/h)^2} - 2 \geq 0.5$$

$$j = \frac{2.5}{1^2} - 2 = 0.5$$

$$I_{st} \geq 56\ \text{in} \times (0.44\ \text{in})^3 \times 0.5 = 2.34\ \text{in}^4$$

Try a pair of stiffener plates, $2\frac{1}{2}$ in $\times \frac{1}{4}$ in as in Fig. 6-6

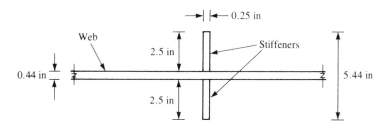

Fig. 6-6

The moment of inertia of the stiffener pair about the web centerline

$$I_{st} = \frac{0.25\ \text{in} \times (5.44\ \text{in})^3}{12} = 3.35\ \text{in}^4 > 2.34\ \text{in}^4 \qquad \text{o.k.}$$

Try a single stiffener plate, $3\frac{1}{2}$ in $\times \frac{1}{4}$ in, as in Fig. 6-7.

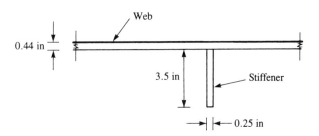

Fig. 6-7

The moment of inertia of the stiffener about the face of the web

$$I_{st} = \frac{0.25 \text{ in} \times (3.5 \text{ in})^3}{3} = 3.57 \text{ in}^4 > 2.34 \text{ in}^4 \qquad \text{o.k.}$$

6.3. See Prob. 6.1 and Fig. 6-3. Change the web thickness to $t_w = \frac{1}{4}$ in. Determine the design moment and shear strengths.

Checking web slenderness, we obtain

$$\left(\frac{h_c}{t_w} = \frac{56 \text{ in}}{0.25 \text{ in}} = 224 \right) > \left(\lambda_r = \frac{970}{\sqrt{F_y}} = \frac{970}{\sqrt{36}} = 161.7 \right)$$

Because the web is slender, the member is classified as a plate girder, and the flexural design provisions of this chapter govern [Eqs. (*A-G2-1*) to (*A-G2-14*)]. (Since $h/t_w = 224 < 260$, the girder web need only be stiffened if an increase in its shear strength is required.)

The flexural design equations can be solved as follows:
For the limit state of LTB

$$\lambda = \frac{L_b}{r_T} = 0 \qquad\qquad (A\text{-}G2\text{-}7)$$

because $L_b = 0$ for continuous bracing.

For the limit state of FLB

$$\lambda = \frac{b_f}{2t_f} = \frac{18 \text{ in}}{2 \times 1 \text{ in}} = 9.0 \qquad\qquad (A\text{-}G2\text{-}11)$$

$$9.0 < \left(\lambda_p = \frac{65}{\sqrt{F_y}} = \frac{65}{\sqrt{36}} = 10.8 \right) \qquad\qquad (A\text{-}G2\text{-}12)$$

Because $\lambda < \lambda_p$ for both LTB and FLB

$$F_{cr} = F_y = 36 \text{ ksi} \qquad\qquad (A\text{-}G2\text{-}4)$$

for this plate girder.

$$R_{PG} = 1 - 0.0005 a_r \left(\frac{h_c}{t_w} - \frac{970}{\sqrt{F_{cr}}} \right) \leq 1.0 \qquad\qquad (A\text{-}G2\text{-}3)$$

The ratio of web area to compression flange area

$$a_r = \frac{56 \text{ in} \times 0.25 \text{ in}}{18 \text{ in} \times 1 \text{ in}} = 0.78$$

$$R_{PG} = 1 - 0.0005 \times 0.78(224 - 161.7) = 0.98$$

The nominal flexural strength M_{nx} is the minimum of

$$M_{nx} = S_{xt} R_{PG} F_y \qquad\qquad (A\text{-}G2\text{-}1)$$

$$M_{nx} = S_{xc} R_{PG} F_{cr} \qquad\qquad (A\text{-}G2\text{-}2)$$

For a doubly symmetric shape, $S_{xt} = S_{xc} = S_x$. From above, $F_{cr} = F_y$ by Eq. (*A-G2-4*). Therefore, both equations for M_n reduce to

$$M_{nx} = S_x R_{PG} F_y$$

in this case.

Determining S_x, we obtain

$$S_x = \frac{I_x}{c}, \quad \text{where} \quad c = \frac{d}{2} = \frac{58 \text{ in}}{2} = 29 \text{ in}$$

The contributions of the two flanges and the web to the moment of inertia I_x are

Elements	$\dfrac{BT^3}{12} + AD^2$	
2 Flanges	$\left[\dfrac{18 \text{ in} \times (1 \text{ in})^3}{12} + (18 \text{ in} \times 1 \text{ in})(28.5 \text{ in})^2\right]2$	$= 29{,}244 \text{ in}^4$
Web	$\dfrac{0.25(56 \text{ in})^3}{12} + 0.$	$= 3{,}659 \text{ in}^4$
I_x		$32{,}903 \text{ in}^4$

$$S_x = \frac{32{,}903 \text{ in}^4}{29 \text{ in}} = 1135 \text{ in}^3$$

$$M_n = S_x R_{PG} F_y = \frac{1135 \text{ in}^3 \times 0.98 \times 36 \text{ kips/in}^2}{12 \text{ in/ft}} = 3337 \text{ kip-ft}$$

The design flexural strength $\phi_b M_n = 0.90 \times 3337$ kip-ft $= 3003$ kip-ft.

Shear strength for an unstiffened web is governed by Eq. [5.12], [5.13], or [5.14], depending on h/t_w.

Here, $h/t_w = 56 \text{ in}/0.25 \text{ in} = 224.0$

$$224 > \left(\frac{523}{\sqrt{F_y}} = \frac{523}{\sqrt{36}} = 87.2\right)$$

Equation [5.14] governs

$$V_n = A_w \frac{132{,}000}{(h/t_w)^2} = \frac{(58 \text{ in} \times 0.25 \text{ in})132{,}000}{(224.0)^2}$$

$$= 38.1 \text{ kips}$$

The design shear strength $\phi_v V_n = 0.90 \times 38.1$ kips $= 34.3$ kips.

6.4. Design web stiffeners for the end panels of the plate girder in Prob. 6.3, to increase shear strength. Assume $a = 24$ in.

Tension field action is not permitted for end panels of girders. The nominal shear strength is obtained from Eq. (A-G3-3) in this chapter: $V_n = 0.6A_w F_t C_v$.

To determine C_v:

$$k = 5 + \frac{5}{(a/h)^2} = 5 + \frac{5}{(24 \text{ in}/56 \text{ in})^2} = 32.2$$

Since

$$\left(\frac{h}{t_w} = \frac{56 \text{ in}}{0.25 \text{ in}} = 224\right) > \left(234\sqrt{\frac{k}{F_y}} = 234\sqrt{\frac{32.2}{36}} = 221.4\right)$$

$$C_v = \frac{44{,}000\,k}{(h/t_w)^2 F_y} \qquad \text{by Eq. } (A\text{-}G3\text{-}6)$$

Substituting for C_v in Eq. (A-G3-3), we have

$$V_n = 0.6A_w F_y \times \frac{44{,}000\,k}{(h/t_w)^2 F_y}$$

$$= A_w \frac{26{,}400\,k}{(h/t_w)^2}$$

$$= \frac{(58 \text{ in} \times 0.25 \text{ in})26{,}400 \times 32.2}{(56 \text{ in}/0.25 \text{ in})^2}$$

$$= 246 \text{ kips}$$

The design shear strength becomes $\phi_v V_n = 0.90 \times 246$ kips $= 221$ kips, a large increase over the 34.3-kip strength of an unstiffened web (in Prob. 6.3).

Stiffener design (with no tension field action) consists of complying with Formula [6.2]: $I_{st} \geq a t_w^3 j$

where
$$j = \frac{2.5}{(a/h)^2} - 2 \geq 0.5$$

$$= \frac{2.5}{(24\ \text{in}/56\ \text{in})^2} - 2 = 11.6$$

$$I_{st} \geq 24\ \text{in} \times (0.25\ \text{in})^3 \times 11.6 = 4.35\ \text{in}^4$$

Among the possible stiffener configurations are

(a) A single stiffener plate 4 in $\times \frac{1}{4}$ in
[The moment of inertia of the single stiffener about the face of the web

$$I_{st} = \frac{0.25\ \text{in} \times (4\ \text{in})^3}{3} = 5.33\ \text{in}^4 > 4.35\ \text{in}^4 \qquad \text{o.k.}]$$

(b) A pair of stiffener plates 3 in $\times \frac{1}{4}$ in
[The moment of inertia of the stiffener pair about the web centerline

$$I_{st} = \frac{0.25 \times (6.25\ \text{in})^3}{12} = 5.09\ \text{in}^4 > 4.35\ \text{in}^5 \qquad \text{o.k.}]$$

6.5. Repeat Prob. 6.4 for an intermediate web panel, including tension field action.

As in Prob. 6.4, $k = 32.2$, $h/t_w = 224$, and C_v is determined from Eq. (A-G3-6).

$$C_v = \frac{44,000\,k}{(h/t_w)^2 F_y} = \frac{44,000 \times 32.2}{(224)^2 \times 36} = 0.78$$

The nominal shear strength (including tension field action) is governed by Eq. (A-G3-2).

$$V_n = 0.6 A_w F_y \left[C_v + \frac{1 - C_v}{1.15\sqrt{1 + (a/h)^2}} \right]$$

$$V_n = 0.6 \times (58\ \text{in} \times 0.25\ \text{in}) \times 36\,\frac{\text{kips}}{\text{in}^2} \left[0.78 + \frac{1 - 0.78}{1.15\sqrt{1 + (24\ \text{in}/56\ \text{in})^2}} \right] = 300\ \text{kips}$$

The design shear strength is $\phi_v V_n = 0.90 \times 300$ kips $= 270$ kips.

Stiffener design taking advantage of tension field action must comply with formulas [6.2], (A-G4-2), and (A-G5-1). The designs in the solution to Prob. 6.4 comply with formula [6.2]. Checking formula (A-G4-2), we obtain

$$A_{st} \geq \frac{F_y}{F_{y,st}} \left[0.15 D h t_w (1 - C_v) \frac{V_u}{\phi_v V_n} - 18 t_w^2 \right] \geq 0$$

Assume $V_u = \phi_v V_n = 270$ kips.

(a) A single stiffener plate 4 in $\times \frac{1}{4}$ in

$$A_{st} \geq \frac{36\ \text{ksi}}{36\ \text{ksi}} \left[0.15 \times 2.4 \times 56\ \text{in} \times 0.25\ \text{in} \times (1 - 0.78) \times \frac{270\ \text{kips}}{270\ \text{kips}} - 18(0.25\ \text{in})^2 \right] = -0.02\ \text{in}^2$$

Any single stiffener plate ($A_{st} > 0$) is satisfactory.

(b) A pair of stiffener plates 3 in $\times \frac{1}{4}$ in

$$A_{st} \geq \frac{36\ \text{ksi}}{36\ \text{ksi}} \left[0.15 \times 1.0 \times 56\ \text{in} \times 0.25\ \text{in} \times (1 - 0.78) \times \frac{270\ \text{kips}}{270\ \text{kips}} - 18(0.25\ \text{in})^2 \right] = -0.66\ \text{in}^2$$

Any pair of stiffener plates ($A_{st} > 0$) is okay.

Regarding criterion $(A\text{-}G5\text{-}1)$ (flexure-shear interaction): $V_u = 270$ kips, $V_n = 300$ kips, $M_n = 3337$ kip-ft (from Prob. 6.3). Let the required flexural strength $M_u = 1500$ kip-ft at the same cross section.

Because
$$\left(\frac{V_u}{M_u} = \frac{270 \text{ kips}}{1500 \text{ kip-ft}} = 0.18/\text{ft}\right) > \left(1.33\frac{V_n}{M_n} = 1.33 \times \frac{300 \text{ kips}}{3337 \text{ kip-ft}} = 0.12/\text{ft}\right)$$

criterion $(A\text{-}G5\text{-}1)$ (flexure-shear interaction) need not be satisfied.

6.6. Determine the minimum web thickness for the plate girder in Fig. 6-3, both with and without web stiffeners; assume A36 steel.

According to the AISC LRFD Specification (App. G), in unstiffened girders h/t_w must be less than 260.

$$\frac{h}{t_w} < 260 \quad \text{implies that} \quad t_w > \frac{h}{260} = \frac{56 \text{ in}}{260} = 0.22 \text{ in}$$

In stiffened girders $(a/h \leq 1.5)$:

$$\frac{h}{t_w} \leq \frac{2000}{\sqrt{F_y}} = \frac{2000}{\sqrt{36}} = 333$$

In stiffened girders $(a/h > 1.5)$:

$$\frac{h}{t_w} \leq \frac{14,000}{\sqrt{F_y(F_y + 16.5)}} = \frac{14,000}{\sqrt{36(36 + 16.5)}} = 322$$

The minimum web thickness:

$$t_w > \frac{h}{333} = \frac{56 \text{ in}}{333} = 0.17 \text{ in}$$

if the stiffeners are closely spaced $(a/h \leq 1.5)$. The theoretical minimum web thicknesses for this plate girder are 0.22 in if not stiffened and 0.17 in if stiffened. However, because of the need to weld (the flange plates and stiffeners) to the web, a web thickness of less than $\frac{1}{4}$ in is inadvisable.

6.7. Repeat Prob. 6.1 (Fig. 6-3) with the following changes: $b_f = 30$ in, $L_b = 40$ ft, and $C_b = 1.75$.

Checking compactness with Table 6-1 (for a doubly symmetric I-shape bending about its major axis):

Flange
$$\lambda = \frac{b}{t} = \frac{b_f}{2t_f} = \frac{30 \text{ in}}{2 \times 1 \text{ in}} = 15.0$$

Flange
$$\lambda_p = \frac{65}{\sqrt{F_y}} = \frac{65}{\sqrt{36}} = 10.8$$

Flange
$$\lambda_r = \frac{106}{\sqrt{F_y - 16.5}} = \frac{106}{\sqrt{36 - 16.5}} = 24.0$$

For the flange, $(\lambda_p = 10.8) < (\lambda = 15.0) < (\lambda_r = 24.0)$.
From Prob. 6.1, for the web (which has not changed)

$$(\lambda_p = 106.7) < (\lambda = 128.0) < (\lambda_r = 161.7)$$

The flanges and web are noncompact; $M_r < M_n < M_p$ for the limit states of FLB and WLB. In both cases, M_{nx} is determined using the linear interpolation Eq. $(A\text{-}F1\text{-}3)$.
Regarding lateral bracing and the limit state of LTB: $\lambda = L_b/r_y$, where $r_y = \sqrt{I_y/A}$. The cross-sectional area $A = (30 \text{ in} \times 1 \text{ in})2 + (56 \text{ in} \times 0.44 \text{ in}) = 84.5 \text{ in}^2$. The contributions of the two flanges

and the web to the moment of inertia I_y are

Elements	$\dfrac{BT^3}{12} + AD^2$
2 Flanges	$\left[\dfrac{1\text{ in} \times (30\text{ in})^3}{12} + 0\right]2 = 4500\text{ in}^4$
Web	$\dfrac{56\text{ in} \times (0.44\text{ in})^3}{12} + 0 = 0.4\text{ in}^4$
I_y	4500 in^4

$$r_y = \sqrt{\dfrac{4500\text{ in}^4}{84.5\text{ in}^2}} = 7.30\text{ in}$$

For LTB,

$$\lambda = \dfrac{L_b}{r_y} = \dfrac{40\text{ ft} \times 12\text{ in/ft}}{7.3\text{ in}} = 65.8$$

For LTB

$$\lambda_p = \dfrac{300}{\sqrt{F_y}} = \dfrac{300}{\sqrt{36}} = 50.0$$

For LTB, λ_r can be determined (as indicated in Table 6-1) from Eqs. (F1-6), (F1-8), and (F1-9) in Chap. 5, as follows.

$$\lambda_r = \dfrac{L_r}{r_y} = \dfrac{X_1}{F_y - F_r}\sqrt{1 + \sqrt{1 + X_2(F_y - F_r)^2}}$$

where

$$X_1 = \dfrac{\pi}{S_x}\sqrt{\dfrac{EGJA}{2}}, \qquad X_2 = 4\dfrac{C_w}{I_y}\left(\dfrac{S_x}{GJ}\right)^2$$

$$F_y - F_r = (36 - 16.5)\text{ ksi} = 19.5\text{ ksi}, \qquad A = 84.5\text{ in}^2$$

$$E = 29{,}000\text{ ksi}, \qquad G = 11{,}200\text{ ksi},$$

$$J \cong \dfrac{\Sigma bt^3}{3} = \dfrac{1}{3}\{[30\text{ in} \times (1\text{ in})^3]2 + [56\text{ in} \times (0.44\text{ in})^3]\} = 21.6\text{ in}^4$$

For I-shaped members, $C_w = I_y/4(d - t_f)^2$. Then

$$X_2 = \dfrac{4[I_y/4(d - t_f)^2]}{I_y}\left(\dfrac{S_x}{GJ}\right)^2 = \left[\dfrac{S_x(d - t_f)}{GJ}\right]^2$$

$$S_x = \dfrac{I_x}{c} = \dfrac{I_x}{d/2} = \dfrac{I_x}{58\text{ in}/2} = \dfrac{I_x}{29\text{ in}}$$

The contributions of the two flanges and the web to the moment of inertia I_x are

Elements	$\dfrac{BT^3}{12} + AD^2$
2 Flanges	$\left[\dfrac{30\text{ in} \times (1\text{ in})^3}{12} + (30\text{ in} \times 1\text{ in})(28.5\text{ in})^2\right]2 = 48{,}740\text{ in}^4$
Web	$\dfrac{0.44\text{ in} \times (56\text{ in})^3}{12} + 0 = 6{,}403\text{ in}^4$
I_x	$55{,}143\text{ in}^4$

$$S_x = \dfrac{55{,}143\text{ in}^4}{29\text{ in}} = 1901\text{ in}^3$$

$$X_1 = \frac{\pi}{1901 \text{ in}^3} \sqrt{\frac{29{,}000 \text{ kips/in}^2 \times 11{,}200 \text{ kips/in}^2 \times 21.6 \text{ in}^4 \times 84.5 \text{ in}^2}{2}} = 900$$

$$X_2 = \left[\frac{1901 \text{ in}^3 \times (58-1) \text{ in}}{11{,}200 \text{ ksi} \times 21.6 \text{ in}^4}\right]^2 = 0.20$$

For LTB,

$$\lambda_r = \frac{900}{19.5} \sqrt{1 + \sqrt{1 + 0.20(19.5)^2}} = 144.3$$

For the limit state of LTB

$$(\lambda_p = 50.0) < (\lambda = 65.8) < (\lambda_r = 144.3)$$

In summary, for all three limit states (LTB, FLB, and WLB), $\lambda_p < \lambda < \lambda_r$; that is, the member is a noncompact beam, and the "noncompact beam" provisions of this chapter apply.

The equations for M_p and M_r are given in Table 6-1 (for a doubly symmetric I shape bending about its major axis)

$$M_{px} = F_y Z_x$$

$$M_{rx} = \begin{cases} (F_y - F_r)S_x & \text{for LTB and FLB} \\ F_y S_x & \text{for WLB} \end{cases}$$

To determine Z_x, we obtain ΣAD.

In calculating Z_x, the upper and lower halves of the web are taken separately.

Elements	AD
2 Flanges	$[(30 \text{ in} \times 1 \text{ in}) \times 28.5 \text{ in}]2 = 1710 \text{ in}^3$
2 half-Webs	$[(28 \text{ in} \times 0.44 \text{ in}) \times 14 \text{ in}]2 = 343 \text{ in}^3$
Z_x	2053 in^3

$$Z_x = 2053 \text{ in}^3$$

Determining flexural strengths, we obtain

$$M_{px} = F_y Z_x = \frac{36 \text{ kips/in}^2 \times 2053 \text{ in}^3}{12 \text{ in/ft}} = 6159 \text{ kip-ft}$$

For LTB and FLB

$$M_r = (F_y - F_r)S_x = \frac{19.5 \text{ kips/in}^2 \times 1901 \text{ in}^3}{12 \text{ in/ft}} = 3089 \text{ kip-ft}$$

For WLB

$$M_{rx} = F_y S_x = \frac{36 \text{ kips/in}^2 \times 1901 \text{ in}^3}{12 \text{ in/ft}} = 5703 \text{ kip-ft}$$

The various results for λ and M are plotted in Fig. 6-8. From the figure, or by solving Eqs. (A-F1-2) and (A-F1-3), it is evident that FLB governs for minimum M_{nx}; $M_{nx} = 5182$ kip-ft.

The design flexural strength $\phi_b M_{nx} = 0.90 \times 5182$ kip-ft $= 4664$ kip-ft.

The design shear strength is 184 kips as in Prob. 6.1.

6.8. Repeat Prob. 6.7 with an additional change. The thickness of the web is $t_w = \frac{1}{4}$ in.

The design shear strength is as in Probs. 6.3 (for an unstiffened web), 6.4, and 6.5 (for a stiffened web).

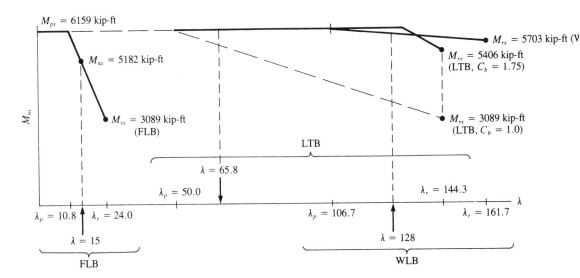

Fig. 6-8

Regarding flexural strength, the plate girder provisions must be applied because

$$\left(\frac{h_c}{t_w} = \frac{56\text{ in}}{0.25\text{ in}} = 224\right) > \left(\frac{970}{\sqrt{F_y}} = \frac{970}{\sqrt{36}} = 161.7\right)$$

The appropriate equations are $(A\text{-}G2\text{-}1)$ to $(A\text{-}G2\text{-}14)$.

For the limit state of LTB, $\lambda = L_b/r_T$

$$\lambda_p = \frac{300}{\sqrt{F_y}} = \frac{300}{\sqrt{36}} = 50.0$$

$$\lambda_r = \frac{756}{\sqrt{F_y}} = \frac{756}{\sqrt{36}} = 126.0$$

Determining r_T, we obtain $r_T = \sqrt{I_y/A}$ of a segment consisting of the compression flange plus one-sixth of the web. (See Fig. 6-9.)

Element	$\dfrac{BT^3}{12} + AD^2$
Flange	$\dfrac{1\text{ in} \times (30\text{ in})^3}{12} + 0 \quad = 2250\text{ in}^4$
$\frac{1}{6}$ Web	$\dfrac{9.3\text{ in} \times (0.25\text{ in})^3}{12} + 0 \ = 0$
I_y	2250 in^4

$$A = (30\text{ in} \times 1\text{ in}) + (9.3\text{ in} \times 0.25\text{ in}) = 32.3\text{ in}^2$$

$$r_T = \sqrt{\frac{2250\text{ in}^4}{32.3\text{ in}^2}} = 8.3\text{ in}$$

$$\lambda = \frac{L_b}{r_T} = \frac{40\text{ ft} \times 12\text{ in/ft}}{8.3\text{ in}} = 57.5$$

For LTB, $(\lambda_p = 50.0) < (\lambda = 57.5) < (\lambda_r = 126.0)$. The value of C_b is normally determined from Eq. [5.10]; however, $C_b = 1.75$ is stated in Prob. 6.7.

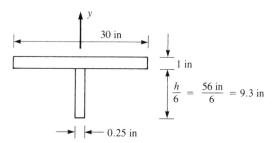

Fig. 6-9

Regarding the limit state of FLB

$$\lambda = \frac{b_f}{2t_f} = \frac{30 \text{ in}}{2 \times 1 \text{ in}} = 15.0$$

$$\lambda_p = \frac{65}{\sqrt{F_y}} = \frac{65}{\sqrt{36}} = 10.8$$

$$\lambda_r = \frac{150}{\sqrt{F_y}} = \frac{150}{\sqrt{36}} = 25.0$$

For FLB, $(\lambda_p = 10.8) < (\lambda = 15.0) < (\lambda_r = 25.0)$; $C_b = 1.0$ for FLB. The critical compression flange stress F_{cr} is the lower value obtained on the basis of LTB and FLB. Because $\lambda_p < \lambda < \lambda_r$ for both LTB and FLB, Eq. (*A-G2-5*) applies in both cases.

$$F_{cr} = C_b F_y \left[1 - \frac{1}{2} \left(\frac{\lambda - \lambda_p}{\lambda_r - \lambda_p} \right) \right] \le F_y$$

For LTB, we obtain

$$D_{cr} = 1.75 \times 36 \text{ ksi} \left[1 - \frac{1}{2} \left(\frac{57.5 - 50.0}{126.0 - 50.0} \right) \right] \le 36 \text{ ksi}$$

$$F_{cr} = 36 \text{ ksi}$$

For FLB

$$F_{cr} = 1.0 \times 36 \text{ ksi} \left[1 - \frac{1}{2} \left(\frac{15.0 - 10.8}{25.0 - 10.8} \right) \right] \le 36 \text{ ksi}$$

$$F_{cr} = 30.7 \text{ ksi}$$

$$R_{PG} = 1 - 0.0005 a_r \left(\frac{h_c}{t_w} - \frac{970}{\sqrt{F_{cr}}} \right) \le 1.0$$

$$a_r = \frac{56 \text{ in} \times 0.25 \text{ in}}{30 \text{ in} \times 1 \text{ in}} = 0.47$$

$$R_{PG} = 1 - 0.0005 \times 0.47 \times \left(\frac{56 \text{ in}}{0.25 \text{ in}} - \frac{970}{\sqrt{30.7}} \right) \lesssim 1.0$$

$$R_{PG} = 0.99$$

For the limit state of tension flange yielding

$$M_{nx} = S_{xt} R_{PG} F_y \qquad\qquad (A\text{-}G2\text{-}1)$$

For the limit state of compression flange buckling,

$$M_{nx} = S_{xc} R_{PG} F_{cr} \qquad\qquad (A\text{-}G2\text{-}2)$$

Because the plate girder is doubly symmetric, $S_{xt} = S_{xc} = S_x$. Also, $(F_{cr} = 30.7 \text{ ksi}) < (F_y = 36 \text{ ksi})$. Eq. (*A-G2-2*) governs.

Determining S_x:

Element	$\dfrac{BT^3}{12} + AD^2$	
2 Flanges	$\left[\dfrac{30 \text{ in} \times (1 \text{ in})^3}{12} + (30 \text{ in} \times 1 \text{ in})(28.5 \text{ in})^2 \right] 2$	$= 48{,}740 \text{ in}^4$
Web	$\dfrac{0.25 \text{ in} \times (56 \text{ in})^3}{12} + 0.$	$= 3{,}659 \text{ in}^4$
I_x		$52{,}399 \text{ in}^4$

$$S_x = \frac{I_x}{c} = \frac{52{,}399 \text{ in}^4}{58 \text{ in}/2} = 1807 \text{ in}^3$$

The nominal flexural strength

$$M_{nx} = S_x R_{PG} F_{cr} = \frac{1807 \text{ in}^3 \times 0.99 \times 30.7 \text{ ksi}}{12 \text{ in/ft}}$$

$$= 4576 \text{ kip-ft}$$

The design flexural strength $\phi_b M_{nx} = 0.90 \times 4576 \text{ kip-ft} = 4119 \text{ kip-ft}$.

Supplementary Problems

For Probs. 6.9 to 6.12, refer to Fig. 6-10 and determine

(a)   Whether the flexural member is a compact beam, noncompact beam, or plate girder.

(b)   The design flexural strength.

(c)   The design shear strength.

Assume A36 steel, $L_b = 0$, $C_b = 1.0$.

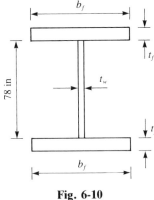

Fig. 6-10

6.9. $b_f = 13 \text{ in}$, $t_f = 2 \text{ in}$, $t_w = \frac{5}{8} \text{ in}$.

   Ans.   (a) Noncompact beam.   (b) $\phi_b M_{nx} = 7829 \text{ kip-ft}$.   (c) $\phi_v V_n = 391 \text{ kips}$.

6.10. $b_f = 13$ in, $t_f = 2$ in, $t_w = \frac{1}{4}$ in.

   Ans.   (*a*) Plate girder.   (*b*) $\phi_b M_{nx} = 5763$ kip-ft.   (*c*) $\phi_v V_n = 25$ kips.

6.11. $b_f = 26$ in, $t_f = 1$ in, $t_w = \frac{5}{8}$ in.

   Ans.   (*a*) Noncompact beam.   (*b*) $\phi_b M_{nx} = 7406$ kip-ft.   (*c*) $\phi_v V_n = 381$ kips.

6.12. $b_f = 26$ in, $t_f = 1$ in, $t_w = \frac{1}{4}$ in.

   Ans.   (*a*) Plate girder.   (*b*) $\phi_b M_{nx} = 5955$ kip-ft.   (*c*) $\phi_v V_n = 24$ kips.

6.13.   Design stiffeners to increase the design shear strength of the plate girder in Prob. 6.12 to 280 kips. Neglect tension field action.

   Ans.   Single 5 in $\times \frac{1}{4}$ in stiffener plates or pairs of 4 in $\times \frac{1}{4}$ stiffener plates, spaced at 2 ft 0 in in either case.

6.14.   For the plate girder with stiffeners in Prob. 6.13, determine the design shear strength if tension field action is included.   *Ans.* $\phi_v V_n = 371$ kips.

Chapter 7

Members in Flexure and Tension

NOTATION

e = eccentricity, in or ft

M = bending moment, kip-in or kip-ft

M_{nx} = nominal flexural strength for x-axis bending, kip-in or kip-ft

M_{ny} = nominal flexural strength for y-axis bending, kip-in or kip-ft

M_{ux} = required flexural strength for x-axis bending, kip-in or kip-ft

M_{uy} = required flexural strength for y-axis bending, kip-in or kip-ft

P = axial tensile force, kips

P_n = nominal tensile strength, kips

P_u = required tensile strength, kips

x = major principal centroidal axis

y = minor principal centroidal axis

$\phi_b M_{nx}$ = design flexural strength for x-axis bending, kip-in or kip-ft

$\phi_b M_{ny}$ = design flexural strength for y-axis bending, kip-in or kip-ft

ϕ_b = resistance factor for flexure = 0.90

$\phi_t P_n$ = design tensile strength, kips

ϕ_t = resistance factor for tension = 0.90 or 0.75 (See Chap. 3.)

INTRODUCTION

This chapter applies to singly and doubly symmetric members subjected to combined axial tension and bending about one or both principal axes. The combination of tension with flexure can result from any of the following:

(1) A tensile force that is eccentric with respect to the centroidal axis of the member, as in Fig. 7-1(a)

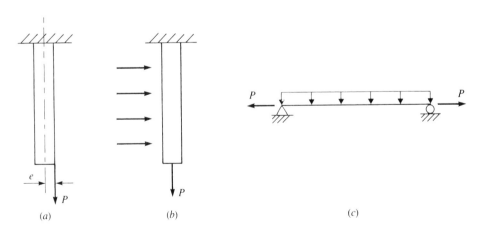

(a) (b) (c)

Fig. 7-1 Combined tension and flexure

(2)   A tension member subjected to lateral force or moment, as in Fig. 7-1(*b*)

(3)   A beam transmitting wind or other axial forces, as in Fig. 7-1(*c*)

INTERACTION FORMULAS

The cross sections of members with combined flexure and tension must comply with Formula (*H1-1a*) or (*H1-1b*), whichever is applicable:

For $(P_u/\phi_t P_n) \geq 0.2$

$$\frac{P_u}{\phi_t P_n} + \frac{8}{9}\left(\frac{M_{ux}}{\phi_b M_{nx}} + \frac{M_{uy}}{\phi_b M_{ny}}\right) \leq 1.0 \qquad\qquad (H1\text{-}1a)$$

For $(P_u/\phi_t P_n) < 0.2$

$$\frac{P_u}{2\phi_t P_n} + \left(\frac{M_{ux}}{\phi_b M_{nx}} + \frac{M_{uy}}{\phi_b M_{ny}}\right) \leq 1.0 \qquad\qquad (H1\text{-}1b)$$

In these interaction formulas, the terms in the numerators (P_u, M_{ux}, and M_{uy}) are the required tensile and flexural strengths calculated from the combinations of factored loads in Chap. 2. The terms in the denominators are as follows: $\phi_t P_n$ is the design tensile strength as determined in Chap. 3, and $\phi_b M_n$ is the design flexural strength as determined in Chap. 5 or 6. The subscript x refers to bending about the major principal centroidal (or x) axis; y refers to the minor principal centroidal (or y) axis.

Interaction formulas (*H1-1a*) and (*H1-1b*) cover the general case of axial force combined with biaxial bending. They are also valid for uniaxial bending (i.e., if $M_{ux} = 0$ or $M_{uy} = 0$), in which case they can be plotted as in Fig. 7-2.

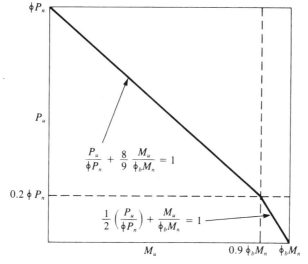

Fig. 7-2 Interaction formulas (*H1-1a*) and (*H1-1b*) modified for axial load combined with bending about one axis only

Solved Problems

7.1.   Find the lightest W8 in A36 steel to support a factored load of 100 kips in tension with an eccentricity of 6 in. The member is 6 ft long and is laterally braced only at the supports; $C_b = 1.0$. Try orientations (*a*) to (*c*) in Fig. 7-3.

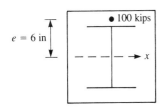 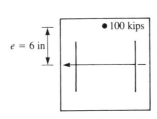 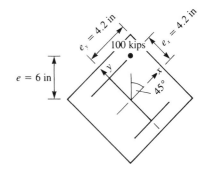

Fig. 7-3

Given

$$P_u = 100 \text{ kips}; \qquad M_u = P_u e = \frac{100 \text{ kips} \times 6 \text{ in}}{12 \text{ in/ft}} = 50 \text{ kip-ft}$$

For orientation (*a*) in Fig. 7.3

$$P_u = 100 \text{ kips}, \quad M_{ux} = 50 \text{ kip-ft}, \quad M_{uy} = 0$$

Try a W8×28: the design tensile strength (for a cross section with no holes)

$$\phi_t P_n = \phi_t F_y A_g \qquad\qquad\qquad \text{[Chap. 3, Eq. } (D1\text{-}1)\text{]}$$
$$= 0.90 \times 36 \text{ ksi} \times 8.25 \text{ in}^2 = 267 \text{ kips}$$

For $(L_b = 6.0 \text{ ft}) < (L_p = 6.8 \text{ ft})$, the design flexural strength for *x*-axis bending

$$\phi_b M_{nx} = \phi_b M_p = \phi_b Z_x F_y \qquad\qquad (\text{Chap. 5, Eq. } [5.7])$$
$$= \frac{0.90 \times 27.2 \text{ in}^3 \times 36 \text{ ksi}}{12 \text{ in/ft}} = 73.4 \text{ kip-ft}$$

which is also the tabulated value for $\phi_b M_p$ for a W8×28 in the Beam Selection Table in Part 3 of the AISC LRFD Manual.

Since
$$\frac{P_u}{\phi_t P_n} = \frac{100 \text{ kips}}{267 \text{ kips}} = 0.37 > 0.2$$

the first of the two interaction formulas applies.

$$\frac{P_u}{\phi_t P_n} + \frac{8}{9} \left(\frac{M_{ux}}{\phi_b M_{nx}} + \frac{M_{uy}}{\phi_b M_{ny}} \right) \leq 1.0$$

$$0.37 + \frac{8}{9} \left(\frac{50 \text{ kip-ft}}{73.4 \text{ kip-ft}} + 0 \right) = 0.37 + 0.61 = 0.98 < 1.0 \qquad \text{o.k.}$$

For orientation (*b*) in Fig. 7-3

$$P_u = 100 \text{ kips}, \quad M_{ux} = 0, \quad M_{uy} = 50 \text{ kip-ft}$$

Again, try a W8×28. For all L_b, the design flexural strength for *y*-axis bending

$$\phi_b M_{ny} = \phi_b M_p = \phi_b Z_y F_y \qquad\qquad (\text{Chap. 5, Eq. } [5.6])$$
$$= \frac{0.90 \times 10.1 \text{ in}^3 \times 36 \text{ ksi}}{12 \text{ in/ft}} = 27.2 \text{ kip-ft}$$

Because $M_{uy} = 50 \text{ kip-ft} > \phi_b M_{ny} = 27.2 \text{ kip-ft}$, a W8×28 is inadequate. Try a W8×48: $A_g = 14.1 \text{ in}^2$,

$Z_y = 22.9 \text{ in}^3$

$$\phi_b M_{ny} = \frac{0.90 \times 22.9 \text{ in}^3 \times 36 \text{ ksi}}{12 \text{ in/ft}} = 61.8 \text{ kip-ft}$$

$$\phi_t P_n = \phi_t F_y A_g = 0.90 \times 36 \frac{\text{kips}}{\text{in}^2} \times 14.1 \text{ in}^2 = 457 \text{ kips}$$

Because $(P_u/\phi_t P_n) = (100 \text{ kips}/457 \text{ kips}) = 0.22 > 0.2$, interaction formula $(H1\text{-}1a)$ again applies.

$$\frac{P_u}{\phi_t P_n} + \frac{8}{9}\left(\frac{M_{ux}}{\phi_b M_{nx}} + \frac{M_{uy}}{\phi_b M_{ny}}\right) \leq 1.0$$

$$0.22 + \frac{8}{9}\left(0 + \frac{50 \text{ kip-ft}}{61.8 \text{ kip-ft}}\right) = 0.22 + 0.72 = 0.94 < 1.0 \qquad \text{o.k.}$$

For orientation (c) in Fig. 7-3, assume that the load is eccentric with respect to both principal axes. Referring to Fig. 7-3(c)

$$e_x = e \cos 45° = 6 \text{ in} \times 0.707 = 4.2 \text{ in}$$

$$e_y = e \sin 45° = 6 \text{ in} \times 0.707 = 4.2 \text{ in}$$

$$M_{ux} = P_u e_x = \frac{100 \text{ kips} \times 4.2 \text{ in}}{12 \text{ in/ft}} = 35.4 \text{ kip-ft}$$

$$M_{uy} = P_u e_y = \frac{100 \text{ kips} \times 4.2 \text{ in}}{12 \text{ in/ft}} = 35.4 \text{ kip-ft}$$

Again, try a W8×48. As above

$$\frac{P_u}{\phi_t P_n} = \frac{100 \text{ kips}}{457 \text{ kips}} = 0.22 > 0.2$$

$$\phi_t M_{ny} = 61.8 \text{ kip-ft}$$

Although the W8×48 is not listed in the Beam Selection Table in the AISC LRFD Manual, L_p and $\phi_b M_{nx}$ can be calculated. From Eq. $(F1\text{-}4)$ (Chap. 5):

$$L_p = \frac{300 r_y}{\sqrt{F_y}} = \frac{300 r_y}{\sqrt{36}} = 50 r_y$$

$$= 50 \times 2.08 \text{ in} = 104 \text{ in} = 8.7 \text{ ft}$$

Since $(L_b = 6.0 \text{ ft}) < (L_p = 8.7 \text{ ft})$

$$\phi_b M_{nx} = \phi_b M_p = \phi_b Z_x F_y \qquad\qquad \text{(Chap. 5, Eq. [5.7])}$$

$$= \frac{0.90 \times 49.0 \text{ in}^3 \times 36 \text{ksi}}{12 \text{ in/ft}} = 132 \text{ kip-ft}$$

In Interaction Formula $(H1\text{-}1a)$

$$0.22 + \frac{8}{9}\left(\frac{35.4 \text{ kip-ft}}{132 \text{ kip-ft}} + \frac{35.4 \text{ kip-ft}}{61.8 \text{ kip-ft}}\right) \leq 1.0$$

$$0.22 + \tfrac{8}{9}(0.27 + 0.57)$$

$$0.22 + 0.75 = 0.97 < 1.0 \qquad \text{o.k.}$$

The most efficient configuration is orientation (a), strong axis bending, which requires a W8×28 as opposed to a W8×48 for the other two cases.

7.2. Determine the maximum axial tension that can be sustained by a continuously braced W10×19 beam with a required flexural strength $M_{ux} = 54$ kip-ft; A36 steel. Given are $M_{ux} = 54$ kip-ft and $M_{uy} = 0$.

For a W10×19

$$\phi_t P_n = \phi_t F_y A_g = 0.90 \times 36 \frac{\text{kips}}{\text{in}^2} \times 5.62 \text{ in}^2 = 182 \text{ kips}$$

Since $L_b = 0. < L_p$, $\phi_b M_{nx} = \phi_b M_p = 58.3$ kip-ft (A36 steel) as listed in the Beam Selection Table in the AISC LRFD Manual.

$$\frac{M_{ux}}{\phi_b M_{nx}} = \frac{54 \text{ kip-ft}}{58.3 \text{ kip-ft}} = 0.93$$

Inspection of Formulas (*H1-1a*) and (*H1-1b*) indicates that $(P_u / \phi_t P_n) < 0.2$ is required. Consequently, the latter interaction formula governs.

$$\frac{P_u}{2\phi_t P_n} + \left(\frac{M_{ux}}{\phi_b M_{nx}} + \frac{M_{uy}}{\phi_b M_{ny}} \right) \leq 1.0$$

$$\frac{P_u}{2 \times 182 \text{ kips}} + (0.93 + 0.) \leq 0$$

$$P_u \leq 26 \text{ kips}$$

The maximum required (or factored) axial tensile force is 26 kips.

7.3.   Check the adequacy of a W10×30 as a simply supported beam carrying the concentrated factored load shown in Fig. 7-4. The beam is of A36 steel and has lateral bracing only at the supports.

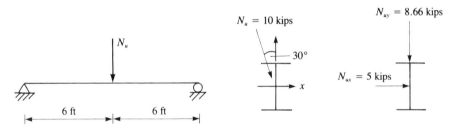

Fig. 7-4

This is a case of biaxial bending with no axial load ($P_u = 0$). Interaction Formula (*H1-1b*) is applicable since $P_u / P_n = 0 < 0.2$.

For $P_u = 0$, Formula (*H1-1b*) reduces to

$$\frac{M_{ux}}{\phi_b M_{nx}} + \frac{M_{uy}}{\phi_b M_{ny}} \leq 1.0$$

As shown in Fig. 7-4, the factored force N_u is skewed with respect to the principal axes. It must first be resolved into components parallel to each principal axis, as follows.

$$N_{uy} = N_u \cos 30° = 10 \text{ kips} \times 0.866 = 8.66 \text{ kips}$$

$$N_{ux} = N_u \sin 30° = 10 \text{ kips} \times 0.500 = 5.0 \text{ kips}$$

The respective bending moments are

$$M_{ux} = \frac{8.66 \text{ kips} \times 12 \text{ ft}}{4} = 26.0 \text{ kip-ft}$$

$$M_{uy} = \frac{5.0 \text{ kips} \times 12 \text{ ft}}{4} = 15.0 \text{ kip-ft}$$

where M_{ux} and M_{uy} are the required flexural strengths for *x*- and *y*-axis bending, respectively.

The design flexural strengths are determined as in Chap. 5. For a simple beam, $C_b = 1.0$. For x-axis bending, $\phi_b M_{nx}$ ($L_b = 12.0$ ft; $C_b = 1.0$) can be determined either directly from the beam graphs in Part 3 of the AISC LRFD Manual or by interpolation of the data in the Beam Selection Table presented therein. The latter procedure is shown in Fig. 7-5.

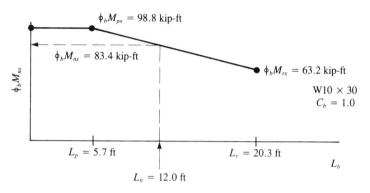

Fig. 7-5

Using either method one obtains $\phi_b M_{nx} = 83.4$ kip-ft for the W10×30.

For y-axis bending (regardless of L_b)

$$\phi_b M_{ny} = \phi_b Z_y F_y = \frac{0.90 \times 8.84 \text{ in}^3 \times 36 \text{ ksi}}{12 \text{ in/ft}} = 23.9 \text{ kip-ft}$$

Substituting in the interaction formula for biaxial bending ($P_u = 0$), we obtain

$$\frac{26.0 \text{ kip-ft}}{83.4 \text{ kip-ft}} + \frac{15.0 \text{ kip-ft}}{23.9 \text{ kip-ft}} \leq 1.0$$

$$0.31 \quad + \quad 0.63 \quad = 0.94 < 1.0 \qquad \text{o.k.}$$

7.4.   A 4-in-diameter standard pipe hanger ($A = 3.17$ in^2, $Z = 4.31$ in^3) supports a factored load of 40 kips. For A36 steel, determine the maximum acceptable eccentricity e; see Fig. 7-6.

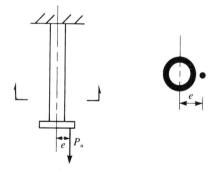

Fig. 7-6

$P_u = 40$ kips. Here

$$\phi_t P_n = \phi_t F_y A_g = 0.90 \times 36 \frac{\text{kips}}{\text{in}^2} \times 3.17 \text{ in} = 103 \text{ kips}$$

Because

$$\frac{P_u}{\phi_t P_n} = \frac{40 \text{ kips}}{103 \text{ kips}} = 0.39 > 0.2$$

use Formula ($H1$-$1a$), which for uniaxial bending becomes

$$\frac{P_u}{\phi_t P_n} + \frac{8}{9} \frac{M_u}{\phi_b M_n} \leq 1.0$$

$M_u = P_u e$. Because it has no "strong" and "weak" axes, a pipe section cannot fail in lateral-torsional buckling. For all L_b,

$$\phi_b M_n = \phi_b M_p = \phi_b Z F_y = 0.90 \times 4.31 \text{ in}^3 \times 36 \frac{\text{kips}}{\text{in}^2} = 140 \text{ kip-in}$$

Substituting in the modified Formula ($H1$-$1a$), we have

$$0.39 + \frac{8}{9} \times \frac{40 \text{ kips} \times e}{140 \text{ kip-in}} \leq 1.0$$

$$e \leq 2.4 \text{ in}$$

Supplementary Problems

7.5. Repeat Prob. 7.4 for $P_u = 20$ kips.   *Ans.* $e \leq 6.3$ in.

7.6. Select the least-weight W12 in A36 steel to resist an axial tension $P_u = 200$ kips combined with $M_{ux} = 100$ kip-ft and $M_{uy} = 50$ kip-ft.   *Ans.*   W12×72.

Chapter 8

Beam-Columns: Combined Flexure and Compression

NOTATION

B_1 = moment magnification factor for beam-columns defined in Eq. (*H1-3*)

B_2 = moment magnification factor for beam-columns defined in Eqs. (*H1-5*) and (*H1-6*)

C_m = coefficient for beam-columns defined in Eq. (*H1-4*)

E = modulus of elasticity of steel = 29,000 ksi

H = horizontal force, kips

I = moment of inertia, in^4

K = the effective length factor

L = story height, in

l = unbraced length, in

M = bending moment, kip-in or kip-ft

M_{lt} = first-order factored moment due to lateral frame translation, kip-in or kip-ft

M_{nt} = first-order factored moment assuming no lateral frame translation, kip-in or kip-ft

M_{nx} = nominal flexural strength for x-axis bending, kip-in or kip-ft

M_{ny} = nominal flexural strength for y-axis bending, kip-in or kip-ft

M_u = required flexural strength including second-order effects, kip-in or kip-ft

M_{ux} = M_u for x-axis bending, kip-in or kip-ft

M_{uy} = M_u for y-axis bending, kip-in or kip-ft

M_1 = smaller end moment in an unbraced length of beam, kip-in or kip-ft

M_2 = larger end moment in an unbraced length of beam, kip-in or kip-ft

m = a factor given in Table 8-1 for use in Eq. [8.2]

P = axial compressive force, kips

P_e = a function of Kl defined by Eq. [8.1], kips

P_n = nominal compressive strength, kips

P_u = required compressive strength, kips

$P_{u,\text{eff}}$ = effective axial load for a beam-column, to be checked against the Column Load Table in AISC LRFD Manual

U = a factor given in Table 8-1 for use in Eq. [8.2]

x = major principal centroidal axis

y = minor principal centroidal axis

Δ_{oh} = translational deflection of the story under consideration, in

$\sum H$ = sum of all horizontal forces producing Δ_{oh}, kips

$\sum P_e, \sum P_u$ = sum for all columns in a story of P_e and P_u, respectively

$\phi_b M_{nx}$ = design flexural strength for x-axis bending, kip-in or kip-ft

$\phi_b M_{ny}$ = design flexural strength for y-axis bending, kip-in or kip-ft

ϕ_b = resistance factor for flexure = 0.90

$\phi_c P_n$ = design compressive strength, kips

ϕ_c = resistance factor for compression = 0.85

INTRODUCTION

This chapter covers singly and doubly symmetric beam-columns: members subjected to combined axial compression and bending about one or both principal axes. The combination of compression with flexure may result from (either)

(a) A compressive force that is eccentric with respect to the centroidal axis of the column, as in Fig. 8-1(a)

(b) A column subjected to lateral force or moment, as in Fig. 8-1(b),

(c) A beam transmitting wind or other axial forces, as in Fig. 8-1(c).

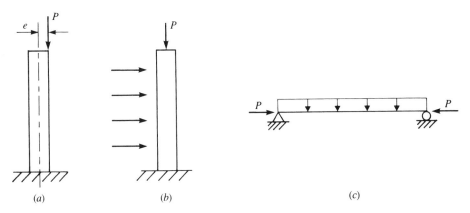

(a) (b) (c)

Fig. 8-1 Combined compression and flexure

INTERACTION FORMULAS

The cross sections of beam-columns must comply with formula ($H1$-$1a$) or ($H1$-$1b$), whichever is applicable.

For $(P_u/\phi_c P_n) \geq 0.2$

$$\frac{P_u}{\phi_c P_n} + \frac{8}{9}\left(\frac{M_{ux}}{\phi_b M_{nx}} + \frac{M_{uy}}{\phi_b M_{ny}}\right) \leq 1.0 \qquad (H1\text{-}1a)$$

For $(P_u/\phi_c P_n) < 0.2$

$$\frac{P_u}{2\phi_c P_n} + \left(\frac{M_{ux}}{\phi_b M_{nx}} + \frac{M_{uy}}{\phi_b M_{ny}}\right) \leq 1.0 \qquad (H1\text{-}1b)$$

Although the interaction formulas for beam-columns appear identical with their counterparts in Chap. 7, there are some significant differences in the definitions of the terms. For beam-columns:

M_{ux}, M_{uy} = required flexural strengths (based on the factored loads) including second-order effects, kip-in or kip-ft

P_u = required compressive strength (based on the factored loads), kips

$\phi_c P_n$ = design compressive strength as determined in Chap. 4, kips

$\phi_b M_{nx}, \ \phi_b M_{ny}$ = design flexural strengths as determined in Chap. 5 or 6, kip-in or kip-ft

ϕ_c = resistance factor for compression = 0.85

ϕ_b = resistance factor for flexure = 0.90

The subscript x refers to bending about the major principal centroidal (or x) axis; y refers to the minor principal centroidal (or y) axis.

SIMPLIFIED SECOND-ORDER ANALYSIS

Second-order moments in beam-columns are the additional moments caused by the axial compressive forces acting on a displaced structure. Normally, structural analysis is first-order; that is, the everyday methods used in practice (whether done manually or by one of the popular computer programs) assume the forces as acting on the original undeflected structure. Second-order effects are neglected. To satisfy the AISC LRFD Specification, second-order moments in beam-columns must be considered in their design.

Instead of rigorous second-order analysis, the AISC LRFD Specification presents a simplified alternative method. The components of the total factored moment determined from a first-order elastic analysis (neglecting secondary effects) are divided into two groups, M_{nt} and M_{lt}.

1. M_{nt}—the required flexural strength in a member assuming there is no lateral translation of the structure. It includes the first-order moments resulting from the gravity loads (i.e., dead and live loads), calculated manually or by computer.

2. M_{lt}—the required flexural strength in a member due to lateral frame translation. In a braced frame, $M_{lt} = 0$. In an unbraced frame, M_{lt} includes the moments from the lateral loads. If both the frame and its vertical loads are symmetric, M_{lt} from the vertical loads is zero. However, if either the vertical loads (i.e., dead and live loads) or the frame geometry is asymmetric and the frame is not braced, lateral translation occurs and $M_{lt} \neq 0$. To determine M_{lt} (a) apply fictitious horizontal reactions at each floor level to prevent lateral translation and (b) use the reverse of these reactions as "sway forces" to obtain M_{lt}. This procedure is illustrated in Fig. 8-2. As is indicated there, M_{lt} for an unbraced frame is the sum of the moments due to the lateral loads and the "sway forces."

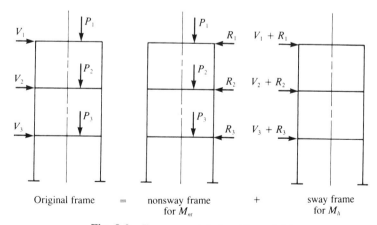

Fig. 8-2   Frame models for M_{nt} and M_{lt}

Once M_{nt} and M_{lt} have been obtained, they are multiplied by their respective magnification factors, B_1 and B_2, and added to approximate the actual second-order factored moment M_u.

$$M_u = B_1 M_{nt} + B_2 M_{lt} \qquad\qquad (H1\text{-}2)$$

As shown in Fig. 8-3, B_1 accounts for the secondary $P - \delta$ effect in all frames (including sway-inhibited), and B_2 covers the $P - \Delta$ effect in unbraced frames. The analytical expressions for B_1 and B_2 follow.

$$B_1 = \frac{C_m}{(1 - P_u/P_e)} \geq 1.0 \qquad (H1\text{-}3)$$

where P_u is the factored axial compressive force in the member, kips

$$P_e = \frac{\pi^2 EI}{(Kl)^2} \qquad [8.1]$$

where $K = 1.0$, I is the moment of inertia (in^4), and l is the unbraced length (in). (Both I and l are taken in the plane of bending only.)

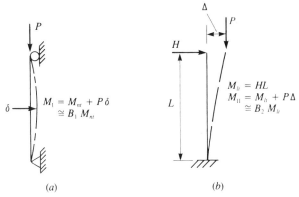

Fig. 8-3 Illustrations of secondary effects. (a) column in braced frame; (b) column in unbraced frame

The coefficient C_m is determined as follows.

(1) For restrained beam-columns not subjected to transverse loads between their supports in the plane of bending

$$C_m = 0.6 - 0.4 \frac{M_1}{M_2} \qquad (H1\text{-}4)$$

where M_1/M_2 is the ratio of the smaller to larger moment at the ends of the portion of the member unbraced in the plane of bending under consideration. If the rotations due to end moments M_1 and M_2 are in opposite directions, then M_1/M_2 is negative; otherwise M_1/M_2 is positive.

(2) For beam-columns subjected to transverse loads between supports, if the ends are *restrained* against rotation, $C_m = 0.85$; if the ends are *unrestrained* against rotation, $C_m = 1.0$.

Two equations are given for B_2 in the AISC LRFD Specification:

$$B_2 = \frac{1}{1 - \Sigma P_u \left(\dfrac{\Delta_{oh}}{\Sigma HL} \right)} \qquad (H1\text{-}5)$$

or

$$B_2 = \frac{1}{1 - \dfrac{\Sigma P_u}{\Sigma P_e}} \qquad (H1\text{-}6)$$

where $\sum P_u$ = required axial strength of all columns in a story (i.e., the total factored gravity load above that level), kips

Δ_{oh} = translational deflection of the story under consideration, in

$\sum H$ = sum of all horizontal forces producing Δ_{oh}, kips

L = story height, in

$\sum P_e$ = summation of P_e for all columns in a story.

Values of P_e are obtained from Eq. [8.1], considering the actual K and l of each column in its plane of bending. Equation (H1-5) is generally the more convenient of the two formulas for evaluating B_2. The quantity Δ_{oh}/L is the *story drift index*. Often, especially for tall buildings, the maximum drift index is a design criterion. Using it in Eq. (H1-5) facilitates the determination of B_2.

For columns with biaxial bending in frames unbraced in both directions, two values of B_1 (B_{1x} and B_{1y}) are needed for each column and two values of B_2 for each story, one for each major direction. Once the appropriate B_1 and B_2 have been evaluated, Eq. (H1-2) can be used to determine M_{ux} and M_{uy} for the applicable interaction formula.

PRELIMINARY DESIGN

The selection of a trial W shape for beam-column design can be facilitated by means of an approximate interaction equation given in the AISC LRFD Manual. Bending moments are converted to equivalent axial loads as follows.

$$P_{u,\text{eff}} = P_u + M_{ux}m + M_{uy}mU \qquad [8.2]$$

where $P_{u,\text{eff}}$ is the effective axial load to be checked against the Column Load Table in Part 2 of the AISC LRFD Manual; P_u, M_{ux}, and M_{uy} are as defined in interaction formulas (H1-1a) and (H1-1b) (P_u, kips; M_{ux}, M_{uy}, kip-ft); and m and U are factors from Table 8-1, adapted from the AISC LRFD Manual.

Table 8-1   Values of m and U for Eq. [8.2]; $F_y = 36$ ksi

KL, ft	m							U
	10	12	14	16	18	20	≥22	
W4	4.3	3.1	2.3	1.9	—	—	—	1.4
W5	4.7	3.8	2.9	2.3	1.8	1.7	—	1.3
W6	3.8	3.2	2.8	2.4	2.3	1.9	1.8	1.9
W8	3.6	3.5	3.4	3.1	2.8	2.4	2.4	1.5
W10	3.1	3.0	3.0	2.9	2.8	2.5	2.4	1.5
W12	2.5	2.5	2.4	2.4	2.4	2.4	2.4	1.5
W14	2.2	2.0	2.0	2.0	2.0	2.0	2.0	1.5

Once a satisfactory trial section has been selected (i.e., $P_{u,\text{eff}} \leq$ the tabulated $\phi_c P_n$), it should be verified with formula (H1-1a) or (H1-1b).

Solved Problems

8.1. In A36 steel, select a W14 section for a beam-column (in a braced frame) with the following combination of factored loads: $P_u = 800$ kips; first-order moments $M_x = 200$ kip-ft, $M_y = 0$, single curvature bending (i.e., equal and opposite end moments); and no transverse loads along the member. The floor-to-floor height is 15 ft.

For a braced frame, $K = 1.0$ for design (see Chap. 4); $K_x L_x = K_y L_y = 1.0 \times 15$ ft $= 15$ ft. Select a trial W14 shape using Eq. [8.2].

$$P_{u,\text{eff}} = P_u + M_{ux} m + M_{uy} mU$$

For a W14 with $KL = 15$ ft $m = 1.0$ and $U = 1.5$, in Table 8-1. Substituting in Eq. [8.2], we obtain

$$P_{u,\text{eff}} = 800 + 200 \times 2.0 + 0 = 1200 \text{ kips}$$

In the AISC Column Load Tables (p. 2-19 of the LRFD Manual) if $F_y = 36$ ksi and $KL = 15$ ft, $\phi_c P_n = 1280$ kips $(>P_{u,\text{eff}} = 1200$ kips) for a W14×159.
   Try a W14×159. To determine M_{ux} (the second-order moment), use Eq. (H1-2).

$$M_u = B_1 M_{nt} + B_2 M_{lt}$$

Because the frame is braced, $M_{lt} = 0$.

$$M_u = B_1 M_{nt} \quad \text{or} \quad M_{ux} = B_1 \times 200 \text{ kip-ft}$$

According to Eq. (H1-3)

$$B_1 = \frac{C_m}{1 - P_u/P_e} \geq 1.0$$

where $C_m = 0.6 - 0.4(M_1/M_2)$ for beam-columns not subjected to lateral loads between supports.
   For $M_1 = M_2 = 200$ kip-ft in single curvature bending (i.e., end moments in opposite directions),

$$\frac{M_1}{M_2} = -\frac{200}{200} = -1.0$$

$$C_m = 0.6 - 0.4(-1.0) = 1.0$$

For a W14×159, $I_x = 1900$ in^4

$$P_l = \frac{\pi^2 E I_x}{(Kl)^2} = \frac{\pi^2 \times 29,000 \text{ kips/in}^2 \times 1900 \text{ in}^4}{(1.0 \times 15 \text{ ft} \times 12 \text{ in/ft})^2} = 16,784 \text{ kips}$$

In Eq. (H1-3)

$$B_1 = \frac{1.0}{1 - 800 \text{ kips}/16,784 \text{ kips}} = 1.05$$

Here, $M_{ux} = 1.05 \times 200$ kip-ft $= 210$ kip-ft, the second-order required flexural strength. (Substituting $M_{ux} = 210$ kip-ft in preliminary design, Eq. [8.2] still leads to a W14×159 as the trial section.)
   Selecting the appropriate beam-column interaction formula, (H1-1a) or (H1-1b), we have

$$\frac{P_u}{\phi_c P_n} = \frac{800 \text{ kips}}{1280 \text{ kips}} = 0.63 > 0.2$$

Use formula (H1-1a), which, for $M_{uy} = 0$, reduces to

$$\frac{P_u}{\phi_c P_n} + \frac{8}{9} \frac{M_{ux}}{\phi_b M_{nx}} \leq 1.0$$

To determine $\phi_b M_{nx}$ (the design flexural strength), refer to Chap. 5 of this text or the Load Factor Design Selection Table for Beams in the AISC LRFD Manual. Since the W14 × 159 is not tabulated therein, the basic equations are used instead. From Eq. [5.10] in Chap. 5:

$$C_b = 1.75 + 1.05 \frac{M_1}{M_2} + 0.3 \left(\frac{M_1}{M_2}\right)^2 \leq 2.3$$

Again, $M_1/M_2 = -1.0$.

$$C_b = 1.75 + 1.05(-1.0) + 0.3(-1.0)^2 = 1.0$$

If $C_b = 1.0$, $M_n = M_p = Z_x F_y$ for bending about the x axis if $L_b \leq L_p$ (see Eq. [5.7]); $L_p = (300 r_y/\sqrt{F_y})$ for W shapes bent about the x axis [Eq. (F1-4)]. For a W14×159, $r_y = 4.0$ in and

$$L_p = \frac{(300 \times 4.0 \text{ in})/(12 \text{ in/ft})}{\sqrt{36}} = 16.7 \text{ ft}$$

Because $(L_b = 15.0 \text{ ft}) < (L_p = 16.7 \text{ ft})$,

$$M_{nx} = Z_x F_y = \frac{287 \text{ in}^3 \times 36 \text{ kips/in}^2}{12 \text{ in/ft}} = 861 \text{ kip-ft}$$

and $\phi_b M_{nx} = 0.90 \times 861 \text{ kip-ft} = 775 \text{ kip-ft}$
Substituting the interaction formula, we obtain

$$0.63 + \frac{8}{9} \times \frac{210 \text{ kip-ft}}{775 \text{ kip-ft}}$$

$$= 0.63 + 0.24 = 0.87 < 1.0 \qquad \text{o.k.}$$

By a similar solution of interaction formula $(H1\text{-}1a)$, it can be shown that a W14×145 is also adequate.

8.2. Assume the beam-column in Prob. 8.1 is turned 90°; that is, $M_x = 0$, $M_y = 200$ kip-ft (first-order moments). Select the appropriate W14 section.

Again, for a braced frame, $K = 1.0$.

$$K_x L_x = K_y L_y = 1.0 \times 15 \text{ ft} = 15 \text{ ft}$$

In selecting a trial W14 shape with Eq. [8.2], $m = 1.0$ and $U = 1.5$ (Table 8-1). Substituting in Eq. [8.2], we obtain

$$P_{u,\text{eff}} = P_u + M_{ux} m + M_{uy} m U$$
$$= 800 + 0 + 200 \times 2.0 \times 1.5 = 1400 \text{ kips}$$

In the Column Load Tables of the AISC LRFD Manual (p. 2-19) if $F_y = 36$ ksi and $KL = 15$ ft, $\phi_c P_n = 1430$ kips ($> P_{u,\text{eff}} = 1400$ kips) for a W14×176.

Try a W14×176. To determine M_{uy} (the second-order moment), use Eq. $(H1\text{-}2)$, which, for a braced frame ($M_{lt} = 0$), becomes $M_u = B_1 M_{nt}$, or $M_{uy} = B_1 \times 200$ kip-ft. As in Prob. 8.1, $C_m = 1.0$ for equal end moments in single curvature bending (i.e., end rotations in opposite directions). Determining P_e for y-axis bending of a W14×176, ($I_y = 838$ in^4)

$$P_e = \frac{\pi^2 E I_y}{(Kl)^2} = \frac{\pi^2 \times 29{,}000 \text{ ksi/in}^2 \times 838 \text{ in}^4}{(1.0 \times 15 \text{ ft} \times 12 \text{ in/ft})^2} = 7403 \text{ kips}$$

In Eq. $(H1\text{-}3)$

$$B_1 = \frac{C_m}{1 - P_u/P_e} = \frac{1.0}{1 - 800 \text{ kips}/7403 \text{ kips}} = 1.12$$

The second-order required flexural strength $M_{uy} = 1.12 \times 200$ kip-ft = 224 kip-ft.
Substituting $M_{uy} = 224$ kip-ft in preliminary design Eq. [8.2]

$$P_{u,\text{eff}} = 800 + 0 + 224 \times 2.0 \times 1.5$$
$$= 1472 \text{ kips}$$
$$> 1430 \text{ kips} = \phi_c P_n \quad \text{for} \quad \text{W14×176}$$
$$< 1570 \text{ kips} = \phi_c P_n \quad \text{for} \quad \text{W14×193}$$

(See p. 2-19 of the AISC LRFD Manual.)

Try a W14×193: $I_y = 931$ in^4

$$P_e = \frac{\pi^2 E I_y}{(Kl)^2} = \frac{\pi^2 \times 29{,}000 \text{ kips/in}^2 \times 931 \text{ in}^4}{(1.0 \times 15 \text{ ft} \times 12 \text{ in/ft})^2} = 8224 \text{ kips}$$

In Eq. (H1-3)

$$B_1 = \frac{C_m}{(1 - P_u/P_e)} = \frac{1.0}{1 - 800 \text{ kips}/8224 \text{ kips}} = 1.11$$

The second-order required flexural strength $M_{uy} = 1.11 \times 200$ kip-ft $= 222$ kip-ft.
    Selecting the appropriate beam-column interaction formula, (H1-1a) or (H1-1b)

$$\frac{P_u}{\phi_c P_n} = \frac{800 \text{ kips}}{1570 \text{ kips}} = 0.51 > 0.2$$

Use formula (H1-1a), which, for $M_{ux} = 0$, reduces to

$$\frac{P_u}{\phi_c P_n} + \frac{8}{9} \frac{M_{uy}}{\phi_b M_{ny}} \leq 1.0$$

To determine $\phi_b M_{ny}$ (the design flexural strength), refer to Chap. 5 of this text. From Eq. [5.6], $M_{ny} = M_p = Z_y F_y$ (for minor-axis bending) regardless of the unbraced length L_b.
    For a W14×193, $Z_y = 180$ in^3

$$M_{ny} = \frac{180 \text{ in}^3 \times 36 \text{ kips/in}^2}{12 \text{ in/ft}} = 540 \text{ kip-ft}$$

and $\phi_b M_{ny} = 0.90 \times 540$ kip-ft $= 486$ kip-ft.
    Substituting in the interaction formula, we obtain

$$0.51 + \frac{8}{9} \times \frac{222 \text{ kip-ft}}{486 \text{ kip-ft}}$$

$$= 0.51 + 0.41 = 0.92 < 1.0 \qquad \text{o.k.}$$

8.3. Select a W14 section (A36 steel) for a beam-column in a braced frame with the factored loads: $P_u = 200$ kips; first-order moments $M_x = 200$ kip-ft, $M_y = 200$ kip-ft. The 15-ft-long beam-column is subjected to transverse loads; its ends are "pinned."

For a braced frame, $K = 1.0$.

$$K_x L_x = K_y L_y = 1.0 \times 15 \text{ ft} = 15 \text{ ft}$$

Select a trial W14 shape using Eq. [8.2]:

$$P_{u,\text{eff}} = P_u + M_{ux} m + M_{uy} m U$$

For a W14 with $KL = 15$ ft; $m = 2.0$ and $U = 1.5$, in Table 8-1. Substituting in Eq. [8.2], we obtain

$$P_{u,\text{eff}} = 200 + 200 \times 1.0 + 200 \times 2.0 \times 1.5 = 1200 \text{ kips}$$

In the Column Load Tables of the AISC LRFD Manual (p. 2-19), if $F_y = 36$ ksi and $KL = 15$ ft, $\phi_c P_n = 1280$ kips ($> P_{u,\text{eff}} = 1200$ kips) for a W14×159.
    Try a W14×159. To determine the required second-order moments, M_{ux} and M_{uy}, use Eq. (H1-2), which, for a braced frame ($M_{lt} = 0$), reduces to

$$M_{ux} = B_{1x} M_{ntx} \quad \text{and} \quad M_{uy} = B_{1y} M_{nty}$$

According to Eq. (H1-3)

$$B_{1x} = \frac{C_{mx}}{1 - P_u/P_{ex}} \geq 1.0$$

$$B_{1y} = \frac{C_{my}}{1 - P_u/P_{ey}} \geq 1.0$$

For a beam-column subjected to transverse loads and with ends unrestrained against rotation, $C_m = 1.0$. Therefore, $C_{mx} = C_{my} = 1.0$.

For a W14×159, $I_x = 1900$ in⁴

$$P_{ex} = \frac{\pi^2 EI_x}{(K_x l_x)^2} = \frac{\pi^2 \times 29{,}000 \text{ kips/in}^2 \times 1900 \text{ in}^4}{(1.0 \times 15 \text{ ft} \times 12 \text{ in/ft})^2} = 16{,}784 \text{ kips}$$

In Eq. (*H1-3*)

$$B_{1x} = \frac{1.0}{1 - 200 \text{ kips}/16{,}784 \text{ kips}} = 1.01$$

$$M_{ux} = 1.01 \times 200 \text{ kip-ft} = 202 \text{ kip-ft}$$

$$I_y = 748 \text{ in}^4$$

$$P_{ey} = \frac{\pi^2 EI_y}{(K_y l_y)^2} = \frac{\pi^2 \times 29{,}000 \text{ kips/in}^2 \times 748 \text{ in}^4}{(1.0 \times 15 \text{ ft} \times 12 \text{ in/ft})^2} = 6608 \text{ kips}$$

In Eq. (*H1-3*)

$$B_{1y} = \frac{1.0}{1 - 200 \text{ kips}/6608 \text{ kips}} = 1.03$$

$$M_{uy} = 1.03 \times 200 \text{ kip-ft} = 206 \text{ kip-ft}$$

The second-order required flexural strengths are $M_{ux} = 202$ kip-ft and $M_{uy} = 206$ kip-ft. (Substituting these values in preliminary design Eq. [*8.2*] reconfirms a W14×159 as the trial section.)

Selecting the appropriate beam-column interaction formula, (*H1-1a*) or (*H1-1b*), we obtain

$$\frac{P_u}{\phi_c P_n} = \frac{200 \text{ kips}}{1280 \text{ kips}} = 0.16 < 0.2$$

Use formula (*H1-1b*):

$$\frac{P_u}{2\phi_c P_n} + \left(\frac{M_{ux}}{\phi_b M_{nx}} + \frac{M_{uy}}{\phi_b M_{ny}}\right) \le 1.0$$

For a simply supported member (i.e., end moments $M_1 = M_2 = 0$), $C_b = 1.0$. In the solution to Prob. 8.1 it was determined that for a W14×159 ($L_b = 15$ ft, $C_b = 1.0$), $\phi_b M_{nx} = 775$ kip-ft.

The value of $\phi_b M_{ny}$ can be determined from Eq. [*5.6*]: $M_{ny} = M_p = Z_y F_y$ (for minor-axis bending) regardless of the unbraced length L_b.

For a W14×159, $Z_y = 146$ in³,

$$M_{ny} = \frac{146 \text{ in}^3 \times 36 \text{ kips/in}^2}{12 \text{ in/ft}} = 438 \text{ kip-ft}$$

$$\phi_b M_{ny} = 0.90 \times 438 \text{ kip-ft} = 394 \text{ kip-ft}$$

Substituting in Interaction formula (*H1-1b*), we obtain

$$\frac{0.16}{2} + \left(\frac{202 \text{ kip-ft}}{775 \text{ kip-ft}} + \frac{206 \text{ kip-ft}}{394 \text{ kip-ft}}\right)$$

$$= 0.08 + 0.26 + 0.52 = 0.86 < 1.0 \qquad \text{o.k.}$$

By a similar solution of interaction formula (*H1-1b*), it can be shown that a W14 × 145 is also adequate.

8.4. In A36 steel, select a W12 section for a beam-column (in a symmetric unbraced frame; $K = 1.2$) with the following factored loads: $P_u = 400$ kips; first-order $M_{ltx} = 100$ kip-ft due to wind, all other moments equal zero. Member length is 12 ft. The allowable story drift index

(Δ_{oh}/L) is $\frac{1}{400}$, or 0.0025, as a result of a total horizontal (unfactored) wind force of 80 kips. The total factored gravity load above this story is 4800 kips.

Given: $P_u = 400$ kips, $M_{uy} = 0$, $M_{ntx} = 0$, $M_{ltx} = 100$ kip-ft, $\sum P_u = 4800$ kips, $\Delta_{oh}/L = 0.0025$, $\sum H = 80$ kips, $KL = 1.2 \times 12$ ft = 14.4 ft.

From Eq. (H1-2), $M_{ux} = B_2 M_{ltx}$, where [according to Eq. (H1-5)]

$$B_2 = \cfrac{1}{1 - \cfrac{\sum P_u}{\sum H}\left(\cfrac{\Delta_{oh}}{L}\right)}$$

$$= \cfrac{1}{1 - \cfrac{4800 \text{ kips}}{80 \text{ kips}}(0.0025)} = 1.18$$

The second-order required flexural strength $M_{ux} = 1.18 \times 100$ kip-ft = 118 kip-ft.

Selecting a trial W12 shape with Eq. [8.2], we obtain

$$P_{u,\text{eff}} = P_u + M_{ux}m + M_{uy}mU$$

where for a W12 ($KL = 14.4$ ft), $m = 2.4$ and $U = 1.5$.

$$P_{u,\text{eff}} = 400 + 118 \times 2.4 + 0 = 683 \text{ kips}$$

By interpolation in the Column Load Tables of the AISC LRFD Manual (p. 2-24), if $F_y = 36$ ksi and $KL = 14.4$ ft, $\phi_c P_n = 732$ kips ($> P_{u,\text{eff}} = 683$ kips) for a W12×96.

Selecting the appropriate beam-column interaction formula, (H1-1a) or (H1-1b), we obtain

$$\frac{P_u}{\phi_c P_n} = \frac{400 \text{ kips}}{732 \text{ kips}} = 0.55 > 0.2$$

Use formula (H1-1a), which, for $M_{uy} = 0$, reduces to

$$\frac{P_u}{\phi_c P_n} + \frac{8}{9}\frac{M_{ux}}{\phi_b M_{nx}} \le 1.0$$

The design flexural strength $\phi_b M_{nx}$ for a W12×96 can be determined from the Beam Selection Table on page 3-15 of the AISC LRFD Manual: because ($L_b = 12$ ft) < ($L_p = 12.9$ ft), $\phi_b M_{nx} = \phi_b M_p = 397$ kip-ft, as tabulated. Substituting in the interaction formula:

$$0.55 + \frac{8}{9} \times \frac{118 \text{ kip-ft}}{397 \text{ kip-ft}} \le 1.0$$

$$0.55 + 0.26 = 0.81 < 1.0 \qquad \text{o.k.}$$

By a similar solution of interaction formula (H1-1a), it can be shown that a W12×87 and a W12×79 are also adequate.

8.5. Assume the beam-column in Prob. 8.4 is turned 90°; i.e., $M_x = 0$, $M_{lty} = 100$ kip-ft, $M_{nty} = 0$. Select the appropriate W12 section.

Given: $P_u = 400$ kips, $M_{ux} = 0$, $M_{nty} = 0$, $M_{lty} = 100$ kip-ft, $\sum P_u = 4800$ kips, $\Delta_{oh}/L = 0.0025$, $\sum H = 80$ kips, $KL = 1.2 \times 12$ ft = 14.4 ft.

From Eq. (H1-2), $M_{uy} = B_2 M_{lty}$, where $B_2 = 1.18$ as in Prob. 8.4. The second-order required flexural strength $M_{uy} = 1.18 \times 100$ kip-ft = 118 kip-ft. Selecting a trial W12 shape with Eq. [8.2], we obtain

$$P_{u,\text{eff}} = P_u + M_{ux}m + M_{uy}mU$$

where for a W12 ($KL = 14.4$ ft), $m = 2.4$, and $U = 1.5$.

$$P_{u,\text{eff}} = 400 + 0 + 118 \times 2.4 \times 1.5 = 825 \text{ kips}$$

By interpolation in the Column Load Tables (p. 2-23 in the AISC LRFD Manual), if $F_y = 36$ ksi and $KL = 14.4$ ft, $\phi_c P_n = 920$ kips ($> P_{u,\text{eff}} = 825$ kips) for a W12×120.

Selecting the appropriate beam-column interaction formula, we obtain

$$\frac{P_u}{\phi_c P_n} = \frac{400 \text{ kips}}{920 \text{ kips}} = 0.43 > 0.2$$

Use formula $(H1\text{-}1a)$, which, for $M_{ux} = 0$, reduces to

$$\frac{P_u}{\phi_c P_n} + \frac{8}{9}\frac{M_{uy}}{\phi_b M_{ny}} \leq 1.0$$

To determine $\phi_b M_{ny}$ (the design flexural strength), refer to Chap. 5 of this text. From Eq. [5.6], $M_{ny} = M_p = Z_y F_y$ (for minor-axis bending) regardless of the unbraced length L_b.

For a W12 × 120, $Z_y = 85.4 \text{ in}^3$, and

$$M_{ny} = \frac{85.4 \text{ in}^3 \times 36 \text{ kips/in}^2}{12 \text{ in/ft}} = 256 \text{ kip-ft}$$

$$\phi_b M_{ny} = 0.90 \times 256 \text{ kip-ft} = 231 \text{ kip-ft}$$

Substitution in the interaction formula yields

$$0.43 + \frac{8}{9} \times \frac{118 \text{ kip-ft}}{231 \text{ kip-ft}}$$

$$= 0.43 + 0.45 = 0.88 < 1.0 \qquad \text{o.k.}$$

8.6. Select a W12 section (A36 steel) for a beam-column in a symmetric unbraced frame with the factored loads: $P_u = 150$ kips; first-order moments $M_{ltx} = 100$ kip-ft, $M_{lty} = 100$ kip-ft, $M_{ntx} = M_{nty} = 0$. The story height is 12 ft; $K_x = K_y = 1.2$. For all columns in the story, $\sum P_u = 3000$ kips, $\sum P_e \cong 60{,}000$ kips for bending about east-west axes, and $\sum P_e \cong 30{,}000$ kips for bending about north-south axes; see Fig. 8-4.

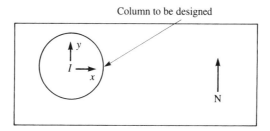

Column to be designed

N

Fig. 8-4

Since $M_{ntx} = M_{nty} = 0$, Eq. $(H1\text{-}2)$ becomes

$$M_{ux} = B_{2x} M_{ltx}$$
$$M_{uy} = B_{2y} M_{lty}$$

where [according to Eq. $(H1\text{-}6)$]

$$B_{2x} = \frac{1}{1 - \sum P_u / \sum P_{ex}}$$

$$B_{2y} = \frac{1}{1 - \sum P_u / \sum P_{ey}}$$

From the statement of the problem, $\sum P_u = 3000$ kips, $\sum P_{ex} \cong 60,000$ kips, and $\sum P_{ey} \cong 30,000$ kips. Substituting, we obtain

$$B_{2x} = \frac{1}{1 - 3000 \text{ kips}/60,000 \text{ kips}} = 1.05$$

$$B_{2y} = \frac{1}{1 - 3000 \text{ kips}/30,000 \text{ kips}} = 1.11$$

The second-order required flexural strengths are

$$M_{ux} = 1.05 \times 100 \text{ kip-ft} = 105 \text{ kip-ft}$$

$$M_{uy} = 1.11 \times 100 \text{ kip-ft} = 111 \text{ kip-ft}$$

Selecting a trial W12 shape with Eq. [8.2], we obtain

$$P_{u,\text{eff}} = P_u + M_{ux}m + M_{uy}mU,$$

where for a W12 ($KL = 1.2 \times 12$ ft $= 14.4$ ft), $m = 2.4$ and $U = 1.5$.

$$P_{u,\text{eff}} = 150 + 105 \times 2.4 + 111 \times 2.4 \times 1.5 = 802 \text{ kips}$$

By interpolation in the Column Load Tables (on p. 2-24 in the AISC LRFD Manual), if $F_y = 36$ ksi and $KL = 14.4$ ft, it follows that $\phi_c P_n = 811$ kips ($>P_{u,\text{eff}} = 802$ kips) for a W12 × 106.
Try a W12 × 106. Select the appropriate beam-column interaction formula.

$$\frac{P_u}{\phi_c P_n} = \frac{150 \text{ kips}}{811 \text{ kips}} = 0.18 < 0.2$$

Use interaction formula (H1-1b):

$$\frac{P_u}{2\phi_c P_n} + \left(\frac{M_{ux}}{\phi_b M_{nx}} + \frac{M_{uy}}{\phi_c M_{ny}}\right) \leq 1.0$$

The design flexural strengths for a W12 × 106 can be determined as follows. Because ($L_b = 12$ ft) < ($L_p = 13.0$ ft), $\phi_b M_{nx} = \phi_b M_p = 443$ kip-ft, as tabulated in the Load Factor Design Selection Table for Beams (on p. 3-15 of the AISC LRFD Manual).
For all values of L_b, $\phi_b M_{ny} = \phi_b M_p = \phi_b Z_y F_y$; $Z_y = 75.1$ in³ for a W12×106.

$$\phi_b M_{ny} = \frac{0.90 \times 75.1 \text{ in}^3 \times 36 \text{ kips/in}^2}{12 \text{ in/ft}} = 203 \text{ kip-ft}$$

Substituting in interaction formula (H1-1b), we obtain

$$\frac{0.18}{2} + \left(\frac{105 \text{ kip-ft}}{443 \text{ kip-ft}} + \frac{111 \text{ kip-ft}}{203 \text{ kip-ft}}\right) \leq 1.0$$

$$0.09 + 0.24 + 0.55 = 0.87 < 1.0 \qquad \text{o.k.}$$

By a similar solution of interaction formula (H1-1b), it can be shown that a W12 × 96 is also adequate.

8.7. Select a W14 section (A36 steel) for a beam-column in an unbraced frame with the factored loads: $P_u = 300$ kips, $M_{ntx} = M_{nty} = 50$ kip-ft, $M_{ltx} = 120$ kip-ft, $M_{lty} = 80$ kip-ft (reverse curvature bending with equal end moments in the same direction in all cases; no transverse loads along the span). The story height is 14 ft; $K_x = K_y = 1.2$. The allowable story drift index is $\frac{1}{500}$, or 0.0020, due to total horizontal (unfactored) wind forces of 100 kips in the north-south direction and 70 kips in the east-west direction (see Fig. 8-4). The total factored gravity load above this level $\sum P_u = 6000$ kips.

Given: $K_x = K_y = 1.2$, $L_x = L_y = 14$ ft.

$$K_x L_x = K_y L_y = 1.2 \times 14 \text{ ft} = 16.8 \text{ ft}$$

The second-order required flexural strengths [from Eq. $(H1\text{-}2)$] are

$$M_{ux} = B_{1x}M_{ntx} + B_{2x}M_{ltx}$$
$$M_{uy} = B_{1y}M_{nty} + B_{2y}M_{lty}$$

where

$$B_{1x} = \frac{C_{mx}}{1 - P_u/P_{ex}} \geq 1.0$$

$$B_{1y} = \frac{C_{my}}{1 - P_u/P_{ey}} \geq 1.0$$

$$B_{2x} = \frac{1}{1 - \dfrac{\sum P_u}{\sum H_y}\left(\dfrac{\Delta_{ohy}}{L}\right)}$$

$$B_{2y} = \frac{1}{1 - \dfrac{\sum P_u}{\sum H_x}\left(\dfrac{\Delta_{ohx}}{L}\right)}$$

Before the selection of a trial section, P_{ex} and P_{ey} (and hence, B_{1x} and B_{1y}) are unknown. Let $B_{1x} = B_{1y} = 1.0$.

$$B_{2x} = \frac{1}{1 - (6000\text{ kips}/100\text{ kips})(0.0020)} = 1.14$$

$$B_{2y} = \frac{1}{1 - (6000\text{ kips}/70\text{ kips})(0.0020)} = 1.21$$

$$M_{ux} = 1.0 \times 50\text{ kip-ft} + 1.14 \times 120\text{ kip-ft} = 187\text{ kip-ft}$$

$$M_{uy} = 1.0 \times 50\text{ kip-ft} + 1.21 \times 80\text{ kip-ft} = 147\text{ kip-ft}$$

Selecting a trial W14 shape with Eq. [8.2] yields

$$P_{u,\text{eff}} = P_u + M_{ux}m + M_{uy}mU$$

where for a W14 ($KL = 16.8$ ft), $m = 2.0$, and $U = 1.5$.

$$P_{u,\text{eff}} = 300 + 187 \times 2.0 + 147 \times 2.0 \times 1.5 = 1115\text{ kips}$$

By interpolation in the Column Load Tables (on p. 2-19 of the AISC LRFD Manual), if $F_y = 36$ ksi and $KL = 16.8$ ft, $\phi_c P_n = 1144$ kips ($>P_{u,\text{eff}} = 1115$ kips) for a W14×145.

Try a W14×145. First, determine B_{1x} and B_{1y}. For reverse curvature bending with equal end moments, $M_1/M_2 = +1.0$. From Eq. $(H1\text{-}4)$, $C_m = 0.6 - 0.4(M_1/M_2) = 0.6 - 0.4(+1.0) = 0.2$; $C_{mx} = C_{my} = 0.2$. In the equation for B_1 $(H1\text{-}3)$, P_e is based on Kl in the plane of bending with $K = 1.0$. (By contrast, $\sum P_e$ in Eq. $(H1\text{-}6)$ for B_2 is based on the actual Kl of each column in its plane of bending). Referring to P_e in Eq. $(H1\text{-}3)$, for a W14×145

$$I_x = 1710\text{ in}^4$$

$$P_{ex} = \frac{\pi^2 EI_x}{(K_x l_x)^2} = \frac{\pi^2 \times 29{,}000\text{ kips/in}^2 \times 1710\text{ in}^4}{(1.0 \times 14\text{ ft} \times 12\text{ in/ft})^2} = 17{,}341\text{ kips}$$

$$I_y = 677\text{ in}^4$$

$$P_{ey} = \frac{\pi^2 EI_y}{(K_y l_y)^2} = \frac{\pi^2 \times 29{,}000\text{ kips/in}^2 \times 677\text{ in}^4}{(1.0 \times 14\text{ ft} \times 12\text{ in/ft})^2} = 6865\text{ kips}$$

$$B_{1x} = \frac{0.2}{1 - 300\text{ kips}/17{,}341\text{ kips}} \geq 1.0$$

$$= 1.0$$

$$B_{1y} = \frac{0.2}{1 - 300\text{ kips}/6865\text{ kips}} \geq 1.0$$

$$= 1.0$$

Since $B_{1x} = B_{1y} = 1.0$ as originally estimated, the resulting second-order required flexural strengths are correct; i.e., $M_{ux} = 187$ kip-ft and $M_{uy} = 147$ kip-ft. Also, the selection of a W14×145 as the trial section is valid.

Selecting the appropriate beam-column interaction formula, $(H1\text{-}1a)$ or $(H1\text{-}1b)$, we obtain

$$\frac{P_u}{\phi_c P_n} = \frac{300 \text{ kips}}{1144 \text{ kips}} = 0.26 > 0.2$$

Use formula $(H1\text{-}1a)$.

$$\frac{P_u}{\phi_c P_n} + \frac{8}{9}\left(\frac{M_{ux}}{\phi_b M_{nx}} + \frac{M_{uy}}{\phi_b M_{ny}}\right) \le 1.0$$

To determine the design flexural strengths $\phi_b M_{nx}$ and $\phi_b M_{ny}$ for a W14×145 ($L_b = 14$ ft)

$$C_b = 1.75 + 1.05\left(\frac{M_1}{M_2}\right) + 0.3\left(\frac{M_1}{M_2}\right)^2 \le 2.3$$

according to Eq. [5.10]. For reverse curvature bending with equal end moments, $M_1/M_2 = +1.0$.

$$C_b = 1.75 + 1.05(+1.0) + 0.3(+1.0)^2 \le 2.3$$

$$= 2.3$$

$$L_p = \frac{300\, r_y}{\sqrt{F_y}} = \frac{300 \times 3.98 \text{ in}}{\sqrt{36} \times 12 \text{ in/ft}} = 16.6 \text{ ft}$$

for a W14×145, according to Eq. $(F1\text{-}4)$ in Chap. 5.

Since $(L_b = 14 \text{ ft}) < (L_p = 16.6 \text{ ft}) < L_m$,

$$\phi_b M_{nx} = \phi_b M_p = \phi_b Z_x F_y$$

$$= \frac{0.90 \times 260 \text{ in}^3 \times 36 \text{ kips/in}^2}{12 \text{ in/ft}} = 702 \text{ kip-ft}$$

$$\phi_b M_{ny} = \phi_b M_p = \phi_b Z_y F_y$$

$$= \frac{0.90 \times 133 \text{ in}^3 \times 36 \text{ kips/in}^2}{12 \text{ in/ft}} = 359 \text{ kip-ft}$$

Substituting in interaction formula $(H1\text{-}1a)$:

$$0.26 + \frac{8}{9}\left(\frac{187 \text{ kip-ft}}{702 \text{ kip-ft}} + \frac{147 \text{ kip-ft}}{359 \text{ kip-ft}}\right) \le 1.0$$

$$0.26 + \frac{8}{9}(0.27 + 0.41) = 0.86 < 1.0 \qquad \text{o.k.}$$

Supplementary Problems

8.8.   Repeat Prob. 8.1 with a W14×145.

Ans.   It is satisfactory.

8.9.   For Prob. 8.2, find the most economical W12.

Ans.   W12×210.

8.10. Repeat Prob. 8.3 with
  (*a*) A W14×145
  (*b*) A W14×132

  Ans. (*a*) Satisfactory. (*b*) Unsatisfactory.

8.11. For Prob. 8.4, find the most economical W14.

  Ans. W14×82.

8.12. For Prob. 8.5, find the most economical W14.

  Ans. W14×99.

8.13. For Prob. 8.6, find the most economical W14.

  Ans. W14×90.

8.14. Repeat Prob. 8.7 with
  (*a*) A W14×132.
  (*b*) A W14×120.

  Ans. (*a*) Satisfactory. (*b*) Unsatisfactory.

Chapter 9

Torsion

NOTATION

A = cross-sectional area of member, in^2

A_w = area of the web, in^2

e = eccentricity with respect to the shear center, in

F_{cr} = critical, or buckling, stress, ksi

F_y = specified minimum yield stress, ksi

f_{nT} = normal stress due to (warping) torsion, ksi

f_{un} = total normal stress under factored loads, ksi

f_{uv} = total shear stress under factored loads, ksi

f_{vST} = shear stress due to St. Venant torsion, ksi

f_{vWT} = shear stress due to warping torsion, ksi

G = shear modulus of elasticity of steel = 11,200 ksi

J = torsional constant, in^4

l = distance from the support, in

M_{ux} = required flexural strength for x-axis bending, kip-in

M_{uy} = required flexural strength for y-axis bending, kip-in

P_u = required axial strength, tension or compression, kips

S_x = elastic section modulus for x-axis bending, in^3

S_y = elastic section modulus for y-axis bending, in^3

T = concentrated torsional moment, kip-in

t = distributed torsional moment, kip-in/linear in

V_u = required shear strength, kips

θ = angle of rotation, radians

ϕ = appropriate resistance factor

INTRODUCTION

This chapter covers torsion, acting alone or in combination with tension, compression, and/or bending. Torsion, or twisting of cross sections, will result from the bending of unsymmetric members. In symmetric members (such as I-shaped beams), torsion will occur when the line of action of a lateral load does not pass through the *shear center*. The emphasis in this chapter is on torsion of symmetric shapes, those most commonly used in construction.

SHEAR CENTER

The shear center of a cross section, which is also the center of rotation, can be located by equilibrium of the internal torsional shear stresses with the external torsional forces. Such a calculation is unnecessary in most cases because the following rules (illustrated in Fig. 9-1) are applicable.

For W and other doubly symmetric shapes, the shear center is located at the centroid.

Singly symmetric cross sections, such as C shapes, have their shear centers on the axis of symmetry, but not at the centroid. (The shear center locations for C sections are given in the Properties Tables in Part 1 of the AISC LRFD Manual.)

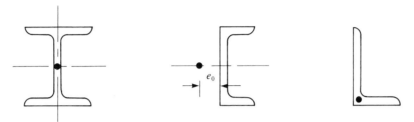

Fig. 9-1   Shear center locations

As shown in Fig. 9-2, the torsional moment, T or t, equals the magnitude of the force multiplied by its distance from the shear center e.

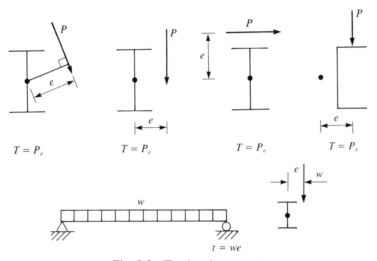

Fig. 9-2   Torsional moments

AVOIDING OR MINIMIZING TORSION*

As is demonstrated later in this chapter, *open sections,* such as W and C shapes, are very inefficient in resisting torsion; thus, torsional rotations can be large and torsional stresses relatively high. It is best to avoid torsion by detailing the loads and reactions to act through the shear center of the member. In the case of spandrel members supporting building facade elements, this may not be possible. Heavy exterior masonry walls and stone panels can impose severe torsional loads on spandrel beams. The following are suggestions for eliminating or reducing this kind of torsion.

1. Wall elements may span between floors. The moment due to the eccentricity of the wall with respect to the edge beams can be resisted by lateral forces acting through the floor diaphragms. No torsion would be imposed on the spandrel beams.

2. If facade panels extend only a partial story height below the floor line, the use of diagonal steel "kickers" may be possible. These light members would provide lateral support to the wall panels. Torsion from the panels would be resisted by forces originating from structural elements other than the spandrel beams.

---

* This section is reprinted with permission from the author's earlier work, *Guide to Load and Resistance Factor Design of Structural Steel Buildings,* American Institute of Steel Contruction (AISC), Chicago, 1986.

3. Even if torsion must be resisted by the edge members, providing intermediate torsional supports can be helpful. Reducing the span over which the torsion acts will reduce torsional stresses. If there are secondary beams framing into a spandrel girder, the beams can act as intermediate torsional supports for the girder. By adding top and bottom moment plates to the connections of the beams with the girder, the bending resistances of the beams can be mobilized to provide the required torsional reactions along the girder.

4. *Closed sections* provide considerably better resistance to torsion than do open sections; torsional rotations and stresses are much lower for box beams than for wide-flange members. For members subjected to torsion, it may be advisable to use box sections or to simulate a box shape by welding one or two side plates to a W shape.

DESIGN CRITERIA

When torsion is present, the provisions in Sec. H2 of the AISC LRFD Specification must be applied. The expressions given therein [Formulas (*H2-1*) to (*H2-3*)] limit the total normal and shear stresses occurring at any point. These stresses may result from torsion alone or from torsion combined with other effects.

AISC formulas (*H2-1*) to (*H2-3*) may be rewritten as follows.

(*1*) For the limit state of yielding under normal stress (i.e., axial tension or compression)

$$f_{un} \leq \phi F_y \qquad [9.1]$$

where $\phi = 0.90$ and

$$f_{un} = \frac{P_u}{A} \pm \frac{M_{ux}}{S_x} \pm \frac{M_{uy}}{S_y} \pm f_{nT} \qquad [9.2]$$

(*2*) For the limit state of yielding under shear stress,

$$f_{uv} \leq 0.6\phi F_y \qquad [9.3]$$

where $\phi = 0.90$ and

$$f_{uv} = \frac{V_u}{A_w} \pm f_{vST} \pm f_{vWT} \qquad [9.4]$$

(*3*) For the limit state of buckling

$$f_{un} \leq \phi_c F_{cr} \qquad [9.5]$$

or

$$f_{uv} \leq \phi_c F_{cr} \qquad [9.6]$$

as applicable; where $\phi_c = 0.85$, F_{cr} is obtained from the appropriate buckling formula [e.g., Eq. (*E2-2*) or (*E2-3*) in Chap. 4] and f_{un} and f_{uv} are the compressive normal and shear stresses resulting from Eqs. [9.2] and [9.4], respectively.

The terms in Expressions. [9.1] to [9.6] are defined as follows.

f_{un} = total axial (or normal) stress under factored loads, ksi

f_{uv} = total shear stress under factored loads, ksi

f_{nT} = normal stress due to torsion, ksi

f_{vST} = shear stress due to St. Venant torsion, ksi

f_{vWT} = shear stress due to warping torsion, ksi

P_u = required axial load strength, tension or compression, kips

M_{ux}, M_{uy} = required flexural strengths for x- and y-axis bending, kip-in

V_u = required shear strength, kips

A = cross-sectional area, in^2

A_w = web area, in^2

S_x, S_y = elastic section moduli for x- and y-axis bending, in^3

The terms *St. Venant* torsion and *warping torsion* are explained below.

ST. VENANT TORSION

When a torsional moment is applied to a circular bar or tube, each cross section rotates in its own plane without warping. Resistance to torsion is provided by shear stresses in the cross-sectional plane. This kind of "pure" torsion is called *St. Venant torsion*. Noncircular cross sections, when subjected to the same torsional moment, tend to warp; that is, plane sections do not remain planar. Theoretically, if warping were totally unrestrained, all cross sections would experience St. Venant torsion only. However, end conditions and geometry restrain warping. In addition to the shear stresses of St. Venant torsion, noncircular cross sections are also subjected to the normal and shear stresses of *warping torsion*.

In Table 9-1, f_{vST}, the shear stress due to St. Venant torsion, is given for various cross-sectional shapes.

Table 9-1   St. Venant Torsion

	Shear Stress f_{vST} (ksi)	Torsional Constant J (in^4)
Closed sections Round bar	$\dfrac{Tr}{J}$	$\dfrac{\pi R^4}{2}$
Round tube	$\dfrac{Tr}{J}$	$\dfrac{\pi}{2}(R_o^4 - R_i^4)$
Rectangular tube	$\dfrac{T}{2bht_1}$ $\dfrac{T}{2bht_2}$	$\dfrac{2t_1t_2b^2h^2}{bt_2 + ht_1}$
Square tube	$\dfrac{T}{2b^2t}$	tb^3
Rectangular bar	$\dfrac{Tt}{J}$	$\dfrac{bt^3}{3}$ (approx.)
Open sections	$\dfrac{Tt_i}{J}$	$\dfrac{\Sigma bt^3}{3}$ (approx.; for exact values, see AISC LRFD Manual, pp. 1-133—1-161)

WARPING TORSION

Warping torsion is most significant for *open sections,* specifically, shapes rolled or fabricated as a series of planes. This is in contrast to *closed sections,* where St. Venant torsion predominates. The subject of torsion for such commonly used open sections as W and C shapes is covered in detail in the AISC publication *Torsional Analysis of Steel Members* (1983). Final design of beams subjected to torsion should be verified with the tables and charts contained therein. However, the simplified procedure presented here may be used for preliminary design.

As shown in Fig. 9-3, the effects of warping torsion on I beams can be approximated by converting the torsional moment T into an equivalent force couple acting on the flanges. The normal and shear stresses due to warping torsion are assumed equal to the corresponding stresses resulting from the bending of each flange acting as a separate beam and subjected to the lateral force T/d'.

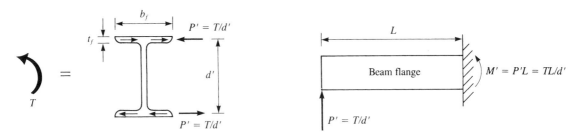

Fig. 9-3   Warping torsion: approximation for W shapes

DEFORMATION

The angle of rotation, in radians, for all types of cross sections is

$$\theta = \frac{Tl}{GJ} \qquad\qquad [9.7]$$

where T = applied torsional moment, kip-in

l = distance from the support, in

G = shear modulus of elasticity of steel = 11,200 ksi

J = torsional constant, in^4

(Values of J for common structural shapes are given in a special section, Torsion Properties, in Part 1 of the AISC LRFD Manual. For cross sections not tabulated, the formulas for J in Table 9-1 may be used.)

Solved Problems

For Probs. 9.1 to 9.4, refer to Fig. 9-4. A twisting moment of 10 kip-ft is applied to the end of a 5-ft shaft in Fig. 9-4(*a*). Determine

The maximum shear stress

The maximum normal stress

The maximum angle of rotation

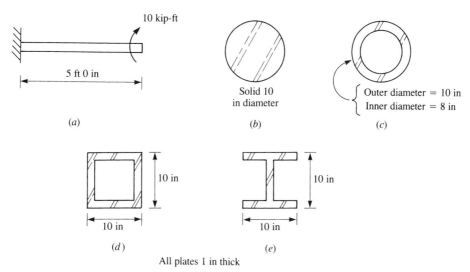

Fig. 9-4

9.1. For the cross section in Fig. 9-4(b).

The only active force in Fig. 9-4(a) is the torsional moment; there are no axial forces or bending moments. Because the round bar in Fig. 9-4(b) does not warp, this is a case of "pure" St. Venant torsion. Normal stresses are zero throughout.

Torsional shear stresses can be determined from Table 9-1. For a round bar

$$f_{vST} = \frac{Tr}{J} \qquad \text{where} \qquad J = \frac{\pi R^4}{2}$$

The maximum shear stresses are at the outer edge, where $r = R = 10\,\text{in}/2 = 5\,\text{in}$.

$$J = \frac{\pi R^4}{2} = \frac{\pi \times (5\,\text{in})^4}{2} = 982\,\text{in}^4$$

The maximum shear stress

$$f_{vST} = \frac{TR}{J} = \frac{(10\,\text{kip-ft} \times 12\,\text{in/ft}) \times 5\,\text{in}}{982\,\text{in}^4} = 0.61\,\text{ksi}$$

According to Eq. [9.7], the maximum angle of rotation occurs at the free end (where $l = 5$ ft). In radians

$$\theta = \frac{Tl}{GJ}$$

$$= \frac{(10\,\text{kips/in}^2 \times 12\,\text{in/ft}) \times (5\,\text{ft} \times 12\,\text{in/ft})}{11{,}200\,\text{kips/in}^2 \times 982\,\text{in}^4}$$

$$= 0.00065\,\text{radian}$$

To convert angles from radians to degrees, recall that a full circle $= 360° = 2\pi$ radians, or $180° = \pi$ radians:

$$\theta = \frac{180°}{\pi\,\text{radians}} \times 0.00065\,\text{radian} = 0.038°$$

9.2. For the cross section in Fig. 9-4(c).

The torsional behavior of a hollow circular shaft is similar to that of a round bar: St. Venant torsion with no warping; no normal stresses.

From Table 9-1, the torsional shear stresses

$$f_{vST} = \frac{T_r}{J}, \qquad \text{where} \quad J = \frac{\pi}{2}(R_o^4 - R_i^4)$$

$$J = \frac{\pi}{2}[(5 \text{ in})^4 - (4 \text{ in})^4] = 580 \text{ in}^4$$

The maximum shear stresses are at the outer edge, where $r = R_o = 5$ in.

$$f_{vST} = \frac{TR_o}{J} = \frac{(10 \text{ kip-ft} \times 12 \text{ in/ft}) \times 5 \text{ in}}{580 \text{ in}^4}$$

$$= 1.04 \text{ ksi}$$

The angle of rotation, in radians

$$\theta = \frac{Tl}{GJ} = \frac{(10 \text{ kip-ft} \times 12 \text{ in/ft})(5 \text{ ft} \times 12 \text{ in/ft})}{11{,}200 \text{ kips/in}^2 \times 580 \text{ in}^4}$$

$$= 0.0011 \text{ radian}$$

In degrees

$$\theta = \frac{180°}{\pi \text{ radians}} \times 0.0011 \text{ radians} = 0.064°$$

9.3. For the cross section in Fig. 9-4(d).

When a square tube is twisted, warping is minor; the normal and shear stresses due to warping are small and are generally neglected.

Referring to Table 9-1, for a square tube the St. Venant torsional shear stresses are

$$f_{vST} = \frac{T}{2b^2t}$$

where b is the distance between the centerlines of the opposite sides, $b = 10 \text{ in} - 1 \text{ in} = 9 \text{ in}$; $t = 1$ in.

$$f_{vST} = \frac{10 \text{ kip-ft} \times 12 \text{ in/ft}}{2 \times (9 \text{ in})^2 \times 1 \text{ in}} = 0.74 \text{ ksi}$$

According to Eq. [9.7], the maximum angle of rotation is at the free end.

$$\theta = \frac{Tl}{GJ}$$

From Table 9-1

$$J = tb^3 = 1 \text{ in} \times (9 \text{ in})^3 = 729 \text{ in}^3$$

In radians

$$\theta = \frac{(10 \text{ kip-ft} \times 12 \text{ in/ft})(5 \text{ ft} \times 12 \text{ in/ft})}{11{,}200 \text{ kips/in}^2 \times 729 \text{ in}^3}$$

$$= 0.00088 \text{ radian}$$

In degrees

$$\theta = \frac{180°}{\pi \text{ radians}} \times 0.00088 \text{ radian} = 0.051°$$

9.4. For the cross section in Fig. 9-4(e).

In *open sections*, such as the I shape in Fig. 9-4(e), the torsional stresses are

        Shear stresses due to St. Venant torsion

        Shear stresses due to warping torsion

        Normal stresses due to warping torsion

The St. Venant shear stresses can be determined from Table 9-1.

$$f_{vST} = \frac{T t_i}{J}$$

where t_i is the thickness of the element under consideration and

$$J = \frac{\Sigma b t^3}{3}$$

In this case, $t_i = 1$ in for the web and both flanges.

$$J = \tfrac{1}{3}[2 \times 10 \text{ in} \times (1 \text{ in})^3 + 8 \text{ in} \times (1 \text{ in})^3] = 9.33 \text{ in}^4$$

The St. Venant shear stresses

$$f_{vST} = \frac{(10 \text{ kip-ft} \times 12 \text{ in/ft}) \times 1 \text{ in}}{9.33 \text{ in}^4} = 12.9 \text{ ksi}$$

To determine the stresses due to warping torsion, the approximation in Fig. 9-3 can be used.

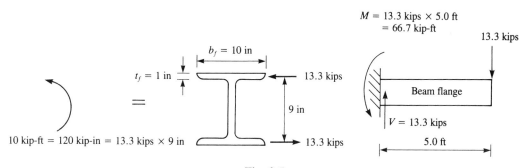

Fig. 9-5

As shown in Fig. 9-5, the torsional moment of 10 kip-ft can be resolved into a force couple of 13.3 kips (equal and opposite forces) on each flange. Each flange is assumed to act as an independent (1 in × 10 in) rectangular beam resisting its 13.3-kip load. The shear $V = 13.3$ kips and maximum moment (at the support) $M = 13.3$ kips × 5.0 ft = 66.7 kip-ft.

For a rectangular member, the maximum shear stress

$$f_{vWT} = \frac{1.5 \, V}{t_f b_f} = \frac{1.5 \times 13.3 \text{ kips}}{1 \text{ in} \times 10 \text{ in}} = 2.0 \text{ ksi}$$

The maximum normal stress

$$f_{nT} = \frac{M}{S}$$

where
$$S = \frac{t_f b_f^2}{6} \quad \text{(the section modulus of the flange)}$$

$$= \frac{1 \text{ in} \times (10 \text{ in})^2}{6} = 16.7 \text{ in}^3$$

$$f_{nT} = \frac{66.7 \text{ kip-ft} \times 12 \text{ in/ft}}{16.7 \text{ in}^3} = 48.0 \text{ ksi}$$

Combining stresses, we obtain the values shown in Fig. 9-6.

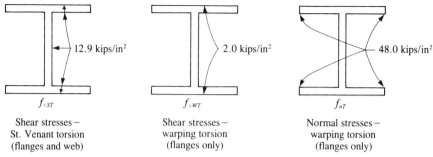

Fig. 9-6

As is shown in Fig. 9-6, the maximum shear stress is in the flanges: $f_{uv} = f_{vST} + f_{vWT} = (12.9 + 2.0)$ ksi = 14.9 ksi. The maximum normal stress is also in the flanges: $f_{un} = f_{nT} = 48.0$ ksi.

The maximum angle of rotation, from Eq. [9.7], is

$$\theta = \frac{Tl}{GJ}$$

where J is as determined above: $J = 9.33$ in^4.

In radians

$$\theta = \frac{(10 \text{ kip-ft} \times 12 \text{ in/ft})(5 \text{ ft} \times 12 \text{ in/ft})}{11{,}200 \text{ kips/in}^2 \times 9.33 \text{ in}^4}$$

$$= 0.069 \text{ radian}$$

In degrees

$$\theta = \frac{180°}{\pi \text{ radians}} \times 0.069 \text{ radians} = 3.9°$$

A comparison of the solutions to Probs. 9.1 to 9.4 indicates that *open sections* are poor in torsional resistance. The stresses and rotations of the I shape are at least an order of magnitude greater than those of the *closed sections* under the same torsional loading.

For the beams in Probs. 9.5 to 9.8, plot the variation along the span of

Flexural shear V

Bending moment M

Torsional moment T

9.5. The cantilever beam in Fig. 9-7(*a*).

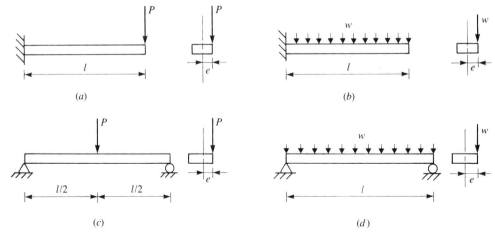

Fig. 9-7

The procedure for drawing the shear V, moment M, and torsion T diagrams is essentially the same:

(a)   Determine the support reactions by statics.

(b)   Plot the appropriate left-handed reaction on the diagram.

(c)   Obtain additional points on the diagram by cutting sections along the beam and solving for the required forces by statics.

(d)   Ascertain closure at the right side of the diagram.

See Fig. 9-8.

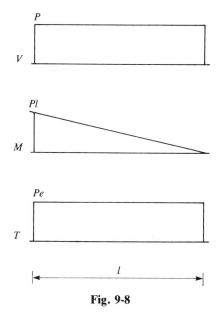

Fig. 9-8

9.6.   The cantilever beam in Fig. 9-7(b).

See Fig. 9-9.

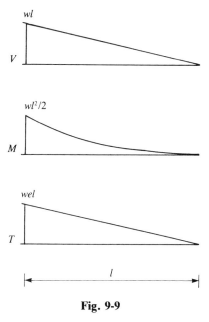

Fig. 9-9

9.7. The simply supported beam in Fig. 9-7(c).

See Fig. 9-10.

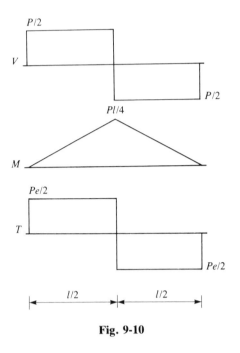

Fig. 9-10

9.8. The simply supported beam in Fig. 9-7(d).

See Fig. 9-11.

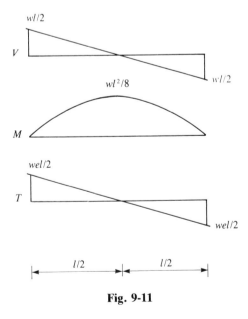

Fig. 9-11

9.9. In A36 steel, select a W shape with side plates to support the wall panel shown in Fig. 9-12. The beam is simply supported and has a span of 20 ft. The wall panel weighs 150 lb/ft^3.

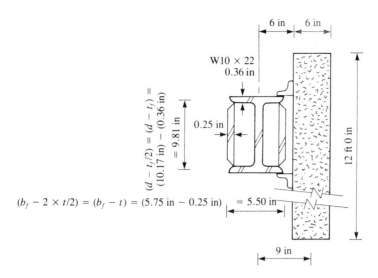

Fig. 9-12

The vertical load on the beam consists of the weights of the wall panel and the beam:

$$w \text{ (wall panel)} = 150\frac{\text{lb}}{\text{ft}^3} \times \frac{6 \text{ in}}{12 \text{ in/ft}} \times 12 \text{ ft} = 900 \text{ lb/ft}$$

$$w \text{ (beam assumed)} \qquad\qquad\qquad = 100 \text{ lb/ft}$$

$$\overline{}$$

$$w \text{ (total)} \qquad\qquad\qquad\qquad = 1000 \text{ lb/ft}$$

$$w = 1000 \text{ lb/ft} = 1.0 \text{ kips/ft}$$

As a result of an eccentricity of 9 in for the wall panel, the torsional moment

$$t = we = 900\frac{\text{lb}}{\text{ft}} \times \frac{9 \text{ in}}{12 \text{ in/ft}} = 675\frac{\text{lb-ft}}{\text{ft}}$$

$$= 0.675 \text{ kip-ft/ft}$$

For the case of dead load only [i.e., Formula (*A4-1*) in Chap. 2], the factored loads are

$$w_u = 1.4w = 1.4 \times 1.0 \text{ kips/ft} = 1.4 \text{ kips/ft}$$

$$t_u = 1.4t = 1.4 \times 0.675 \text{ kip-ft/ft} = 0.945 \text{ kip-ft/ft}$$

A W shape with side plates is a box section with negligible warping torsion. The problem of designing this beam for flexure combined with torsion can be divided into the following components. Flexure is resisted by the W shape; the flexural normal stresses by the flanges; and the flexural shear, by the web. The torsion (which in this case involves mainly St. Venant shear stresses) is resisted by a "box" consisting of the flanges and side plates.

The shear, moment, and torsion diagrams for this case [corresponding to Fig. 9-7(*d*)] appear in Fig. 9-11. The location of the maximum moment (and, hence, the maximum flexural normal stresses) is at midspan. Flexural and torsional shear are maximum at the end supports.

Design for flexure.

$$M_u = \frac{w_u l^2}{8} = \frac{1.4 \text{ kips/ft} \times (20 \text{ ft})^2}{8} = 70 \text{ kip-ft}$$

Because a box shape will not experience lateral torsional buckling, $\phi_b M_n = \phi_b M_p$. From p. 3-16 of the AISC LRFD Manual, for a W10×22, $\phi_b M_p = 70.2$ kip-ft > 70 kip-ft required. Try a W10×22.

Check flexural shear. From the shear diagram in Fig. 9-11, the maximum flexural shear is

$$V_u = \frac{w_u l}{2} = \frac{1.4 \text{ kips/ft} \times 20 \text{ ft}}{2} = 14 \text{ kips}$$

From p. 3-33 of the AISC LRFD Manual, for a W10×22, $\phi_v V_n = 47.4 \text{ kips} > 14 \text{ kips}$ required. The W10×22 is okay.

Regarding torsional shear, try $\frac{1}{4}$-in side plates. The maximum torsional moment (as shown in Fig. 9-11) is

$$T_u = \frac{w_u e l}{2} = \frac{t_u l}{2} = 0.945 \frac{\text{kip-ft}}{\text{ft}} \times \frac{20 \text{ ft}}{2} = 9.45 \text{ kip-ft}$$

The torsional shear stresses for a rectangular tube (from Table 9-1) are

$$f_{vST} = \frac{T}{2bht}$$

For the side plates (where $t = 0.25$ in)

$$f_{vST} = \frac{9.45 \text{ kip-ft} \times 12 \text{ in/ft}}{2 \times 5.50 \text{ in} \times 9.81 \text{ in} \times 0.25 \text{ in}} = 4.2 \text{ ksi}$$

For the flanges (where $t = 0.36$)

$$f_{vST} = \frac{9.45 \text{ kip-ft} \times 12 \text{ in/ft}}{2 \times 5.50 \times 9.81 \times 0.36 \text{ in}} = 2.9 \text{ ksi}$$

In both cases, the torsional shear stresses are within the limits set by Formula [9.3]:

$$f_{uv} \le 0.6\phi F_y = 0.6 \times 0.90 \times 36 \text{ ksi} = 19.4 \text{ ksi}$$

Use a W10×22 beam with $\frac{1}{4}$-in side plates.

9.10. For the beam in Prob. 9.9, select a W shape without side plates.

The major differences between a box section and a W shape acting as beams are in the resistance to torsion. Unlike the box beam in Prob. 9.9, a W section will experience significant warping torsion. As a result

(1) Normal stresses due to warping torsion are superimposed on the flexural normal stresses. (Both types of normal stresses are maximum in the flanges at midspan of the member.)

(2) Shear stresses due to warping torsion are superimposed on the shear stresses from St. Venant torsion. (Both are maximum at the supports; the former occur only in the flanges, while the latter occur in the web as well.)

(3) Also, the web shear stresses from St. Venant torsion add to the flexural shear stresses. (Both are maximum at the supports; the later are primarily in the web.)

Warping Torsion
Figure 9-13, which corresponds to Fig. 9-3, approximates the effects of warping torsion on the W14×99 beam. The uniformly distributed factored torque $t_u = 0.945$ kip-ft/ft (obtained in the solution to Prob. 9.9) is resolved into equal-and-opposite uniform loads on the flanges. Each flange is assumed to be a laterally loaded beam spanning between the end supports.

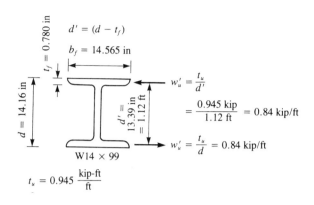 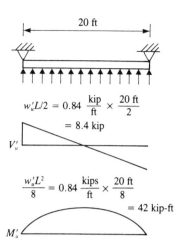

Fig. 9-13

From Fig. 9-13, the equivalent uniform lateral flange load is 0.84 kip/ft and the resulting maximum shear and moment are $V'_u = 8.4$ kips and $M'_u = 42$ kip-ft, respectively.

The maximum warping normal stress is

$$f_{nT} = \frac{M'_u}{S'}$$

where

$$S' = \frac{t_f b_f^2}{6} \quad \text{(section modulus of flange)}$$

$$= \frac{0.78 \text{ in} \times (14.565 \text{ in})^2}{6} = 27.6 \text{ in}^3$$

$$f_{nT} = \frac{42 \text{ kip-ft} \times 12 \text{ in/ft}}{27.6 \text{ in}^3} = 18.3 \text{ ksi}$$

The maximum warping shear stress is

$$f_{vWT} = \frac{1.5 \, V'_u}{b_f t_f} \quad \text{(for shear on a rectangular shape)}$$

$$= \frac{1.5 \times 8.4 \text{ kips}}{14.565 \text{ in} \times 0.78 \text{ in}} = 1.1 \text{ ksi}$$

St. Venant Torsion

As given in Table 9-1 for open sections, the shear stresses due to St. Venant torsion are $f_{vST} = Tt_i/J$.

For a W14×99, $J = 5.37$ in^4, as tabulated under Torsional Properties in Part 1 of the AISC LRFD Manual. For a W14×99, $t_f = 0.78$ in and $t_w = 0.485$ in. Maximum $T_u = 9.45$ kip-ft, as determined in Prob. 9.9.

In the flanges

$$f_{vST} = \frac{9.45 \text{ kip-ft} \times 0.78 \text{ in} \times 12 \text{ in/ft}}{5.37 \text{ in}^4} = 16.5 \text{ ksi}$$

In the web

$$f_{vST} = \frac{9.45 \text{ kip-ft} \times 0.485 \text{ in} \times 12 \text{ in/ft}}{5.37 \text{ in}^4} = 10.2 \text{ ksi}$$

Flexure

From Prob. 9.9, as a result of flexure: maximum $M_{ux} = 70$ kip-ft and maximum $V_u = 14$ kips. The corresponding flexural normal and shear stresses are M_{ux}/S_x and V_u/A_w.

From Part 1 of the AISC LRFD Manual, the required properties of a W14×99 are

$$S_x = 157 \text{ in}^3$$

$$A_w = dt_w = 14.16 \text{ in} \times 0.485 \text{ in} = 6.87 \text{ in}^2$$

Then

$$\frac{M_{ux}}{S_x} = \frac{70 \text{ kip-ft} \times 12 \text{ in/ft}}{157 \text{ in}^3} = 5.4 \text{ ksi}$$

$$\frac{V_u}{A_w} = \frac{14 \text{ kips}}{6.87 \text{ in}^2} = 2.0 \text{ ksi}$$

Combining Stresses

(1) Normal stresses (maximum in the flanges at midspan). From Eq. [9.2]

$$f_{un} = \frac{P_u}{A} \pm \frac{M_{ux}}{S_x} \pm \frac{M_{uy}}{S_y} \pm f_{nT}$$

$$= 0 + 5.4 \text{ ksi} + 0 + 18.3 \text{ ksi} = 23.7 \text{ ksi}$$

$$\phi F_y = 0.90 \times 36 \text{ ksi} = 32.4 \text{ ksi}$$

$$(f_{un} = 23.7 \text{ ksi}) < (F_y = 32.4 \text{ ksi}) \qquad \text{o.k.}$$

(2) Flange shear stresses (maximum at the supports). Because flexural shear is negligible in the flanges of a W shape, Eq. [9.4] reduces to

$$f_{uv} = f_{vST} + f_{vWT}$$

$$= 16.5 \text{ ksi} + 1.1 \text{ ksi} = 17.6 \text{ ksi}$$

$$0.6\phi F_y = 0.6 \times 32.4 \text{ ksi} = 19.4 \text{ ksi}$$

$$(f_{uv} = 17.6 \text{ ksi}) < (0.6\phi F_y = 19.4 \text{ ksi}) \qquad \text{o.k.}$$

(3) Web shear stresses (maximum at the supports): Warping shear stresses are zero in the web of a W section. Equation [9.4] becomes

$$f_{uv} = \frac{V_u}{A_w} \pm f_{vST}$$

$$= 2.0 \text{ ksi} + 10.2 \text{ ksi} = 12.2 \text{ ksi}$$

$$0.6\phi F_y = 19.4 \text{ ksi} \qquad \text{(as above)}$$

$$(f_{uv} = 12.2 \text{ ksi}) < (0.6\phi F_y = 19.4 \text{ ksi}) \qquad \text{o.k.}$$

Regarding the limit state of buckling, because a W14×99 is compact in A36 steel, local buckling need not be considered. However, if the 20-ft member is not laterally braced, lateral-torsional buckling should be checked using Formula [9.5]: $f_{un} \le \phi_c F_{cr}$, where $\phi_c = 0.85$. To determine F_{cr}, use the ratios

$$\frac{F_{cr}}{F_y} \approx \frac{\phi_b M_n}{\phi_b M_p}$$

For a simply supported member ($C_b = 1.0$), the beam graphs (in Part 3 of the AISC LRFD Manual) indicate for a W14×99

$$\phi_b M_n = 450 \text{ kip-ft} \qquad (L_b = 20 \text{ ft})$$

$$\phi_b M_p = 467 \text{ kip-ft} \qquad (L_b \le L_p = 15.5 \text{ ft})$$

From this ratio, it follows that

$$\frac{F_{cr}}{36 \text{ ksi}} = \frac{450 \text{ kip-ft}}{467 \text{ kip-ft}}$$

$$F_{cr} = 34.7 \text{ ksi}$$

Formula [9.5] becomes $f_{un} \le 0.85 \times 34.7 \text{ ksi} = 29.5 \text{ ksi}$. Because $f_{un} = 23.7 \text{ ksi} < 29.5 \text{ ksi}$, the W14×99 beam is satisfactory.

Supplementary Problems

9.11. Design a box beam (A36 steel, 20 ft long) to carry the $150 \, lb/ft^3$ wall panel shown in Fig. 9-12. Determine the magnitudes and locations of the maximum normal and shear stresses.

Ans. $10 \, in \times 10 \, in \times \frac{3}{8} \, in$.

$$f_{un} = \frac{M_{ux}}{S_x} = 18.8 \, \text{ksi}$$

$$f_{uv} = \frac{V_u}{A_w} + f_{vST} = 14.0 \, \text{ksi}$$

9.12. If $F_y = 50 \, \text{ksi}$, select a W shape to carry the wall panel in Fig. 9-12.

Ans.   W14 × 90.

In Probs. 9.13 to 9.15, a uniform torque of 1.0 kip-ft/ft is applied to the shaft shown in Fig. 9-14. Determine the maximum shear and normal stresses.

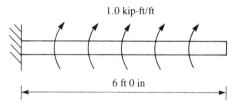

1.0 kip-ft/ft

6 ft 0 in

Fig. 9-14

9.13. Round bar, 3-in diameter.

Ans. $f_{vST} = 13.6 \, \text{ksi}, \, f_n = 0$.

9.14. Standard pipe, 3-in diameter.

Ans. $f_{vST} = 20.9 \, \text{ksi}, \, f_n = 0$.

9.15. Square tube, 3 in × 3 in × $\frac{1}{4}$ in thick.

Ans. $f_{vST} = 19.0 \, \text{ksi}, \, f_n = 0$.

Chapter 10

Composite Members

NOTATION

A_B = bearing area of concrete, in^2

A_c = cross-sectional area of concrete, in^2

A_r = cross-sectional area of longitudinal reinforcing bars, in^2

A_s = cross-sectional area of structural steel, in^2

A_{sc} = cross-sectional area of a shear stud, in^2

b = width of a rectangular steel tube, in

C_b = bending coefficient, defined in Eq. [5.10]

c_1 = 1.0 for concrete-filled pipe and tubing; 0.7 for concrete-encased sections [Eq. (12-1)]

c_2 = 0.85 for concrete-filled pipes and tubing; 0.6 for concrete-encased sections [Eq. (12-1)]

c_3 = 0.4 for concrete-filled pipe and tubing; 0.2 for concrete-encased sections [Eq. (12-2)]

D = outer diameter of pipe sections, in

E = modulus of elasticity of steel = 29,000 ksi

E_c = modulus of elasticity of concrete [Eq. [10.1]), ksi

E_m = modified modulus of elasticity for the design of composite compression members, ksi

F_{cr} = critical compressive stress, ksi

F_{my} = modified yield stress for the design of composite compression members, ksi

F_u = minimum specified tensile strength of a stud shear connector, ksi

F_y = specified minimum yield stress of the structural steel shape, ksi

F_{yr} = specified minimum yield stress of the longitudinal reinforcing bars, ksi

f_c' = specified compressive strength of the concrete, ksi

H_s = stud length (Fig. 10-2), but not to exceed $(h_r + 3)$, in

h_c = steel beam web dimension defined in Fig. 5-2, in

h_r = nominal steel deck rib height (Fig. 10-2), in

K = effective length factor for columns

L_b = unbraced length of beam, ft

L_c = length of channel shear connector, in

L_m = limiting unbraced length for full plastic bending capacity $(C_b > 1.0)$, ft

L_p = limiting unbraced length for full plastic bending capacity $(C_b = 1.0)$, ft

l = unbraced length of the member, in

M_n = nominal flexural strength of member, kip-in or kip-ft

N_r = number of studs in one rib at a beam intersection, but not to exceed 3

n = number of shear connectors required between a section of maximum moment and the nearest section of zero moment

P_e = elastic buckling load, defined in Eq. [10.9], kips

P_n = nominal axial strength of member, kips

P_{nc} = the part of P_n resisted by the concrete, kips

P_u = required axial strength, kips

Q_n = shear capacity of one connector, kips

$\Sigma\, Q_n$ = summation of Q_n between the point of maximum moment and the nearest point of zero moment, kips

r_m = modified radius of gyation for composite columns, in

t = thickness of steel, in

t_f = flange thickness, in

t_w = web thickness, in

V_n = total horizontal shear transferred between sections of maximum and zero moments, kips

w = unit weight of concrete, lb/ft^3

w_r = as defined in Fig. 10-2, in

λ_c = column slenderness parameter

ϕ_B = resistance factor for bearing on concrete = 0.60

$\phi_b M_n$ = design flexural strength, kip-in or kip-ft

ϕ_b = resistance factor for bending

$\phi_c P_n$ = design strength of compression member, kips

$\phi_c P_{nc}$ = the portion of the design compressive strength of a composite column resisted by the concrete, kips

ϕ_c = resistance factor for axial compression = 0.85

INTRODUCTION

Composite members consist of rolled or built-up structural steel shapes and concrete. Examples of composite members shown in Fig. 10-1 (p. 125) include (a) concrete-encased steel columns, (b) concrete-filled steel columns, (c) concrete-encased steel beams, and (d) steel beams interactive with and supporting concrete slabs. In contrast with classical structural steel design, which considers only the strength of the steel, composite design assumes that the steel and concrete work together in resisting loads. The inclusion of the contribution of the concrete results in more economical designs, as the required quantity of steel can be reduced.

The provisions for the design of composite columns, beams, and beam-columns discussed in this chapter are from Chap. I of the AISC LRFD Specification. Design aids are provided in Part 4 of the AISC LRFD Manual.

COLUMNS AND OTHER COMPRESSION MEMBERS

The design of composite compression members is similar to that of noncomposite columns. The equations for composite design (Eqs. [10.2] to [10.6], below) are the same as Eq. (E2-1) to (E2-4) in Chap. 4, with the following exceptions: in the design of the structural steel section in a composite member, a modified yield stress F_{my} and a modified modulus of elasticity E_m are used to account for the contributions of the concrete and the longitudinal reinforcing bars.

$$F_{my} = F_y + c_1 F_{yr}\frac{A_r}{A_s} + c_2 f'_c\frac{A_c}{A_s} \qquad (12\text{-}1)$$

$$E_m = E + c_3 E_c\frac{A_c}{A_s} \qquad (12\text{-}2)$$

where
$$E_c = w^{1.5}\sqrt{f'_c} \qquad [10.1]$$

and F_{my} = modified yield stress for the design of composite columns, ksi

F_y = specified minimum yield stress of the structural steel shape, ksi

F_{yr} = specified minimum yield stress of the longitudinal reinforcing bars, ksi

f'_c = specified compressive strength of the concrete, ksi

E_m = modified modulus of elasticity for the design of composite columns, ksi

E = modulus of elasticity of steel = 29,000 ksi

E_c = modulus of elasticity of concrete, ksi

w = unit weight of concrete, lb/ft^3

A_c = cross-sectional area of concrete, in^2

A_r = cross-sectional area of longitudinal reinforcing bars, in^2

A_s = cross-sectional area of structural steel, in^2

For concrete-filled pipe and tubing: $c_1 = 1.0$, $c_2 = 0.85$, and $c_3 = 0.4$. For concrete-encased shapes $c_1 = 0.7$, $c_2 = 0.6$, and $c_3 = 0.2$. Utilizing F_{my} and E_m as defined above, the design strength of axially loaded composite columns is $\phi_c P_n$, where $\phi_c = 0.85$ and

$$P_n = A_s F_{cr} \qquad [10.2]$$

If $\lambda_c \leq 1.5$ (inelastic column buckling)

$$F_{cr} = (0.658^{\lambda_c^2}) F_{my} \qquad [10.3]$$

or

$$F_{cr} = [\exp(-0.419\lambda_c^2)] F_{my} \qquad [10.4]$$

where $\exp(x) = e^x$.

If $\lambda_c > 1.5$ (elastic column buckling)

$$F_{cr} = \left(\frac{0.877}{\lambda_c^2}\right) F_{my} \qquad [10.5]$$

where

$$\lambda_c = \frac{Kl}{r_m \pi} \sqrt{\frac{F_{my}}{E_m}} \qquad [10.6]$$

and A_s = cross-sectional area of structural steel, in^2

K = effective length factor, discussed in Chap. 4

l = unbraced length of the member, in

r_m = radius of gyration of the steel shape, but not less than 0.3 times the overall thickness of the composite cross section in the plane of buckling, in

In Sec. I2, the AISC LRFD Specification places the following restrictions on composite columns.

(a)   The cross-sectional area of structural steel $A_s \geq 4$ percent of the total area of the composite cross section. Otherwise, design as a reinforced concrete column.

(b)   Concrete encasement of steel shall be reinforced with longitudinal bars and lateral ties. Maximum spacing of lateral ties shall be two-thirds of the least dimension of the composite cross section. The minimum cross-sectional area of all reinforcement (lateral and longitudinal) shall be 0.007 in^2 per inch of bar spacing. A clear concrete cover of at least 1.5 in must be provided outside all reinforcement at the perimeter.

(c)   Minimum design f'_c is 3 ksi for normal-weight concrete, and 4 ksi for lightweight concrete. Maximum design f'_c is 8 ksi.

(d)   For both structural and reinforcing steel, design $F_y \leq 55$ ksi.

(e) The wall thicknesses of structural steel members filled with concrete

$$t \geq b \sqrt{\frac{F_y}{3E}} \qquad \text{for each face of width } b \text{ in rectangular tubes,}$$

$$t \geq D \sqrt{\frac{F_y}{8E}} \qquad \text{for pipes of outside diameter } D$$

(f) If a composite cross section includes two or more steel shapes, the shapes shall be connected with batten plates, tie plates, or lacing to prevent buckling of each shape before hardening of the concrete.

(g) The part of the design compressive strength resisted by the concrete $\phi_c P_{nc}$ must be developed by direct bearing at connections.

$$\phi_c P_{nc} \leq 1.7 \phi_B f'_c A_B \qquad\qquad\qquad [10.7]$$

where $\phi_B = 0.60 =$ the resistance factor in bearing on concrete and $A_B =$ the bearing area, in².

The design of composite columns can be accomplished through the Composite Column Tables in Part 4 of the AISC LRFD Manual for the cross sections tabulated therein, or the above equations for all cross sections.

BEAMS AND OTHER FLEXURAL MEMBERS

The most common case of a composite flexural member is a steel beam interacting with a concrete slab, as shown in Fig. 10-1(d). The slab can be either a solid reinforced concrete slab or a concrete slab on a corrugated metal deck. In either case, stud or channel shear connectors are essential to ensure composite action. (When designed in accordance with this section, a beam is composite regardless of the type of deck. A steel deck is designated as a composite deck when it contains embossments on its upper surfaces to bond it to the concrete slab; the beams supporting it may or may not be composite in this case.)

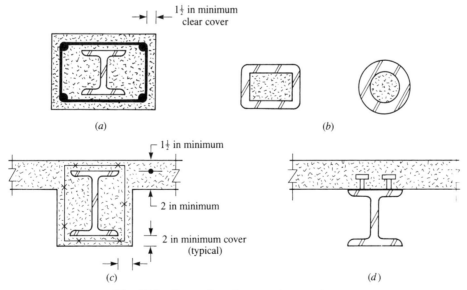

Fig. 10-1 Examples of composite members

Three criteria determine the *effective width* of a concrete slab acting compositely with a steel beam. On either side of the beam centerline, the effective width of concrete slab cannot exceed (a) one-eighth of the beam spin, (b) one-half of the distance to the centerline of the adjacent beam, or (c) the distance to the edge of the slab.

The horizontal shear forces between the steel beam and concrete slab, to be transferred by the shear connectors, are as follows.

In regions of *positive moment*, between the points of zero and maximum positive moments (e.g., between a support point and midspan on a uniformly loaded, simply supported beam), the smallest of (1) $0.85f'_c A_c$ (the maximum possible compressive force in the concrete), (2) $A_s F_y$ (the maximum possible tensile force in the steel), and (3) ΣQ_n (the capacity of the shear connectors).

In regions of *negative moment*, between the points of zero and maximum negative moments (e.g., between the free end and the support on a cantilever beam), the smaller of (4) $A_r F_{yr}$ (the maximum possible tensile force in the reinforcement) and (5) ΣQ_n (the capacity of the shear connectors).

When sufficient shear connectors are provided (in accordance with the section on shear connectors below) to allow condition 1, 2, or 4 above to govern, there is *full composite action*. However, if the number of shear connectors is reduced and condition 3 or 5 governs, the result is *partial composite action*.

DESIGN FLEXURAL STRENGTH

For *positive moment*, the design flexural strength $\phi_b M_n$ is determined as follows.

If $h_c/t_w \le 640/\sqrt{F_y}$ (i.e., the web of the steel beam is compact, which is true for all rolled W shapes in A36 steel), $\phi_b = 0.85$, and M_n is calculated from the *plastic stress distribution* on the composite section. The assumptions are (*a*) a uniform compressive stress of $0.85f'_c$ and zero tensile strength in the concrete, (*b*) a uniform steel stress of F_y in the tension area and compression area (if any) of the steel section, and (*c*) that the net tensile force in the steel section equals the compressive force in the concrete slab.

If $h_c/t_w > 640/\sqrt{F_y}$ (i.e., the web of the steel beam is not compact), $\phi_b = 0.90$, and M_n is calculated from the *elastic stress distribution*, considering the effects of shoring. The assumptions are (*a*) the strains in the steel and concrete are proportional to the distance from the neutral axis; (*b*) steel stress, tension or compression, equals strain times E, but cannot exceed F_y; (*c*) concrete compressive stress equals strain times E_c, but cannot exceed $0.85f'_c$; and (*d*) tensile strength is zero in the concrete.

For *negative moments* the design flexural strength $\phi_b M_n$ is determined by most engineers according to the provisions in Chap. 5, neglecting composite action. However, if the steel beam is compact and adequately braced (i.e., $L_b \le L_p$ for $C_b = 1.0$, or $L_b \le L_m$ for $C_b > 1.0$) and the slab reinforcement is properly developed, the negative flexural design strength may be determined as follows: $\phi_b = 0.85$, and M_n is calculated from the *plastic stress distribution* on the composite section. The assumptions are

(*a*) a tensile stress of F_{yr} in all adequately developed longitudinal reinforcing bars within the effective width of the concrete slab

(*b*) no tensile strength in the concrete

(*c*) a uniform stress of F_y in the tension and compression areas of the steel section and

(*d*) that the net compressive force in the steel section equals the total tensile force in the reinforcement

The issue of *shoring* is important in composite design. If temporary shores are used during construction to help the steel beams support the newly poured "wet" concrete, design is as outlined above, with the composite section resisting the total factored load, dead plus live. If shoring is not anticipated, the bare steel beam must also be checked for adequacy to support the wet concrete and other construction loads (properly factored) in accordance with the requirements of Chap. 5.

Because of beam stress redistribution under full plastification, the total factored load for unshored construction can still be assumed to act on the composite section, whenever design with a *plastic stress distribution* is allowed by the AISC LRFD Specification. However, if an *elastic stress distribution* is required, (1) the unshored loads applied prior to curing of the concrete (defined as attaining 75 percent of f'_c) must be taken by the steel beam alone, and (2) only the subsequent loads can be resisted by composite action. In the latter case, the total flexural stress at any point in the steel beam is a superposition of the two effects.

SHEAR CONNECTORS

Acceptable as shear connectors are headed steel studs of minimum four stud diameters in length and rolled steel channels. The nominal strength of a single *stud* shear connector in a solid concrete slab is

$$Q_n = 0.5A_{sc}\sqrt{f'_c E_c} \leq A_{sc}F_u \qquad (15\text{-}1)$$

where A_{sc} is the cross-sectional area of the stud, in^2, and F_u is the minimum specified tensile strength of the stud, ksi.

The nominal strength of a single *channel* shear connector in a solid concrete slab is

$$Q_n = 0.3(t_f + 0.5t_w)L_c\sqrt{f'_c E_c} \qquad (15\text{-}2)$$

where t_f = flange thickness of the channel, in

t_w = web thickness of the channel, in

L_c = length of the channel, in

The number of shear connectors required between a section of maximum moment and the nearest section of zero moment is

$$n = \frac{V_h}{Q_n} \qquad [10.8]$$

where Q_n = the shear capacity of one connector [as determined from Eq. (15-1) or (15-2)], kips and V_h = the total horizontal shear force to be transferred, kips.

As discussed above, in regions of positive moment, V_h = the minimum of ($0.85f'_c A_c$, $A_s F_y$, and ΣQ_n), while in regions of negative moment, V_h = the minimum of ($A_r F_{yr}$ and ΣQ_n).

Shear connectors may be uniformly distributed between the points of maximum and zero moment. However, when a concentrated load is present, enough connectors must be placed between the point of concentrated load and the point of zero moment to adequately develop the moment capacity required at the concentrated load.

The following restrictions on the placement and spacing of shear connectors are imposed by the AISC LRFD Specification:

(a) Minimum 1-in lateral concrete cover, except when installed in a steel deck

(b) Diameter of studs ≤2.5 times the thickness of the flange to which they are welded, unless they are located over the web

(c) Minimum center-to-center spacing of studs, longitudinally along the supporting beam, six diameters in solid slabs and four diameters in decks; laterally, four diameters in all cases

(d) Maximum center-to-center spacing of shear connectors of eight times the total slab thickness

SPECIAL PROVISIONS FOR STEEL DECKS

When a metal deck is used, the diameter of the shear studs must not exceed $\frac{3}{4}$ in. The studs may be welded to the steel beam either through the deck (which is the usual practice) or through holes punched in the deck. Additional restrictions affecting the studs and deck (from Sec. I3.5 of the AISC LRFD Specification) are shown in Fig. 10-2, which is reproduced (with permission) from the Commentary on the AISC LRFD Specification.

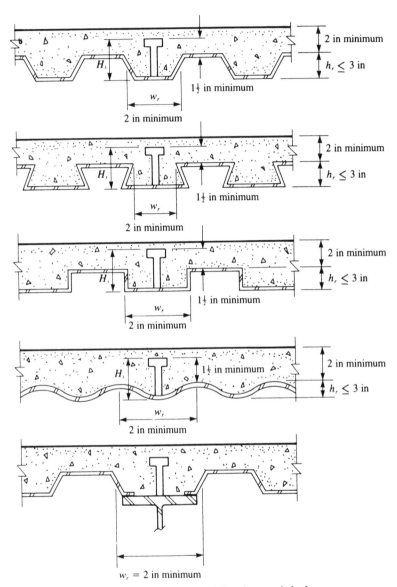

Fig. 10-2 Special provision for steel decks

When the *deck ribs are perpendicular to the steel beam*

(a) The concrete below the top of the steel deck is ignored in calculating A_c and other section properties.

(b) The longitudinal spacing of shear studs ≤32 in.

(c) The nominal strength of each shear stud [i.e., the middle term in Expression (*I5-1*), above] is multiplied by the reduction factor

$$\frac{0.85}{\sqrt{N_r}} \left(\frac{w_r}{h_r}\right) \left(\frac{H_s}{h_r} - 1.0\right) \le 1.0 \qquad (13\text{-}1)$$

where N_r = the number of studs in one rib at a beam intersection (≤ 3 in this formula, even if more than three studs are present) and w_r, h_r, and H_s are as defined in Fig. 10-2, in inches. In calculations, $H_s \leq (h_r + 3)$ must be used.

(d) The steel deck must be anchored to all supporting members at a spacing ≤ 16 in. Welded studs or arc spot (puddle) welds are satisfactory for this purpose.

When the *deck ribs are parallel to the steel beam*

(a) The concrete below the top of the steel deck is included in calculating A_c and other section properties.

(b) The deck may be cut longitudinally at a rib and separated to form a concrete haunch over the supporting steel beam, as shown at the bottom of Fig. 10-2.

(c) When $h_r \geq 1.5$ in, $w_r \geq 2$ in for the first stud in the transverse direction plus four stud diameters for each additional stud.

(d) When $w_r/h_r < 1.5$, the nominal strength of each shear stud [i.e., the middle term in Expression (15-1), above] must be multiplied by the reduction factor

$$0.6 \frac{w_r}{h_r} \left(\frac{H_s}{h_r} - 1.0 \right) \leq 1.0 \qquad (13\text{-}2)$$

CONCRETE-ENCASED BEAMS

The special case of a concrete-encased beam [shown in Fig. 10-1(c)], where shear connectors are not required for composite action, is as follows. A beam totally encased in concrete cast with the slab may be assumed bonded to the concrete if

(a) Concrete cover of the sides and soffit of the beam is at least 2 in.

(b) The top of the beam is at least $1\frac{1}{2}$ in below and 2 in above the bottom of the slab.

(c) The concrete encasement has sufficient welded wire mesh or bar reinforcing steel to prevent spalling of the concrete.

The design flexural strength of concrete-encased beams is $\phi_b M_n$, where $\phi_b = 0.90$ and M_n is calculated from either (a) the *elastic stress distribution on the composite section*, considering the effects of shoring, or (b) the *plastic stress distribution on the bare steel section* (i.e., $M_n = M_p = ZF_y$). Either way, there is no need to consider local buckling or lateral-torsional buckling of the steel beam because such buckling is inhibited by the encasement.

BEAM-COLUMNS: COMBINED FLEXURE AND COMPRESSION

Doubly and singly symmetric composite beam-columns are designed by the method presented in Chap. 8 for ordinary beam-columns [including Interaction Formulas (H1-1a) and (H1-1b), and simplified Second-Order Analysis Equations (H1-2) to (H1-6)], but with the following exceptions.

In Eqs. (H1-1a) and (H1-1b), $\phi_c P_n$ is as defined in this chapter for composite columns; similarly $\phi_b M_n$, where $\phi_b = 0.85$ and M_n is the nominal flexural strength calculated from the plastic stress distribution on the composite cross section. However, if $(P_u/\phi_c P_n) < 0.3$, M_n is determined by linear interpolation between M_n (calculated from the plastic stress distribution on the composite cross section) at $(P_u/\phi_c P_n) = 0.3$ and M_n for the appropriate composite beam (e.g., a concrete-encased beam) at $P_u = 0$.

In Eqs. (H1-3) and (H1-6)

$$P_e = A_s \frac{F_{my}}{\lambda_c^2} \qquad [10.9]$$

where A_s, F_{my}, and λ_c are as defined in this chapter. See Eqs. (12-1) and [10.6].

Beam-columns must conform with the minimum requirements for composite columns, listed as items (a) to (g) earlier in this chapter, under the heading Columns and Other Compression Members. If shear connectors are required for a beam (i.e., when $P_u = 0$), they must be provided for that member whenever $(P_u / \phi_c P_n) < 0.3$.

DESIGN SHEAR STRENGTH

The design shear strength for composite beams is taken as the shear strength of the steel web, as for noncomposite beams. The equations for shear strength in Chaps. 5 and 6 are, therefore, valid for composite flexural members.

Solved Problems

10.1. Select a 6-in concrete-filled pipe column for a required axial compressive strength of 200 kips, where $KL = 10.0$ ft, $F_y = 36$ ksi, $f'_c = 3.5$ ksi, normal weight (145 lb/ft³) concrete. See Prob. 4.11.

In Prob. 4.11, a noncomposite 6-in extrastrong pipe was required for the same conditions.
Try a 6-in standard-weight concrete-filled pipe. (See Fig. 10-3.)

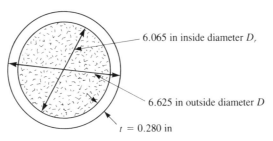

6.065 in inside diameter D_r

6.625 in outside diameter D

$t = 0.280$ in

Fig. 10-3

Check minimum wall thickness of pipe:

$$t \geq D \sqrt{\frac{F_y}{8E}} = 6.625 \text{ in} \sqrt{\frac{36 \text{ ksi}}{8 \times 29{,}000 \text{ ksi}}} = 0.083 \text{ in}$$

$$t = 0.280 \text{ in} > 0.083 \text{ in} \qquad \text{o.k.}$$

Check minimum cross-sectional area of steel pipe:

$$A_s = \pi (R^2 - R_i^2) = \frac{\pi}{4}(D^2 - D_i^2)$$

$$= \frac{\pi}{4}[(6.625 \text{ in})^2 - (6.065 \text{ in})^2] = 5.6 \text{ in}^2$$

$$A_c = \pi R_i^2 = \frac{\pi}{4} D_i^2 = \frac{\pi}{4} \times (6.065 \text{ in})^2 = 28.9 \text{ in}^2$$

$$\frac{A_s}{A_s + A_c} = \frac{5.6 \text{ in}^2}{5.6 \text{ in}^2 + 28.9 \text{ in}^2} = 0.16 > 4\% \qquad \text{o.k.}$$

In the absence of reinforcing bars, Eqs. $(12\text{-}1)$ and $(12\text{-}2)$ become

$$F_{my} = F_y + c_2 f_c' \frac{A_c}{A_s}$$

$$E_m = E + c_3 E_c \frac{A_c}{A_s}$$

where $E_c = w^{1.5}\sqrt{f_c'}$, $c_2 = 0.85$, $c_3 = 0.4$.

The modulus of elasticity of the concrete

$$E_c = 145^{1.5}\sqrt{3.5} = 3267 \text{ ksi}$$

The modified yield stress for composite design is

$$F_{my} = 36 \text{ ksi} + 0.85 \times 3.5 \text{ ksi} \times \frac{28.9 \text{ in}^2}{5.6 \text{ in}^2}$$

$$= 51.4 \text{ ksi}$$

The modified modulus of elasticity for composite design is

$$E_m = 29{,}000 \text{ ksi} + 0.4 \times 3267 \text{ ksi} \times \frac{28.9 \text{ in}^2}{5.6 \text{ in}^2}$$

$$= 35{,}744 \text{ ksi}$$

The radius of gyration of a hollow circular shape

$$r = \frac{\sqrt{D^2 + D_i^2}}{4} \quad \text{(See AISC LRFD Manual, p. 7-21.)}$$

$$= \frac{\sqrt{(6.625 \text{ in})^2 + (6.065 \text{ in})^2}}{4} = 2.25 \text{ in}$$

for the bare steel pipe.

The modified radius of gyration for composite design

$$r_m = r \ge 0.3D \text{ (the overall dimension)}$$

$$= 2.25 \text{ in} \ge (0.3 \times 6.625 \text{ in} = 1.99 \text{ in})$$

$$= 2.25 \text{ in}$$

The slenderness parameter

$$\lambda_c = \frac{Kl}{r_m \pi} \sqrt{\frac{F_{my}}{E_m}}$$

$$= \frac{10.0 \text{ ft} \times 12 \text{ in/ft}}{2.25 \text{ in} \times \pi} \sqrt{\frac{51.4 \text{ ksi}}{35{,}744 \text{ ksi}}} = 0.64$$

Because $\lambda_c < 1.5$

$$F_{cr} = (0.658^{\lambda_c^2})F_{my}$$

$$= 0.658^{(0.64)^2} \times 51.4 \text{ ksi} = 43.2 \text{ ksi}$$

The design compressive strength

$$\phi_c P_n = \phi_c A_s F_{cr}$$

$$= 0.85 \times 5.6 \text{ in}^2 \times 43.2 \text{ kips/in}^2$$

$$= 205 \text{ kips} > 200 \text{ kips required}$$

($\phi_c P_n = 205$ kips for this case is also tabulated on p. 4-100 of the AISC LRFD Manual.)
The 6-in standard-weight concrete-filled pipe-column is satisfactory.

10.2. Determine the design compressive strength of a W8$\times$40 (A36 steel) encased in a 16 in $\times$ 16 in ($f_c' = 3.5$ ksi) normal-weight concrete column in Fig. 10-4. Reinforcement is four No. 7 (Grade 60) bars longitudinally, and No. 3 ties at 10 in horizontally; $K_x L_x = K_y L_y = 15.0$ ft.

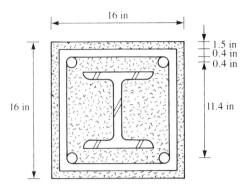

Fig. 10-4

Checking minimum requirements

(*a*)   For a W8×40, $A_s = 11.7 \text{ in}^2$, total area = 16 in × 16 in = 256 in^2

$$\frac{11.7 \text{ in}^2}{256 \text{ in}^2} = 4.6\% > 4\% \text{ minimum} \qquad\qquad \text{o.k.}$$

(*b*)   Lateral tie spacing = 10 in

$$< \tfrac{2}{3} \times 16 \text{ in outer dimension} = 10.7 \text{ in} \qquad \text{o.k.}$$

Minimum clear cover = 1.5 in   o.k.

Horizontal No. 3 bars: $A_r = 0.11 \text{ in}^2$ per bar

$$> 0.007 \text{ in}^2 \times 10 \text{ in spacing} = 0.07 \text{ in}^2 \qquad \text{o.k.}$$

Vertical No. 7 bars: $A_r = 0.60 \text{ in}^2$ per bar

$$> 0.007 \text{ in}^2 \times 11.4 \text{ in spacing} = 0.08 \text{ in}^2 \qquad \text{o.k.}$$

(*c*) $3.0 \text{ ksi} < (f'_c = 3.5 \text{ ksi}) < 8.0 \text{ ksi}$ for normal weight concrete   o.k.

(*d*)   Use $F_{yr} = 55 \text{ ksi}$ for reinforcement in calculations, even though actual $F_{yr} = 60 \text{ ksi}$ for Grade 60 bars.

Determine F_{my} and E_m:

$$F_{my} = F_y + c_1 F_{yr} \frac{A_r}{A_s} + c_2 f'_c \frac{A_c}{A_s}$$

where A_r = the cross-sectional area of four No. 7 longitudinal bars = $4 \times 0.6 \text{ in}^2 = 2.4 \text{ in}^2$
   A_s = cross-sectional area of W8×40 = 11.7 in^2
   A_c = 16 in × 16 in − $(11.7 \text{ in}^2 + 2.4 \text{ in}^2) = 242 \text{ in}^2$

For concrete-encased shapes, $c_1 = 0.7$ and $c_2 = 0.6$.

$$F_{my} = 36 \text{ ksi} + 0.7 \times 55 \text{ ksi} \times \frac{2.4 \text{ in}^2}{11.7 \text{ in}^2} + 0.6 \times 3.5 \text{ ksi} \times \frac{242 \text{ in}^2}{11.7 \text{ in}^2}$$

$$= 87.3 \text{ ksi}$$

$$E_m = E + c_e E_c \frac{A_c}{A_s}$$

where $c_3 = 0.2$ for concrete-encased shapes
   $E_c = w^{1.5}\sqrt{f'_c} = 145^{1.5}\sqrt{3.5} = 3267 \text{ ksi}$ for 3.5-ksi normal-weight (145 lb/ft^3) concrete
   $E_m = 29{,}000 \text{ ksi} + 0.2 \times 3267 \text{ ksi} \times 242 \text{ in}^2/11.7 \text{ in}^2 = 42{,}513 \text{ ksi}$

The modified radius of gyration

$$r_m = r_y(W8\times40) \geq 0.3 \times 16 \text{ in (overall dimension)}$$
$$= 2.04 \text{ in} \geq 4.80 \text{ in}$$
$$= 4.80 \text{ in}$$

The slenderness parameter

$$\lambda_c = \frac{Kl}{r_m\pi}\sqrt{\frac{E_{my}}{E_m}}$$
$$= \frac{15.0 \text{ ft} \times 12 \text{ in/ft}}{4.80 \text{ in} \times \pi}\sqrt{\frac{87.3 \text{ ksi}}{42,513 \text{ ksi}}} = 0.54$$

The critical stress

$$F_{cr} = (0.658^{\lambda_c^2})F_{my}$$
$$= 0.658^{(0.54)^2} \times 87.3 \text{ ksi} = 77.2 \text{ ksi}$$

The design compressive strength

$$\phi_c P_n = \phi_c A_s F_{cr}$$
$$= 0.85 \times 11.7 \text{ in}^2 \times 77.2 \text{ kips/in}^2$$
$$= 768 \text{ kips}$$

($\phi_c P_n = 768$ kips for this case is also tabulated on p. 4-73 of the AISC LRFD Manual.)

The 768-kip design strength is considerably more than the 238-kip design strength of a noncomposite W8×40 column under the same conditions. See Prob. 4.12.

10.3. Determine the design compressive strength of the composite column in Prob. 10.2 if $f'_c = 5.0$ ksi.

As in Prob. 10.2, the minimum requirements for a composite column are satisfied; $A_r = 2.4$ in^2, $A_s = 11.7$ in^2, $A_c = 242$ in^2, $c_1 = 0.7$, $c_2 = 0.6$, $c_3 = 0.2$.

$$F_{my} = F_y + c_1 F_{yr}\frac{A_r}{A_s} + c_2 f'_c\frac{A_c}{A_s}$$
$$= 36 \text{ ksi} + 0.7 \times 55 \text{ ksi} \times \frac{2.4 \text{ in}^2}{11.7 \text{ in}^2} + 0.6 \times 5.0 \text{ ksi} \times \frac{242 \text{ in}^2}{11.7 \text{ in}^2}$$
$$= 105.9 \text{ ksi}$$
$$E_c = w^{1.5}\sqrt{f'_c} = 145^{1.5}\sqrt{5.0} = 3904 \text{ ksi}$$
$$E_m = E + c_3 E_c\frac{A_c}{A_s}$$
$$= 29,000 \text{ ksi} + 0.2 \times 3904 \text{ ksi} \times \frac{242 \text{ in}^2}{11.7 \text{ in}^2}$$
$$= 45,150 \text{ ksi}$$

$r_m = 4.80$ in as in Prob. 10.2.

$$\lambda_c = \frac{Kl}{r_m\pi}\sqrt{\frac{F_{my}}{E_m}}$$
$$= \frac{15.0 \text{ ft} \times 12 \text{ in/ft}}{4.80 \text{ in} \times \pi}\sqrt{\frac{105.9 \text{ ksi}}{45,150 \text{ ksi}}} = 0.58$$

$$F_{cr} = (0.0658^{\lambda_c^2})F_{my}$$
$$= 0.658^{(0.58)^2} \times 105.9 \text{ ksi} = 92.1 \text{ ksi}$$
$$\phi_c P_n = \phi_c A_s F_{cr}$$
$$= 0.85 \times 11.7 \text{ in}^2 \times 92.1 \text{ ksi}$$
$$= 916 \text{ kips}$$

(as also tabulated on p. 4-85 of the AISC LRFD Manual).

10.4. Assume all the column load in Prob. 10.3 enters the composite column at one level. Determine A_B, the required bearing area of concrete.

$$\phi_c P_{nc} = \phi_c P_n - \phi_c P_{ns}$$

In other words, the part of the design compressive strength resisted by the concrete equals the total design compresive strength of the composite column minus the portion resisted by the steel.

In this case, $\phi_c P_n = 916$ kips and $\phi_c P_{ns} = 238$ kips.

$$\phi_c P_{nc} = 916 \text{ kips} - 238 \text{ kips} = 678 \text{ kips}$$

According to formula [10.7]

$$\phi_c P_{nc} \leq 1.7 \phi_B f_c' A_B$$

or

$$A_B \geq \frac{\phi_c P_{nc}}{1.7 \phi_B f_c'} = \frac{678 \text{ kips}}{1.7 \times 0.60 \times 5 \text{ ksi}} = 133 \text{ in}^2$$

The required concrete-bearing area of 133 in^2 can be satisfied by applying the load to a 12 in × 12 in bearing plate placed on the column.

For Probs. 10.5 to 10.9, determine

(*a*) The effective width of concrete slab for composite action
(*b*) V_h (the total horizontal shear force to be transferred) for full composite action
(*c*) The number of $\frac{3}{4}$-in-diameter shear studs required if $F_u = 60$ ksi

10.5. A W18×40 interior beam is shown in Fig. 10-5. Steel is A36, beam span is 30 ft 0 in, and beam spacing is 10 ft 0 in. The beams are to act compositely with a 5-in normal-weight concrete slab; $f_c' = 5.0$ ksi.

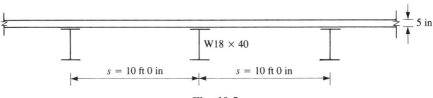

Fig. 10-5

(*a*) For an interior beam, the effective slab width on either side of the beam centerline is the minimum of

$$\frac{L}{8} = \frac{30.0 \text{ ft}}{8} = 3.75 \text{ ft} = 45 \text{ in}$$

$$\frac{s}{2} = \frac{10.0 \text{ ft}}{2} = 5.00 \text{ ft}$$

The effective slab width is 2 × 45 in = 90 in.

(*b*) In positive moment regions, V_h for full composite action is the smaller of

$$0.85f'_cA_c = 0.85 \times 5\text{ ksi} \times (90\text{ in} \times 5\text{ in})$$
$$= 1913\text{ kips}$$
$$A_sF_y = 11.8\text{ in}^2 \times 36\text{ ksi} = 425\text{ kips}$$
$$V_h = 425\text{ kips}$$

(*c*) The nominal strength of a single shear stud [from Eq. (*15-1*)] is

$$Q_n = 0.5A_{sc}\sqrt{f'_cE_c} \le A_{sc}F_u$$

For a $\frac{3}{4}$-in-diameter stud,

$$A_{sc} = \pi\left(\frac{0.75\text{ in}}{2}\right)^2 = 0.44\text{ in}^2$$
$$E_c = w^{1.5}\sqrt{f'_c} = 145^{1.5}\sqrt{5.0} = 3904\text{ ksi}$$
$$F_u = 60\text{ ksi}$$
$$Q_n = 0.5 \times 0.44\text{ in}^2\sqrt{5.0\text{ ksi} \times 3904\text{ ksi}} \le 0.44\text{ in}^2 \times 60\text{ ksi}$$
$$= 30.9\text{ kips} \le 26.4\text{ kips}$$
$$= 26.4\text{ kips per stud}$$

The number of shear connectors between the points of zero and maximum moments is

$$n = \frac{V_h}{Q_n} = \frac{425\text{ kips}}{26.4\text{ kips/stud}}$$
$$= 16.1\text{ or }17\text{ studs}$$

For the beam shown in Fig. 10-6, the required number of shear studs is $2n = 2 \times 17 = 34$.

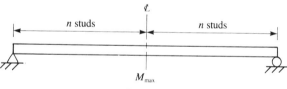

Fig. 10-6

Assuming a single line of shear studs (over the beam web), stud spacing $= 30.0\text{ ft}/34 = 0.88\text{ ft} = 10.6\text{ in}$. This is greater than the six-stud diameter (or $6 \times \frac{3}{4}\text{ in} = 4.5\text{ in}$) minimum spacing, and less than the eight slab thickness (or $8 \times 5\text{ in} = 40\text{ in}$) maximum spacing, which is satisfactory.

10.6. A W24×68 edge beam is shown in Fig. 10-7. Steel is A36, and the beam span is 32 ft 0 in. The beam is to act compositely with a 4-in lightweight concrete (110 lb/ft^3) slab; $f'_c = 3.5\text{ ksi}$.

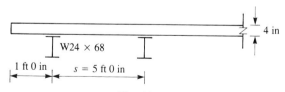

Fig. 10-7

(*a*) For the edge beam in Fig. 10-7, the effective slab width on the exterior (or left) side of the beam centerline is the minimum of $L/8 = 32.0\text{ ft}/8 = 4.0\text{ ft.}$ or distance to edge of slab $= 1.0\text{ ft} = 12\text{ in}$.

The effective slab width on the interior (or right) side of the beam centerline is the minimum of

$$\frac{L}{8} = \frac{32.0 \text{ ft}}{8} = 4.0 \text{ ft}$$

$$\frac{s}{2} = \frac{5.0 \text{ ft}}{2} = 2.5 \text{ ft} = 30 \text{ in}$$

The effective slab width is (12 in + 30 in) = 42 in.

(b)   In the positive moment regions, V_h for full composite action is the smaller of

$$0.85 f_c' A_c = 0.85 \times 3.5 \text{ ksi} \times (42 \text{ in} \times 4 \text{ in}) = 500 \text{ kips}$$

$$A_s F_y = 20.1 \text{ in}^2 \times 36 \text{ ksi} = 724 \text{ kips}$$

$$V_h = 500 \text{ kips}$$

(c)   The nominal strength of a single shear stud [from Eq. (15-1)] is

$$Q_n = 0.5 A_{sc} \sqrt{f_c' E_c} \leq A_{sc} F_u$$

$F_u = 60 \text{ ksi}$ $A_{sc} = 0.44 \text{ in}^2$ for $\frac{3}{4}$-in-diameter studs

$$E_c = w^{1.5} \sqrt{f_c'} = 110^{1.5} \sqrt{3.5} = 2158 \text{ ksi}$$

$$Q_n = 0.5 \times 0.44 \text{ in}^2 \sqrt{3.5 \text{ ksi} \times 2158 \text{ ksi}} \leq 0.44 \text{ in}^2 \times 60 \text{ ksi}$$

$$= 19.1 \text{ kips} \leq 26.4 \text{ kips}$$

$$= 19.1 \text{ kips per stud}$$

The number of shear connectors between the points of zero and maximum moments is $n = V_h/Q_n = 500 \text{ kips}/19.1 \text{ kips per stud} = 26.1$ or 27 studs. For the beam shown in Fig. 10-6, the required number of shear studs is $2n = 2 \times 27 = 54$.

Assuming a single line of shear studs (over the beam web), stud spacing = 32.0 ft/54 = 0.59 ft = 7.1 in. This is greater than the six stud diameter (or $6 \times \frac{3}{4}$ in = 4.5 in) minimum spacing, and less than the eight slab thickness (or 8×4 in = 32 in) maximum spacing, which is satisfactory.

10.7.   Assume the beams in Fig. 10-5 are cantilever beams: A36 steel, with a cantilever span of 8 ft 0 in. Slab reinforcement is No. 4 bars ($A_r = 0.20 \text{ in}^2$ per bar) at 1 ft 0 in center-to-center. Bars are Grade 60 steel.

(a)   For an interior beam, the effective slab width on either side of the beam centerline is the minimum of

$$\frac{L}{8} = \frac{8.0 \text{ ft}}{8} = 1.0 \text{ ft}$$

$$\frac{s}{2} = \frac{10.0 \text{ ft}}{2} = 5.0 \text{ ft}$$

The effective slab width is $2 \times 1.0 \text{ ft} = 2.0 \text{ ft}$.

(b)   In negative-moment regions (such as cantilevers): $V_h = A_r F_{yr}$ for full composite action, where A_r and F_{yr} are the cross-sectional area and minimum yield stress of the reinforcement, respectively. Because the slab is in tension, the concrete cannot participate in composite action.

For an effective slab width of 2.0 ft

$$A_r = \frac{0.20 \text{ in}^2}{\text{bar}} \times \frac{1 \text{ bar}}{\text{ft}} \times 2.0 \text{ ft width} = 0.40 \text{ in}^2$$

$$V_h = 0.40 \text{ in}^2 \times 60 \text{ ksi} = 24 \text{ kips}$$

(c)   The nominal strength of a single shear stud is $Q_n = 26.4 \text{ kips}$. Although $n = V_h/Q_n = 24 \text{ kips}/26.4 \text{ kips per stud} = 0.9$ would indicate that one stud is satisfactory, the actual number of shear studs is governed by the maximum spacing of eight times the slab thickness:

$$n = \frac{\text{span}}{\text{maximum spacing}}$$

$$= \frac{8.0\,\text{ft} \times 12\,\text{in/ft}}{8 \times 5\,\text{in}} = 2.4 \text{ or } 3 \text{ shear studs}$$

10.8. Repeat Prob. 10.5 with the following modification: The 5-in normal-weight concrete slab (shown in Fig. 10-5) consists of 2 in of concrete on a 3-in steel deck, with ribs spanning perpendicular to the W18×40 steel beam. See Fig. 10-8.

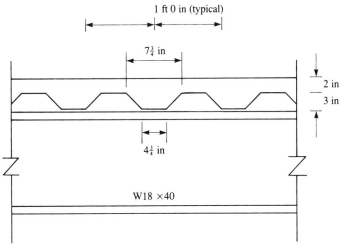

Fig. 10-8

Verifying compliance with the special provisions for steel decks (Fig. 10-2):

Nominal deck rib height $h_r = 3$ in maximum

Slab thickness above steel deck $= 2$ in minimum

Average width of concrete rib $w_r = (4.75 + 7.25)\,\text{in}/2 = 6.0\,\text{in} > 2$ in minimum

Shear stud diameter $= 0.75$ in maximum

Height of shear stud $H_s \geq (h_r + 1.5\,\text{in}) = (3.0 + 1.5)\,\text{in} = 4.5$ in

Use $4\tfrac{1}{2}$-in-long $\tfrac{3}{4}$-in-diameter shear studs.

(*a*) The effective slab width is 90 in, as in Prob. 10.5.

(*b*) Because the deck ribs are perpendicular to the steel beam, the concrete below the top of the steel deck is ignored in calculating A_c and other section properties. In regions of positive moment, V_h for full composite action is the smaller of

$$0.85 f'_c A_c = 0.85 \times 5\,\text{ksi} \times (90\,\text{in} \times 2\,\text{in}) = 765 \text{ kips}$$

$$A_s F_y = 11.8\,\text{in}^2 \times 36\,\text{ksi} = 425 \text{ kips}$$

$$V_h = 425 \text{ kips}$$

(*c*) For a solid slab, the nominal strength of a single shear stud (as determined in Prob. 10.5) is

$$Q_n = 0.5 A_{sc}\sqrt{f'_c E_c} \leq A_{sc} F_u$$

$$= 30.7 \text{ kips} \leq 26.4 \text{ kips} \qquad\qquad (15\text{-}1)$$

When the deck ribs are perpendicular to the steel beam, the middle term of Expression (*15-1*) is multiplied by the reduction factor

$$\frac{0.85}{\sqrt{N_r}}\left(\frac{w_r}{h_r}\right)\left(\frac{H_s}{h_r}-1.0\right)\le 1.0 \qquad (13\text{-}1)$$

From the solution to this problem, $w_r = 6$ in, $h_r = 3$ in, $H_s = 4.5$ in. Assume the number of stud connectors in one rib at a beam intersection $N_r = 2$. The reduction factor in expression (13-1) is

$$\frac{0.85}{\sqrt{2}}\times\frac{6\,\text{in}}{3\,\text{in}}\left(\frac{4.5\,\text{in}}{3\,\text{in}}-1.0\right)=0.60$$

Then

$$Q_n = 30.7\,\text{kips}\times 0.60\le 26.4\,\text{kips}$$
$$= 18.5\,\text{kips}\le 26.4\,\text{kips}$$
$$= 18.5\,\text{kips per stud}$$

The maximum number of shear connectors between the points of zero and maximum moments is $n = V_h/Q_n = 425\,\text{kips}/18.5\,\text{kips}$ per stud $= 23$ studs. As indicated by Fig. 10-6, the required minimum number of shear studs is $2n = 2\times 23 = 46$.

Because the deck ribs are spaced at 1 ft 0 in center-to-center, as shown in Fig. 10-8, there are 30 ribs for the 30-ft beam span. It is advisable to place two shear studs per rib, for a total of 60 studs.

The reader can verify that the minimum center-to-center spacing of shear studs in deck ribs of four diameters (i.e., $4\times 0.75\,\text{in} = 3\,\text{in}$) in any direction allows the two studs in each rib to be placed longitudinally or transversely in the case at hand (a W18×40 beam and a deck with a 4.75-in rib width at the bottom).

10.9. Repeat Prob. 10.6 with the following modification: The 4-in lightweight concrete slab (shown in Fig. 10-7) consists of 2 in of concrete on a 2-in steel deck, with ribs spanning perpendicular to the W24×68 steel beam. See Fig. 10-9.

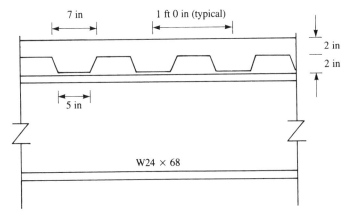

Fig. 10-9

Verifying compliance with the special provisions for steel decks (Fig. 10-2):

Nominal deck rib height $h_r = 2$ in < 3 in maximum

Slab thickness above steel deck $= 2$ in minimum

Average width of concrete rib $w_r = (5+7)\,\text{in}/2 = 6\,\text{in} > 2\,\text{in}$ minimum

Shear stud diameter $= 0.75$ in maximum

Height of shear stud $H_s \ge (h_r + 1.5\,\text{in}) = (2.0 + 1.5)\,\text{in} = 3.5\,\text{in}$

Use $3\frac{1}{2}$-in long $\frac{3}{4}$-in-diameter shear studs (*a*)   The effective slab width is 42 in, as in Prob. 10.6.

(*b*)   Because the deck ribs are perpendicular to the steel beam, the concrete below the top of the steel deck is ignored in calculating A_c.

   In regions of positive moment, V_h for full composite action is the smaller of

$$0.85 f'_c A_c = 0.85 \times 3.5 \text{ ksi} \times (42 \text{ in} \times 2 \text{ in}) = 250 \text{ kips}$$

$$A_s F_y = 20.1 \text{ in}^2 \times 36 \text{ ksi} = 724 \text{ kips}$$

$$V_h = 250 \text{ kips}$$

(*c*)   For a solid slab, the nominal strength of a single shear stud (as determined in Prob. 10.6) is

$$Q_n = 0.5 A_{sc} \sqrt{f'_c E_c} \le A_{sc} F_u$$

$$= 19.1 \text{ kips} \le 26.4 \text{ kips} \qquad\qquad (15\text{-}1)$$

If the deck ribs are perpendicular to the steel beam, the middle term of expression (*15-1*) is multiplied by the reduction factor

$$\frac{0.85}{\sqrt{N_r}} \left(\frac{w_r}{h_r}\right) \left(\frac{H_s}{h_r} - 1.0\right) \le 1.0 \qquad\qquad (13\text{-}1)$$

From the solution to this problem, $w_r = 6$ in, $h_r = 2$ in, $H_s = 3.5$ in. The reduction factor in expression (*13-1*) is

$$\frac{0.85}{\sqrt{N_r}} \left(\frac{6 \text{ in}}{2 \text{ in}}\right) \left(\frac{3.5 \text{ in}}{2 \text{ in}} - 1.0\right) \le 1.0$$

Regardless of the number of shear studs in one rib at a beam intersection (i.e., $N_r = 1$, 2, or 3), the reduction factor equals 1.0.

$$Q_n = 19.1 \text{ kips} \times 1.0 = 19.1 \text{ kips per stud}$$

The minimum number of shear connectors between the points of zero and maximum moments is $n = V_h / Q_n = 250 \text{ kips}/19.1 \text{ kips per stud} = 13.1$ or 14 studs.

   As indicated by Fig. 10-6, the required minimum number of shear studs is $2n = 2 \times 14 = 28$. Because the deck ribs are spaced at 1 ft 0 in center-to-center, as shown in Fig. 10-9, there are 32 ribs for the 32-ft beam span. It is advisable to place one shear stud per rib, for a total of 32 studs.

10.10. Determine the design flexural strength of the W18×40 beam in Prob. 10.5 with full composite action. Assume the beam is shored during construction.

Because the beam is shored, the entire load acts on a composite member. From the Properties Tables for W Shapes in Part 1 of the AISC LRFD Manual, for a W18×40

$$\left(\frac{h_c}{t_w} = 51.0\right) < \left(\frac{640}{\sqrt{F_y}} = \frac{640}{\sqrt{36}} = 106.7\right)$$

The design flexural strength is $\phi_b M_n$, where $\phi_b = 0.85$ and M_n is calculated from the plastic stress distribution on the composite section.

   From the solution to Prob. 10.5: the maximum possible compressive force in the concrete slab $C = 0.85 f'_c A_c = 1913$ kips; the maximum possible tensile force in the steel beam $T = A_s F_y = 425$ kips. To satisfy equilibrium, it is necessary that $C = T = 425$ kips. The plastic stress distribution is as shown in Fig. 10-10, with the plastic neutral axis (PNA) in the slab. In Fig. 10-10, $C = 0.85 f'_c ba$, where a is the depth of the compression block (in) and b is the effective slab width (in).

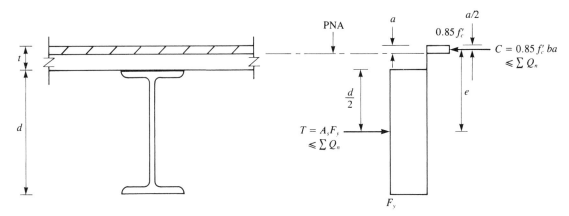

Fig. 10-10

From Prob. 10.5, $f_c' = 5.0$ ksi, $b = 90$ in.

Then,
$$a = \frac{C}{0.85 f_c' b} = \frac{425 \text{ kips}}{0.85 \times 5.0 \dfrac{\text{kips}}{\text{in}^2} \times 90 \text{ in}} = 1.11 \text{ in}$$

The nominal flexural strength
$$M_n = Te = T\left(\frac{d}{2} + t - \frac{a}{2}\right)$$

$$= 425 \text{ kips} \times \left(\frac{17.90 \text{ in}}{2} + 5 \text{ in} - \frac{1.11 \text{ in}}{2}\right)$$

$$= 425 \text{ kips} \times 13.39 \text{ in}$$

$$= 5693 \text{ kip-in} = 474 \text{ kip-ft}$$

The design flexural strength for full composite action is $\phi_b M_n = 0.85 \times 474$ kip-ft $= 403$ kip-ft.

This is nearly double the ($\phi_b M_p =$) 212-kip-ft design compressive strength of a noncomposite W18×40 beam of the same A36 steel (assuming adequate lateral bracing; i.e., $L_b \leq L_p$). (The composite beam is braced by the shear studs, spaced at 10.6 in, embedded in the concrete.)

10.11. Determine the design flexural strength of the W18×40 beam in Prob. 10.8. The 5-in-thick solid concrete slab (in Fig. 10-5) is replaced with 2 in of solid concrete on a 3-in steel deck with ribs perpendicular to the beam as shown in Fig. 10-8. Assume the beam is shored during construction.

When the deck ribs are perpendicular to the beam, the concrete below the top of the deck is neglected. In the case at hand, only the upper 2 in of concrete can be considered effective.

In Prob. 10.10, the PNA was located at 1.11 in below the top of the slab. (See Fig. 10-10.) All the concrete below the PNA is assigned zero strength because it is in tension. The solution to this problem is identical with that of Prob. 10.10; thus, a slab on a steel deck is equivalent to a solid slab if the deck is entirely within the tension zone of the concrete.

10.12. Repeat Prob. 10.10. Assume the beam is not shored during construction.

The solution to Probs. 10.10 and 10.11 (where the *plastic* stress distribution is used to determine M_n) is also valid for unshored construction. However, the bare steel beam must be checked for adequacy to support all loads applied prior to the concrete attaining 75 percent of its specified strength f_c'.

The construction loads on the noncomposite W18 × 40 beam in Prob. 10.10 (see Fig. 10-5) are

Dead Load

Beam $= 40\,\text{lb/ft}$

$\text{Slab} = 150\,\dfrac{\text{lb}}{\text{ft}^3} \times \dfrac{5\,\text{in thick}}{12\,\text{in/ft}} \times 10.0\,\text{ft wide}$ $= \dfrac{625\,\text{lb/ft}}{665\,\text{lb/ft}}$

Construction Live Load (assumed)

$= 20\,\dfrac{\text{lb}}{\text{ft}^2} \times 10.0\,\text{ft wide}$ $= 200\,\text{lb/ft}$

The factored uniform load is $1.2D + 1.6L$:

$$w_u = 1.2 \times 665\,\frac{\text{lb}}{\text{ft}} + 1.6 \times 200\,\frac{\text{lb}}{\text{ft}} = 1118\,\frac{\text{lb}}{\text{ft}} = 1.12\,\text{kips/ft}$$

The required strength $M_u = w_u L^2/8$.

$$M_u = \frac{1.12\ \text{kips/ft} \times (30.0\,\text{ft})^2}{8} = 126\,\text{kip-ft}$$

$< \phi_b M_n$ for the W18×40 alone, if $L_b \leq 16\,\text{ft}$. (See AISC LRFD Manual, p. 3-74.) The unshored noncomposite W18×40 beam is adequate during construction if it is laterally supported at least at one point (midspan).

10.13. Assume the moment diagram in Fig. 10-11 represents the required flexural strength of the composite W18×40 beam in Probs. 10.5 and 10.10. Determine the distribution of shear studs along the span.

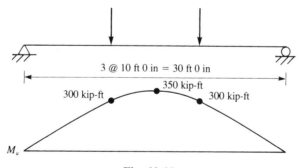

Fig. 10-11

In the solution to Prob. 10.10 it was determined that the design flexural strength of this composite beam for full composite action is $\phi_b M_n = 403\,\text{kip-ft}$. Since the required flexural strength $M_u \leq 350\,\text{kip-ft}$ throughout the span, try partial composite action. Instead of the $(2n =)$ 34 shear studs determined for Prob. 10.5(c) for full composite action, try $(2n =)$ 28 shear studs; i.e., $n = 14$ shear studs on each side of the midspan maximum-moment section.
Check spacing.

$$s = \frac{30.0\,\text{ft} \times 12\,\text{in/ft}}{28\,\text{studs}} = 12.9\,\text{in}$$

$< (8t = 8 \times 5\,\text{in} =)$ 40 in maximum spacing   o.k.

For partial composite action, the horizontal shear transferred by the studs between the points of zero and maximum moments $V_h = \sum Q_n = n Q_n = 14$ studs × 26.4 kips/stud = 370 kips. [The value $Q_n = 26.4$ kips per stud was determined in the solution to Prob. 10.5(c).]

Referring to Fig. 10-10

$$C = 0.85f'_c ba \leq \Sigma\, Q_n = 370 \text{ kips}$$

$$a = \frac{C}{0.85f'_c b} = \frac{370 \text{ kips}}{0.85 \times 5.0 \text{ kips/in}^2 \times 90 \text{ in}} = 0.97 \text{ in}$$

$$M_n = T_e = C_e = C\left(\frac{d}{2} + t - \frac{a}{2}\right)$$

$$= 370 \text{ kips} \times \left(\frac{17.90 \text{ in}}{2} + 5 \text{ in} - \frac{0.97 \text{ in}}{2}\right)$$

$$= 370 \text{ kips} \times 13.47 \text{ in}$$

$$= 4983 \text{ kip-in} = 415 \text{ kip-ft}$$

The design flexural strength for partial composite action is $\phi_b M_n = 0.85 \times 415 \text{ kip-ft} = 353 \text{ kip-ft}$ >350 kip-ft required. This is okay.

Try a uniform distribution of shear studs and check the design flexural strength at the concentrated loads, where the required strength is 300 kip-ft. (See Fig. 10-12.)

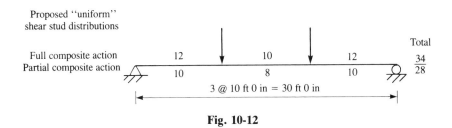

Fig. 10-12

At the points of concentrated load (partial composite action), $n = 10$ and

$$V_n = \Sigma\, Q_n = nQ_n = 10 \text{ studs} \times 26.4 \frac{\text{kips}}{\text{stud}} = 264 \text{ kips}$$

Referring to Fig. 10-10

$$C = 0.85f'_c ba \leq \Sigma\, Q_n = 264 \text{ kips}$$

$$a = \frac{C}{0.85f'_c b} = \frac{264 \text{ kips}}{0.85 \times 5.0 \text{ kips/in}^2 \times 90 \text{ in}} = 0.69 \text{ in}$$

$$M_n = Te = Ce = C\left(\frac{d}{2} + t - \frac{a}{2}\right)$$

$$= 264 \text{ kips} \times \left(\frac{17.90 \text{ in}}{2} + 5 \text{ in} - \frac{0.69 \text{ in}}{2}\right)$$

$$= 264 \text{ kips} \times 13.60 \text{ in}$$

$$= 3592 \text{ kip-in} = 299 \text{ kip-ft}$$

The design flexural strength for partial composite action is $\phi_b M_n = 0.85 \times 299 \text{ kip-ft} = 254 \text{ kip-ft}$ < 300 kip-ft required. Not adequate.

Try $n = 12$ shear studs from the end supports to the points of concentrated load

$$V_n = nQ_n = 12 \text{ studs} \times 26.4 \frac{\text{kips}}{\text{stud}} = 317 \text{ kips}$$

Referring to Fig. 10-10

$$a = \frac{C}{0.85 f'_c b} = \frac{317 \text{ kips}}{0.85 \times 5.0 \text{ kips/in}^2 \times 90 \text{ in}} = 0.83 \text{ in}$$

$$M_n = C\left(\frac{d}{2} + t - \frac{a}{2}\right)$$

$$= 317 \text{ kips} \times \left(\frac{17.90 \text{ in}}{2} + 5 \text{ in} - \frac{0.83 \text{ in}}{2}\right)$$

$$= 317 \text{ kips} \times 13.4 \text{ in}$$

$$= 4291 \text{ kip-in} = 358 \text{ kip-ft}$$

$\phi_b M_n = 0.85 \times 358$ kip-ft $= 304$ kip-ft > 300 kip-ft required. This is okay. (See Fig. 10-13.)

The *correct* shear stud distributions are

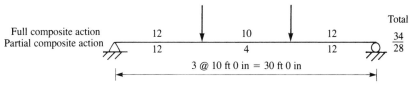

Fig. 10-13

Verifying that the four studs between the concentrated loads satisfy the limitation on maximum spacing (of eight slab thicknesses), we obtain

$$s = \frac{10.0 \text{ ft} \times 12 \text{ in/ft}}{4 \text{ studs}} = 30 \text{ in}$$

$$< 8t = 8 \times 5 \text{ in} = 40 \text{ in} \qquad \text{o.k.}$$

10.14. Determine the design flexural strength of the W24×68 beam in Prob. 10.6 with full composite action. Assume the beam is not shored during construction.

From the Properties Tables for W shapes in Part 1 of the AISC LRFD Manual, for a W24×68

$$\left(\frac{h_c}{t_w} = 52.0\right) < \left(\frac{640}{\sqrt{F_y}} = \frac{640}{\sqrt{36}} = 106.7\right)$$

Thus, the web is compact. Accordingly, the design flexural strength is $\phi_b M_n$, where $\phi_b = 0.85$ and M_n is calculated from the plastic stress distribution on the composite section. However, the absence of shoring necessitates that the noncomposite steel beam be checked for adequacy to support all loads applied before the concrete has reached 75 percent of its specified strength f'_c.

(a) Design flexural strength (M_n) of the composite beam. From the solution to Prob. 10.6, the maximum possible compressive force in the concrete slab $C_c = 0.85 f'_c A_c = 500$ kips; the maximum possible tensile force in the steel beam $T = A_s F_y = 724$ kips.

To satisfy equilibrium, $T = C$. The steel can be either in tension only, or in partial tension and compression, whereas the concrete cannot be in tension. The solution is $T = C = (500 + 724)$ kips/2 $= 612$ kips. The plastic stress distribution is as shown in Fig. 10-14. Because the net compressive force in the steel is less than the beam flange yield force (i.e., [$C_s = (612 - 500)$ kips $= 112$ kips] $\leq [b_f t_f F_y = 8.965$ in $\times 0.585$ in $\times 36$ kips/in$^2 = 189$ kips]), the plastic neutral axis (PNA) is located in the upper beam flange.

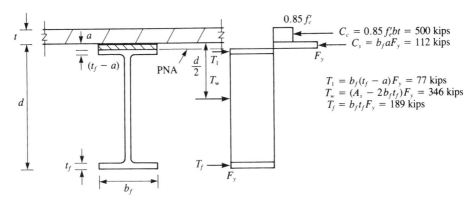

Fig. 10-14

The distance from the top of the beam to the PNA

$$a = \frac{C_s}{b_f F_y} = \frac{112 \text{ kips}}{8.965 \text{ in} \times 36 \text{ kips/in}^2} = 0.347 \text{ in}$$

The contribution to M_n from each element of beam or slab = element (tensile or compressive) force $\times$ the distance of element force from the PNA.

Contributions to M_n from

Compression in the slab $= C_c\left(\dfrac{t}{2} + a\right)$

$= 500 \text{ kips} \times \left(\dfrac{4 \text{ in}}{2} + 0.347 \text{ in}\right) \qquad\qquad = 1174 \text{ kip-in}$

Compression in upper beam flange $= C_s\dfrac{a}{2}$

$= 112 \text{ kips} \times \dfrac{0.347 \text{ in}}{2} \qquad\qquad = 19 \quad \text{kip-in}$

Tension in upper beam flange $= \dfrac{T_1(t_f - a)}{2}$

$= 77 \text{ kips} \times \dfrac{(0.585 - 0.347) \text{ in}}{2} \qquad\qquad = 9 \quad \text{kip-in}$

Tension in beam web $= T_w\left(\dfrac{d}{2} - a\right)$

$= 346 \text{ kips} \times \left(\dfrac{23.73 \text{ in}}{2} - 0.347 \text{ in}\right) \qquad = 3985 \text{ kip-in}$

Tension in lower beam flange $= T_f\left(d - \dfrac{t_f}{2} - a\right)$

$= 189 \text{ kips} \times \left(23.73 \text{ in} - \dfrac{0.585 \text{ in}}{2} - 0.347 \text{ in}\right) \quad = 4364 \text{ kip-in}$

$\overline{}$

9551 kip-in

$M_n = 9551 \text{ kip-in} = 796 \text{ kip-ft}$.

The design flexural strength $\phi_b M_n = 0.85 \times 796 \text{ kip-ft} = 677 \text{ kip-ft}$. This compares with $\phi_b M_p = 478 \text{ kip-ft}$ for a noncomposite W26×68 beam.

(b) Unshored steel beam supporting construction loads.

Dead Load

Beam   = 68 lb/ft

$$\text{Slab} = 150\,\frac{\text{lb}}{\text{ft}^3} \times \frac{4 \text{ in thick}}{12 \text{ in/ft}} \times \left(1.0 + \frac{5.0}{2}\right) \text{ ft wide} \quad = \frac{175 \text{ lb/ft}}{243 \text{ lb/ft}}$$

Construction Live Load (assumed)

$$= 20\,\frac{\text{lb}}{\text{ft}^2} \times \left(1.0 + \frac{5.0}{2}\right) \text{ ft wide} \qquad = 70 \text{ lb/ft}$$

The factored uniform load is $1.2D + 1.6L$:

$$w_u = 1.2 \times 243\,\frac{\text{lb}}{\text{ft}} + 1.6 \times 70\,\frac{\text{lb}}{\text{ft}} = 404 \text{ lb/ft}$$

$$= 0.40 \text{ kips/ft}$$

The required strength is $M_u = w_u L^2/8$.

$$M_u = \frac{0.40 \text{ kips/ft} \times (32.0 \text{ ft})^2}{8} = 52 \text{ kip-ft}$$

$< \phi_b M_n$ for the W24×68 even if $L_b =$ the full 32-ft span. (See AISC LRFD Manual, p. 3-71.) The unshored noncomposite W24 × 68 beam is adequate during construction even if it is not laterally braced.

10.15. Determine the design flexural strength of the W24×68 beam in Prob. 10.9. The 4-in solid concrete slab (in Fig. 10-7) is replaced with 2 in of solid concrete on a 2-in steel deck with ribs perpendicular to the beam, as shown in Fig. 10-9.

In the solution to Prob. 10.14 it was determined that

(a) Because the web of a W24×68 beam is compact, the design flexural strength is $\phi_b M_n$, where $\phi_b = 0.85$ and M_n is calculated from the plastic stress distribution on the composite section.

(b) The unshored noncomposite W24×68 beam can adequately support the 4-in solid concrete slab in Fig. 10-7. (It can surely carry the lighter 2-in solid slab on 2-in deck.)

Regarding M_n, from the solution to Prob. 10.9 the maximum possible compressive force in the concrete slab $C_c = 0.85 f'_c A_c = 250$ kips; the maximum possible tensile force in the steel beam $T = A_s F_y = 724$ kips. To satisfy equilibrium, $T = C = (250 + 724)$ kips$/2 = 487$ kips. The plastic stress distribution is as shown in Fig. 10-15. Because the net compressive force in the steel is greater than the beam flange yield force (i.e., $[C_s = (487 - 250) \text{ kips} = 237 \text{ kips}] > [b_f t_f F_y = 8.965 \text{ in} \times 0.585 \text{ in} \times 36 \text{ kips/in}^2 = 189 \text{ kips}]$), the plastic neutral axis (PNA) is located in the web. Ignoring the web fillets of the beam, the distance from the

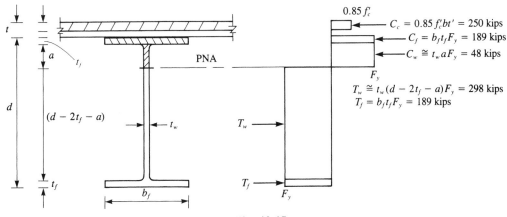

Fig. 10-15

bottom of the upper beam flange to the PNA is approximately

$$a \cong \frac{C_w}{t_w F_y} = \frac{48 \text{ kips}}{0.415 \text{ in} \times 36 \text{ kips/in}^2} = 3.2 \text{ in}$$

The contribution to M_n from each element of beam or slab = element (tensile or compressive) force × the distance of element force from the PNA.

Contributions to M_n from

Compression in the slab $= C_c \left(a + t_f + t - \dfrac{t'}{2} \right)$

$= 250 \text{ kips} \times \left(3.2 + 0.585 + 4.0 - \dfrac{2.0}{2} \right) \text{ in} \quad = 1696 \quad \text{kip-in}$

Compression in upper beam flange $= C_f \left(a + \dfrac{t_f}{2} \right)$

$= 189 \text{ kips} \times \left(3.2 + \dfrac{0.585}{2} \right) \text{ in} \qquad\qquad = 660 \qquad \text{kip-in}$

Compression in beam web $= C_w \dfrac{a}{2}$

$= 48 \text{ kips} \times \dfrac{3.2 \text{ in}}{2} \qquad\qquad\qquad = 77 \qquad \text{kip-in}$

Tension in beam web $= T_w \dfrac{d - 2t_f - a}{2}$

$= 298 \text{ kips} \times \dfrac{(23.73 - 2 \times 0.585 - 3.2) \text{ in}}{2} \quad = 2885 \quad \text{kip-in}$

Tension in lower beam flange $= T_f (d - \frac{3}{2} t_f - a)$

$= 189 \text{ kips} \times (23.73 - \frac{3}{2} \times 0.585 - 3.2) \text{ in} \quad = 3714 \quad \text{kip-in}$

$\overline{\qquad\qquad 9032 \quad \text{kip-in}}$

$M_n = 9032 \text{ kip-in} = 753 \text{ kip-ft}$.

The design flexural strength $\phi_b M_n = 0.85 \times 753 \text{ kip-ft} = 640 \text{ kip-ft}$. In comparison with the 677 kip-ft design flexural strength in Prob. 10.14, the 640 kip-ft determined herein represents a mere 5 percent reduction. The inability of the 2 in of concrete within the deck to participate in composite action is not very significant.

10.16. Assume the concrete-encased W8×40 in Prob. 10.2 and Fig. 10-4 is a beam. Determine the design flexural strengths $\phi_b M_{nx}$ and $\phi_b M_{ny}$ for bending about the major and minor axes.

As indicated in this chapter, in the section entitled Concrete-Encased Beams, concrete encasement satisfying the stated minimum requirements prevents both local and lateral-torsional buckling of the beam. Of the two methods given in the AISC LRFD Specification for determining $\phi_b M_n$ for concrete-encased beams, the simpler one is based on the plastic stress distribution on the steel section alone.

For x-axis bending (regardless of L_b)

$$\phi_b M_{nx} = \phi_b M_p = \phi_b Z_x F_y$$
$$= \frac{0.90 \times 39.8 \text{ in}^3 \times 36 \text{ kips/in}^2}{12 \text{ in/ft}}$$
$$= 107 \text{ kip-ft}$$

For y-axis bending (regardless of L_b)

$$\phi_b M_{ny} = \phi_b M_p = \phi_b Z_y F_y$$
$$= \frac{0.90 \times 18.5 \text{ in}^3 \times 36 \text{ kips/in}^2}{12 \text{ in/ft}}$$
$$= 50 \text{ kip-ft}$$

10.17. Assume the concrete-encased W8×40 in Prob. 10.2 and Fig. 10-4 is a beam-column (i.e., subjected to combined flexure and compression). Determine the design flexural strengths $\phi_b M_{nx}$ and $\phi_b M_{ny}$ for use in the interaction formulas.

For composite beam-columns, $\phi_b M_n$ is determined as follows: $\phi_b = 0.85$, and M_n is calculated from the plastic stress distribution on the composite cross section. However, if $(P_u/\phi_c P_n) < 0.3$, M_n is determined by linear interpolation between M_n (calculated as just described) at $(P_u/\phi_c P_n) = 0.3$, and M_n for a composite beam at $P_u = 0$.

A formula is given in the Commentary on the AISC LRFD Specification (p. 6-175 in the AISC LRFD Manual) for the determination of M_n for composite beam-columns where $0.3 \leq (P_u/\phi_c P_n) < 1.0$:

$$M_n = M_p = ZF_y + \frac{1}{3}(h_2 - 2c_r)A_r F_{yr} + \left(\frac{h_1}{2} - \frac{A_w F_y}{1.7 f'_c h_1}\right) A_w F_y \qquad (C\text{-}I4\text{-}1)$$

where A_w = web area of the encased steel shape, in^2; 0 for concrete-filled tubes

   Z = plastic section modulus of the steel shape, in^2

   c_r = average distance from the tension and compression faces to the nearest longitudinal reinforcing bars, in

   h_1 = width of the composite cross section perpendicular to the plane of bending, in

   h_2 = width of the composite cross section parallel to the plane of bending, in

From Prob. 10.2 and Fig. 10-4: $h_1 = h_2 = 16$ in, $c_r = [1\frac{1}{2} + \frac{3}{8} + (\frac{7}{8}/2)]$ in $= 2.3$ in, $A_r = 4 \times 0.60$ in^2 (for each No. 7 bar) $= 2.4$ in^2. Also, $f'_c = 3.5$ ksi, $F_y = 36$ ksi, $F_{yr} = 60$ ksi, $Z_x = 39.8$ in^3, $Z_y = 18.5$ in^3, $A_w = (A_s - 2b_f t_f) = (11.7$ in$^2 - 2 \times 8.070$ in $\times 0.560$ in$) = 2.66$ in^2.

For $0.3 \leq (P_u/\phi_c P_n) < 1.0$:

$$M_{nx} = 39.8 \text{ in}^3 \times 36 \frac{\text{kips}}{\text{in}^2} + \frac{1}{3} \times (16 \text{ in} - 2 \times 2.3 \text{ in})$$
$$\times 2.4 \text{ in}^2 \times 60 \frac{\text{kips}}{\text{in}^2} + \left(\frac{16 \text{ in}}{2} - \frac{2.66 \text{ in}^2 \times 36 \text{ ksi}}{1.7 \times 3.5 \text{ kips/in}^2 \times 16 \text{ in}}\right)$$
$$\times 2.66 \text{ in}^5 \times 36 \frac{\text{kips}}{\text{in}^2}$$
$$= 2650 \text{ kip-in} = 221 \text{ kip-ft}$$
$$\phi_b M_{nx} = 0.85 \times 221 \text{ kip-ft} = 188 \text{ kip-ft}$$

$$M_{ny} = 18.5 \text{ in}^3 \times 36 \frac{\text{kips}}{\text{in}^2} + \frac{1}{3} \times (16 \text{ in} - 2 \times 2.3 \text{ in})$$
$$\times 2.4 \text{ in}^2 \times 60 \frac{\text{kips}}{\text{in}^2} + \left(\frac{16 \text{ in}}{2} - \frac{2.66 \text{ in}^2 \times 36 \text{ ksi}}{1.7 \times 3.5 \text{ kips/in}^2 \times 16 \text{ in}}\right)$$
$$\times 2.66 \text{ in}^2 \times 36 \frac{\text{kips}}{\text{in}^2}$$
$$= 1883 \text{ kip-in} = 157 \text{ kip-ft}$$
$$\phi_b M_{ny} = 0.85 \times 157 \text{ kip-ft} = 134 \text{ kip-ft}$$

For $P_u = 0$, $M_n = ZF_y$ (as in Prob. 10.16 for the same concrete-encased member)

$$\phi_b M_{nx} = 0.85 Z_x F_y = \frac{0.85 \times 39.8 \text{ in}^3 \times 36 \text{ kips/in}^2}{12 \text{ in/ft}}$$

$$= 101 \text{ kip-ft}$$

$$\phi_b M_{ny} = 0.85 Z_y F_y = \frac{0.85 \times 18.5 \text{ in}^3 \times 36 \text{ kips/in}^2}{12 \text{ in/ft}}$$

$$= 47 \text{ kip-ft}$$

The results are plotted in Fig. 10-16.

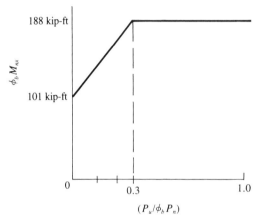
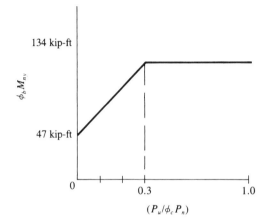

Fig. 10-16

10.18. The built-up beam in Prob. 6.1 and Fig. 6-3 acts compositely with a solid normal-weight concrete floor slab ($f'_c = 5.0$ ksi, effective width = 100 in, thickness = 4 in). Assuming full composite action and shored construction, determine the design flexural strength $\phi_b M_{nx}$.

A review of the solution to Prob. 6.1 indicates that the web of the beam is noncompact.

$$\left(\frac{h_c}{t_w} = 128.0 \right) > \left(\frac{640}{\sqrt{F_y}} = 106.7 \right)$$

Accordingly, the design flexural strength is determined as follows: $\phi_b = 0.90$, and M_n is calculated from the superposition of elastic stresses, considering the effects of shoring. Corresponding elastic stress diagrams for the shored and unshored cases are shown in Fig. 10-17, where

S_s = section modulus of the bare steel beam, in^3

$S_{tr,b}$, $S_{tr,t}$ = section moduli of the transformed section, in^3

n = modular ratio = E/E_c

M_{u1} = required flexural strength due to the (factored) loads applied before the concrete has attained 75 percent of f'_c

M_{u2} = required flexural strength due to the (factored) loads applied after the concrete has achieved 75 percent of f'_c

M_u = total required flexural strength = ($M_{u1} + M_{u2}$)

If construction is shored, all loads are resisted by composite action. The two limitations on flexural strength are the maximum stresses in the steel and concrete. From Fig. 10-17, the limiting conditions are

$$M_u \leq \phi_b M_n = \phi_b S_{tr,b} F_y$$

$$M_u \leq \phi_b M_n = \phi_b n S_{tr,t} (0.85 f'_c)$$

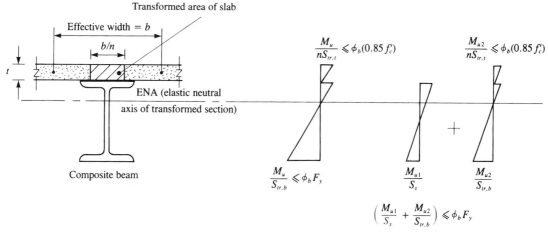

Fig. 10-17

The modular ratio $n = E/E_c$.

$$E_c = w^{1.5}\sqrt{f_c'} = 145^{1.5}\sqrt{5.0} = 3904 \text{ ksi}$$

$$n = \frac{29,000 \text{ ksi}}{3904 \text{ ksi}} = 7.4$$

The transformed section for this composite beam is shown in Fig. 10-18.

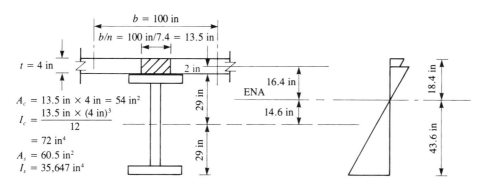

Fig. 10-18

Locating the elastic neutral axis (ENA), relative to the centroid of the steel beam

$$\bar{y} = \frac{y_c A_c}{A_c + A_s} = \frac{(29+2) \text{ in} \times 54 \text{ in}^2}{(54 + 60.5) \text{ in}^2} = 14.6 \text{ in}$$

By the parallel axis theorem, the moment of inertia of the transformed section about the ENA

$$I_{tr} = \sum (I_{CG} + AD^2)$$

$$= I_s + A_s D_s^2 + I_c + A_c D_c^2$$

$$= 35,647 \text{ in}^4 + 60.5 \text{ in}^2 \times (14.6 \text{ in})^2$$

$$+ 72 \text{ in}^4 + 54 \text{ in}^2 \times (16.4 \text{ in})^2$$

$$= 63,139 \text{ in}^4$$

The required section moduli are

$$S_{tr,b} = \frac{63{,}139 \text{ in}^4}{43.6 \text{ in}} = 1448 \text{ in}^3$$

$$S_{tr,t} = \frac{63{,}139 \text{ in}^4}{18.4 \text{ in}} = 3431 \text{ in}^3$$

The design flexural strength of the composite section $\phi_b M_n$ = the minimum of

$$\phi_b S_{tr,b} F_y = \frac{0.90 \times 1448 \text{ in}^3 \times 36 \text{ kips/in}^2}{12 \text{ in/ft}} = 3910 \text{ kip-ft}$$

$$\phi_b n S_{tr,t}(0.85 f_c') = \frac{0.90 \times 7.4 \times 3431 \text{ in}^3 \times (0.85 \times 5 \text{ kips/in}^2)}{12 \text{ in/ft}}$$

$$= 8093 \text{ kip-ft}$$

The design flexural strength $\phi_b M_n = 3910$ kip-ft.

Shear stud requirements for this noncompact composite member are the same as those for compact members.

Supplementary Problems

10.19. Select an 8 in × 8 in concrete-filled structural steel tube for a required axial compressive strength of 500 kips. Assume $KL = 12.0$ ft, $F_y = 46$ ksi, $f_c' = 3.5$ ksi, normal-weight (145 lb/ft^3) concrete.

Ans. TS $8 \times 8 \times \frac{1}{2}$.

10.20. Determine the design compressive strength of a W14×120 (A36 steel) encased in a 24 in × 24 in ($f_c' = 5.0$ ksi) normal-weight concrete column. Reinforcement is four No. 10 (Grade 60) bars longitudinally and No. 3 ties at 16 in horizontally. Assume $K_x L_x = K_y L_y = 13.0$ ft.

Ans. $\phi_c P_n = 2500$ kips.

10.21. For the column in Prob. 10.20, select a bearing plate to transfer to the concrete the load it must resist.

Ans. 18 in × 18 in.

For Probs. 10.22 and 10.23, determine

(a) The effective slab width for composite action

(b) V_h (the total horizontal shear force to be transferred) for full composite action

(c) The number of $\frac{3}{4}$-in-diameter shear studs required if $F_u = 60$ ksi

10.22. A W24×55 interior beam is shown in Fig. 10-19. Steel is A36, beam span is 32 ft 0 in, and beam spacing is 12 ft 0 in. The beams are to act compositely with a 5-in normal-weight concrete slab, consisting of 2 in of solid concrete on a 3-in steel deck, with ribs perpendicular to the beam; $f_c' = 5$ ksi, $Q_n = 18.5$ kips per stud.   *Ans.* (a) $b = 96$ in. (b) $V_h = 583$ kips. (c) $2n = 64$ shear studs.

10.23. A W24×55 edge beam is shown in Fig. 10-19. Steel is A36, and the beam span is 30 ft 0 in. The beam is to act compositely with the concrete and deck described in Prob. 10.22.

Ans. (a) $b = 51$ in. (b) $V_h = 434$ kips. (c) $2n = 48$ shear studs.

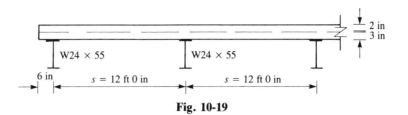

Fig. 10-19

10.24. Determine the design flexural strength $\phi_b M_n$ for the W24×55 interior composite beam in Prob. 10.22. Assume full composite action.   *Ans.* $\phi_b M_n = 781$ kip-ft.

10.25. Determine the design flexural strength $\phi_b M_n$ for the W24×55 edge composite beam in Prob. 10.23. Assume full composite action. *Ans.* $\phi_b M_n = 715$ kip-ft.

10.26. If the concrete-encased W14×120 in Prob. 10.20 is a beam-column with $P_u/\phi_c P_n > 0.3$, determine $\phi_b M_{nx}$ and $\phi_b M_{ny}$.   *Ans.* $\phi_b M_{nx} = 920$ kip-ft, $\phi_b M_{ny} = 623$ kip-ft.

10.27. Assuming the concrete-encased W14×120 in Prob. 10.20 is a beam (i.e., $P_u = 0.$), determine $\phi_b M_{nx}$ and $\phi_b M_{ny}$.   *Ans.* $\phi_b M_{nx} = 572$ kip-ft, $\phi_b M_{ny} = 275$ kip-ft.

Chapter 11

Connections

NOTATION

A_{BM} = cross-sectional area of the base material, in^2

A_H = as defined in Eq. [11.10], in^2

A_g = gross area subjected to tension, in^2

A_n = net area subjected to tension, in^2

A_{ns} = net area subjected to shear, in^2

A_{pb} = projected bearing area, in^2

A_{vg} = gross area subjected to shear, in^2

A_w = effective cross-sectional area of the weld, in^2

A_1 = area of steel bearing on a concrete support, in^2

A_2 = maximum area of supporting surface that is geometrically similar to and concentric with the loaded area, in^2

B = width of column base plate, in

b_f = width of column flange, in

C = distance between the centers of bolt holes, in

C' = clear distance between holes, in

C_1, C_2, C_3 = tabulated values for use in Eqs. [11.2] to [11.4], in

c = as defined in Eq. [11.11], in

d = nominal bolt diameter, in = depth of column section, in

d_h = diameter of the standard size hole, in

F_{BM} = nominal strength of the base material, ksi

F_{EXX} = nominal tensile strength of the weld metal, ksi

F_u = specified minimum tensile strength, ksi

F_w = nominal strength of the weld electrode, ksi

F_y = specified minimum yield stress, ksi

f'_c = the specified compressive strength of the concrete, ksi

L = distance in the line of force from the center of a bolt hole to an edge, in

m = as defined in Fig. 11-6, in

N = length of column base plate, in

n = as defined in Fig. 11-6, in

P = force transmitted by one fastener to the critical connected part, kips

P_o = as defined in Eq. [11.9]

P_p = nominal strength for bearing on concrete, kips

P_u = required column axial strength, kips

R_n = nominal strength, kips

t = thickness of the connected part, in

t_f = thickness of column flange, in

t_p = thickness of plate, in

ϕ = resistance factor

ϕ_c = resistance factor for bearing on concrete

ϕF_{BM} = design strength of the base material, ksi

ϕF_w = design strength of the weld electrode, ksi

ϕP_p = design strength for bearing on concrete, kips

ϕR_n = design strength, kips

INTRODUCTION

The types of connections used in steel structures are too numerous to cover fully in a single chapter. However, the provisions of Chap. J in the AISC LRFD Specification are the basis for connection design in LRFD. The present chapter has a twofold purpose: (1) to outline the basic LRFD Specification requirements for connections and (2) to provide some common examples of connection design. For additional information, the reader is referred to Part 5 of the AISC LRFD Manual, which contains nearly 200 pages of data on connections. Although there are a number of excellent books on structural steel connections, nearly all are based on allowable stress design (ASD). It is anticipated that similar books based on LRFD will be published in the next few years.

The most common connectors for steel structures are welds and bolts, which are discussed in the following sections.

WELDS

Of the various welding procedures, four are acceptable in structural work: shielded metal arc, submerged arc, flux-core arc, and gas metal arc. All four involve fusion welding by an electric arc process; that is, the heat of an electric arc simultaneously melts an electrode (or welding rod) and the adjacent steel in the parts being joined. The joint is formed from the cooling and solidification of the fused material. The American Welding Society *Structural Welding Code-Steel* (AWS D1.1) specifies the electrode classes and welding processes that can be used to achieve "matching" weld

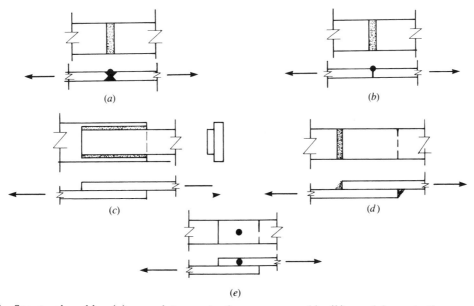

Fig. 11-1 Structural welds: (*a*) complete-penetration groove weld; (*b*) partial-penetration groove weld; (*c*) longitudinal fillet weld; (*d*) transverse fillet weld; (*e*) plug or slot weld

metal, that is, weld metal that has a nominal tensile strength F_{EXX} similar to that of the base steel being connected.

As illustrated in Fig. 11-1, three types of structural welds are normally used in building construction: groove (complete and partial penetration), fillet (longitudinal and transverse), and plug or slot welds. The design strength of welds is the lower value of

$$\phi F_{BM} A_{BM} \qquad \text{and} \qquad \phi F_w A_w$$

Table 11-1 Design Strength of Welds

Types of Weld and Stress	Material	Resistance Factor ϕ	Nominal Strength F_{BM} or F_w	Required Weld Strength Level
Complete-Penetration Groove Weld				
Tension normal to effective area	Base	0.90	F_y	"Matching" weld must be used
Compression normal to effective area	Base	0.90	F_y	Weld metal with a strength level equal to or less than "matching" may be used
Tension or compression parallel to axis of weld				
Shear on effective area	Base Weld electrode	0.90 0.80	$0.60F_y$ $0.60F_{EXX}$	
Partial-Penetration Groove Welds				
Compression normal to effective area	Base	0.90	F_y	Weld metal with a strength level equal to or less than "matching" weld metal may be used
Tension or compression parallel to axis of weld				
Shear parallel to axis of weld	Base Weld electrode	0.75	$0.60F_{EXX}$	
Tension normal to effective area	Base Weld Electrode	0.90 0.80	F_y $0.60F_{EXX}$	
Fillet Welds				
Stress on effective area	Base Weld electrode	0.75	$0.60F_{EXX}$	Weld metal with a strength level equal to or less than "matching" weld metal may be used
Tension or compression parallel to axis of weld	Base	0.90	F_y	
Plug or Slot Welds				
Shear parallel to faying surfaces (on effective area)	Base Weld electrode	0.75	$0.60F_{EXX}$	Weld metal with a strength level equal to or less than "matching" weld metal may be used

when applicable, where

F_{BM} = nominal strength of the base material, ksi

F_w = nominal strength of the weld electrode, ksi

A_{BM} = cross-sectional area of the base material, in^2

A_w = effective cross-sectional area of the weld, in^2

ϕ = resistance factor.

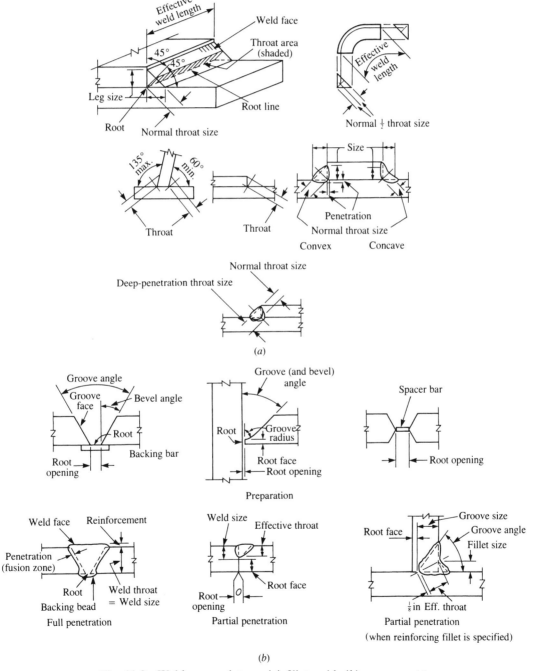

Fig. 11-2   Weld nomenclature: (*a*) fillet weld; (*b*) groove weld

Values for ϕ, F_{BM}, and F_w are given in Table 11-1, which is Table J2.3 in the AISC LRFD Specification.* A_w, the effective cross-sectional areas of weld to be used in conjunction with F_w are the effective length times the effective throat thickness, for groove and fillet welds; and the nominal cross-sectional area of the hole or slot, for plug welds. The nomenclature for fillet and groove welds is shown in Fig. 11-2, reprinted from the AISC publication *Engineering for Steel Construction* (1984).* Minimum sizes of groove and fillet welds are given in Tables 11-2 and 11-3, which are Tables J2.4 and J2.5 in the AISC LRFD Specification.* For both groove and fillet welds, the tabulated minimum weld size is determined by the thicker of the two parts joined. However, the weld size should not exceed the thickness of the thinner part joined. Additional restrictions on welds are given in Sec. J2 of the AISC LRFD Specification.

Table 11-2 Minimum Effective Throat Thickness of Partial-Penetration Groove Welds

Material Thickness of Thicker Part Joined, t, in	Minimum Effective Throat Thickness,* in
$t \le \frac{1}{4}$	$\frac{1}{8}$
$\frac{1}{4} < t \le \frac{1}{2}$	$\frac{3}{16}$
$\frac{1}{2} < t \le \frac{3}{4}$	$\frac{1}{4}$
$\frac{3}{4} < t \le 1\frac{1}{2}$	$\frac{5}{16}$
$1\frac{1}{2} < t \le 2\frac{1}{4}$	$\frac{3}{8}$
$2\frac{1}{4} < t \le 6$	$\frac{1}{2}$
$t > 6$	$\frac{5}{8}$
* Leg dimension.	

Table 11-3 Minimum Size of Fillet Welds

Material Thickness of Thicker Part Joined, t, in	Minimum Size of Fillet Weld,* in
$t \le \frac{1}{4}$	$\frac{1}{8}$
$\frac{1}{4} < t \le \frac{1}{2}$	$\frac{3}{16}$
$\frac{1}{2} < t \le \frac{3}{4}$	$\frac{1}{4}$
$t > \frac{3}{4}$	$\frac{5}{16}$
* Leg dimension of fillet welds.	

Most common welded connections used in buildings have been designated by AISC and AWS as *prequalified,* that is, exempt from tests and qualification if they have been properly designed and detailed. Examples of prequalified welded joints and standard welding symbols are given in the AISC LRFD Manual, beginning on page 5-177.

BOLTS

Bolts consist of a cylindrical shank (partially threaded to receive a nut) with an attached head. High-strength bolts, type A325 or A490, are required in most structural applications; they must be sufficiently tightened to achieve the minimum bolt tension values listed in Table 11-4 (which is Table J3.1 in the AISC LRFD Specification*). For those cases not included in Sec. J1.9 of the AISC

LRFD Specification, ordinary A307 machine bolts may be used; they are tightened to a "snug-tight" condition only. High-strength bolts must comply with the Research Council on Structural Connections *Specification for Structural Joints Using ASTM A325 or A490 Bolts,* which appears in Part 6 of the AISC LRFD Manual.

Table 11-4   Minimum Bolt Tension, kips*

Bolt Size, in	A325 Bolts	A490 Bolts
$\frac{1}{2}$	12	15
$\frac{5}{8}$	19	24
$\frac{3}{4}$	28	35
$\frac{7}{8}$	39	49
1	51	64
$1\frac{1}{8}$	56	80
$1\frac{1}{4}$	71	102
$1\frac{3}{8}$	85	121
$1\frac{1}{2}$	103	148

* Equal to 0.70 of minimum tensile strength of bolts, rounded off to nearest kip, as specified in ASTM specifications for A325 and A490 bolts with UNC threads.

Bolts may be loaded in tension (i.e., parallel to their axes), shear (i.e., perpendicular to their axes), or a combination of shear and tension. The strengths of A307, A325, and A490 bolts are given in the accompanying tables as follows.

This Chapter	AISC LRFD Specification Ref.*	Subject
Table 11-5	Table J3.2	Design tensile strength; design shear strength
Table 11-6	Table J3.3	Tensile stress limit for combined shear and tension
Table 11-7	Table J3.4	Nominal slip-critical shear strength of high-strength bolts

* Reproduced with the permission of AISC.

For bolts loaded in tension only, the design tensile strength is equal to ϕ multiplied by the nominal tensile strength, as given in Table 11-5. For bolts loaded in shear only, the design shear strength is equal to ϕ multiplied by the nominal shear strength, given in Table 11-5. If a combination of tension and shear acts on a bolt, the maximum tensile stress is determined from Table 11-6 and the maximum shear stress, from Table 11-5. In all cases, stresses (in ksi) are converted to forces by multiplying by the nominal cross-sectional area of the bolt (ignoring the threads).

A special category of *slip-critical* joints is recognized by the AISC LRFD Specification. Where joint slippage is undesirable (e.g., if there are frequent load reversals, leading to the possibility of fatigue), the designer may specify "slip-critical" high-strength bolts. Because this is a serviceability criterion, the (unfactored) service loads are used in conjunction with Table 11-7. If the load combination includes either wind or seismic load together with live load, the total service load may be multiplied by 0.75. To determine the design shear strength, the nominal values in Table 11-7 are multiplied by $\phi = 1.0$ (except $\phi = 0.85$ for long-slotted holes if the load is parallel to the slot). If a bolt in a slip-critical connection is subjected to a service tensile force T, the nominal shear strength

Table 11-5   Design Strength of Fasteners

Description of Fasteners	Tensile Strength		Shear Strength in Bearing-Type Connections	
	Resistance Factor ϕ	Nominal Strength, ksi	Resistance Factor ϕ	Nominal Strength ksi
A307 bolts	0.75	45.0	0.60	27.0
A325 bolts, when threads are *not* excluded from shear planes		90.0	0.65	54.0
A325 bolts, when threads *are* excluded from shear planes		90.0		72.0
A490 bolts, when threads are *not* excluded from shear planes		112.5		67.5
A490 bolts, when threads *are* excluded from the shear planes		112.5		90.0
Threaded parts meeting the requirements of Sec. A3, when threads are *not* excluded from the shear planes		$0.75F_u$		$0.45F_u$
Threaded parts meeting the requirements of Sec. A3, when threads *are* excluded from the shear planes		$0.75F_u$		$0.60F_u$
A502, Grade 1, hot-driven rivets		45.0		36.0
A502, Grades 2 and 3, hot-driven rivets		60.0		48.0

Table 11-6   Tension Stress Limit (F_t), ksi, for Fasteners in Bearing-Type Connections

Description of Fasteners	Threads Included in the Shear Plane	Threads Excluded from the Shear Plane
A307 bolts	$39 - 1.8f_v \leq 30$	
A325 bolts	$85 - 1.8f_v \leq 68$	$85 - 1.4f_v \leq 68$
A490 bolts	$106 - 1.8f_v \leq 84$	$106 - 1.4f_v \leq 84$
Threaded parts A449 bolts over $1\frac{1}{2}$-in diameter	$0.73F_u - 1.8f_v \leq 0.56F_u$	$0.73F_u - 1.4f_v \leq 0.56F_u$
A502 Grade 1 rivets	$44 - 1.3f_v \leq 34$	
A502 Grade 2 rivets	$59 - 1.3f_v \leq 45$	

in Table 11-7 is multiplied by the reduction factor $(1 - T/T_b)$, where T_b is the minimum pretension force for that bolt in Table 11-4.

Table 11-7   Nominal Slip-Critical Shear Strength of High-Strength Bolts*

Type of Bolt	Nominal Shear Strength, ksi		
	Standard-Size Holes	Oversized and Short-Slotted Holes	Long-Slotted Holes†
A325	17	15	12
A490	21	18	15

* Class A (slip coefficient 0.33). Clean mill scale and blast cleaned surfaces with class A coatings. For design strengths with other coatings, see RCSC *Load and Resistance Factor Design Specification for Structural Joints Using ASTM A325 or A490 Bolts.*
† Tabulated values are for the case of load application transverse to the slot. When the load is parallel to the slot, multiply tabulated values by 0.85.

Bolt bearing strength, minimum spacing, and minimum edge distance depend on the dimensions of the bolt holes. Nominal dimensions for standard, oversize, short-slotted, and long-slotted holes are given in Table 11-8 (Table J3.5 in the AISC LRFD Specification*). Unlike standard holes, use of the other types of holes requires approval of the designer and is subject to the restrictions in Sec. J3.7 of the AISC LRFD Specification.

Table 11-8   Nominal Hole Dimensions, in

Bolt Diameter, in	Hole Dimensions, in			
	Standard (Dia.)	Oversize (Dia.)	Short-Slot (Width × Length)	Long-Slot (Width × Length)
$\frac{1}{2}$	$\frac{9}{16}$	$\frac{5}{8}$	$\frac{9}{16} \times \frac{11}{16}$	$\frac{9}{16} \times 1\frac{1}{4}$
$\frac{5}{8}$	$\frac{11}{16}$	$\frac{13}{16}$	$\frac{11}{16} \times \frac{7}{8}$	$\frac{11}{16} \times 1\frac{9}{16}$
$\frac{3}{4}$	$\frac{13}{16}$	$\frac{15}{16}$	$\frac{13}{16} \times 1$	$\frac{13}{16} \times 1\frac{7}{8}$
$\frac{7}{8}$	$\frac{15}{16}$	$1\frac{1}{16}$	$\frac{15}{16} \times 1\frac{1}{8}$	$\frac{15}{16} \times 2\frac{3}{16}$
1	$1\frac{1}{16}$	$1\frac{1}{4}$	$1\frac{1}{16} \times 1\frac{5}{16}$	$1\frac{1}{16} \times 2\frac{1}{2}$
$\geq 1\frac{1}{8}$	$d + \frac{1}{16}$	$d + \frac{5}{16}$	$(d + \frac{1}{16}) \times (d + \frac{3}{8})$	$(d + \frac{1}{16}) \times (2.5 \times d)$

Two bolt-spacing schemes are possible.

(1)   In the preferred scheme,

$$C \geq 3d \quad \text{and} \quad L \geq 1.5d$$

where C = distance between the centers of bolt holes, in

L = distance in the line of force, from the center of a bolt hole to an edge, in

d = nominal diameter of the bolt, in.

The design bearing strength ϕR_n *for each of two or more bolts in the line of force* must be checked (even if the connection is slip-critical); $\phi = 0.75$. For standard or short-slotted

* Reproduced with the permission of AISC.

holes,

$$R_n = 2.4 \, dtF_u \qquad (J3\text{-}1a)$$

For long-slotted holes perpendicular to the load

$$R_n = 2.0 \, dtF_u \qquad (J3\text{-}1b)$$

If deformation of the bolt hole need not be considered, then, in all cases

$$R_n = 3.0 \, dtF_u \qquad (J3\text{-}1d)$$

In these equations, t is the thickness of the connected part, in, and F_u is the specified tensile strength of the connected part, ksi.

(2)　In the alternate scheme, the distance between the centers of bolt holes

$$C \geq \begin{cases} 2.67d & [11.1] \\ \dfrac{P}{\phi F_u t} + \dfrac{d_h}{2} + C_1 & [11.2] \end{cases}$$

$$C' \geq d$$

$$L \geq \begin{cases} \dfrac{P}{\phi F_u t} + C_2 & [11.3] \\ C_3 + C_2 & [11.4] \end{cases}$$

The design bearing strength must be checked (regardless of whether the connection is slip-critical). Where $L < 1.5d$, the design bearing strength (for each of one or more bolts in the line of force) is ϕR_n, where $\phi = 0.75$ and

$$R_n = LtF_u \qquad (J3\text{-}1c)$$

In the preceding equations

P = force transmitted by one fastener to the critical connected part, kips

d_h = diameter of the standard size hole, in

C' = clear distance between holes, in

$C_1 = 0$ for standard holes; otherwise use the value in Table 11-9 (Table J3.6 in the AISC LRFD Specification*)

Table 11-9　Values of Spacing Increment C_1, in

Nominal Diameter of Fastener	Oversize Holes	Slotted Holes		
		Perpendicular to Line of Force	Parallel to Line of Force	
			Short Slots	Long Slots*
$\leq \frac{7}{8}$	$\frac{1}{8}$	0	$\frac{3}{16}$	$1\frac{1}{2}d - \frac{1}{16}$
1	$\frac{3}{16}$	0	$\frac{1}{4}$	$1\frac{7}{16}$
$\leq 1\frac{1}{8}$	$\frac{1}{4}$	0	$\frac{5}{16}$	$1\frac{1}{2}d - \frac{1}{16}$

* When length of slot is less than maximum allowed in Table 11-8, C_1 may be reduced by the difference between the maximum and actual slot lengths.

* Reproduced with the permission of AISC.

$C_2 = 0$ for standard holes; otherwise use the value in Table 11-10 (Table J3.8 in the AISC LRFD Specification*)

Table 11-10   Values of Edge Distance Increment C_2, in

Nominal Diameter of Fastener, in	Oversized Holes	Slotted Holes		
		Perpendicular to Edge		Parallel to Edge
		Short Slots	Long Slots*	
$\leq \frac{7}{8}$	$\frac{1}{16}$	$\frac{1}{8}$		
1	$\frac{1}{8}$	$\frac{1}{8}$	$\frac{3}{4}d$	0
$\leq 1\frac{1}{8}$	$\frac{1}{8}$	$\frac{3}{16}$		

* When length of slot is less than maximum allowable (see Table 11-8), C_2 may be reduced by one-half the difference between the maximum and actual slot lengths.

C_3 = the value in Table 11-11 (Table J3.7 in the AISC LRFD Specification*)

Table 11-11 C_3: Minimum Edge Distance, in (Center of Standard Hole to Edge of Connected Part)

Nominal Rivet or Bolt Diameter, in	At Sheared Edges	At Rolled Edges of Plates, Shapes or Bars or Gas Cut Edges
$\frac{1}{2}$	$\frac{7}{8}$	$\frac{3}{4}$
$\frac{5}{8}$	$1\frac{1}{8}$	$\frac{7}{8}$
$\frac{3}{4}$	$1\frac{1}{4}$	1
$\frac{7}{8}$	$1\frac{1}{2}$	$1\frac{1}{8}$
1	$1\frac{3}{4}$	$1\frac{1}{4}$
$1\frac{1}{8}$	2	$1\frac{1}{2}$
$1\frac{1}{4}$	$2\frac{1}{4}$	$1\frac{5}{8}$
$>1\frac{1}{4}$	$1\frac{3}{4} \times$ diameter	$1\frac{1}{4} \times$ diameter

Regardless of which bolt spacing scheme is selected, the maximum edge distance is

$$L \leq \begin{cases} 12t \\ 6\text{ in} \end{cases}$$

CONNECTING ELEMENTS AND MAIN MEMBERS AT CONNECTIONS

Connecting elements include stiffeners, gusset plates, angles, brackets, and the panel zones of beam-to-column connections. Considering the possible modes of failure, the following limit states should be examined for applicability to connecting elements and the adjacent parts of main

* Reproduced with the permission of AISC.

members. The design strength is ϕR_n, where

    (*1*)   For tensile yielding

$$\phi = 0.90$$
$$R_n = A_g F_y$$

    (*J5-1*)

    (*2*)   For tensile fracture

$$\phi = 0.75$$
$$R_n = A_n F_u \qquad \text{where } A_n \le 0.85 A_g$$

    (*J5-2*)

    (*3*)   For shear yielding

$$\phi = 0.90$$
$$R_n = 0.6 A_{vg} F_y$$

    (*J5-3*)

    (*4*)   For shear fracture

$$\phi = 0.75$$
$$R_n = 0.6 A_{ns} F_u$$

    (*J4-1*)

    (*5*)   For block shear rupture

$$\phi = 0.75$$

$R_n =$ the greater value of

$$\begin{cases} 0.6 A_{vg} F_y + A_n F_u \\ 0.6 A_{ns} F_u + A_g F_y \end{cases}$$

    (*C-J4-1*)
    (*C-J4-2*)

In the preceding equations:

    A_g = gross area subjected to tension, in^2
    A_n = net area subjected to tension, in^2
    A_{vg} = gross area subjected to shear, in^2
    A_{ns} = net area subjected to shear, in^2

An explanation of *block shear rupture* follows. At beam end connections where the top flange is coped (as in Fig. 11-3) and in similar situations, one plane is subjected to shear while a perpendicular plane is subjected to tension. Failure can occur in one of two ways: fracture of the (net) section in tension accompanied by yielding of the (gross) section in shear [Eq. (*C-J4-1*)], or fracture of the (net) section in shear accompanied by yielding of the (gross) section in tension [Eq. (*C-J4-2*)]. The design strength is based on the larger-capacity failure mode, which governs.

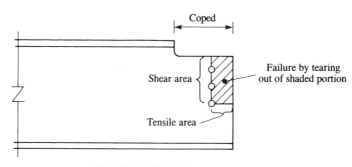

Fig. 11-3 Block shear rupture

TYPICAL CONNECTIONS

The discussion in the earlier sections of this chapter concerned the *design strengths* of the components of connections: the connectors (i.e., welds and bolts) and the connecting elements (stiffeners, gusset plates, etc.). The *required strength* of a connection is determined from an analysis of the entire structure with the factored loads acting on it. A detailed analysis of the connection produces required strengths for its components.

Analysis, design, and construction must follow consistent assumptions. Connections, for example, may or may not transfer moment. Whichever assumption was made by the engineer must be communicated to the contractor. Use of a type of connection not intended in the analysis and design will cause a redistribution of internal forces in the structure, leading to overstress and possible failure.

Examples of shear and moment connections for beams are shown in Figs. 11-4 and 11-5. The groove-welded splice in Fig. 11-4(*a*) develops the full strength of the beam and transfers the full moment and shear. However, the shear splice in Fig. 11-4(*b*) is not capable of transferring any significant moment. Unless otherwise specified on the design drawings, splices are groove-welded with full-penetration welds. Regarding beam end connections, the simple connections in Fig. 11-5(*a*) will only transmit shear. To transfer moment requires moment connections similar to the ones shown in Fig. 11-5(*b*). When not indicated otherwise, beam-to-beam and beam-to-column connections are assumed to be simple shear connections. Where moment connections are required, they should be specified together with their required flexural strengths.

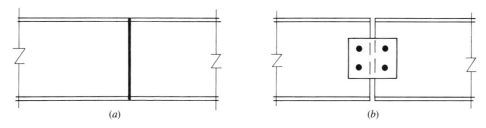

Fig. 11-4   Beam splices: (*a*) groove-welded moment splice; (*b*) bolted shear splice

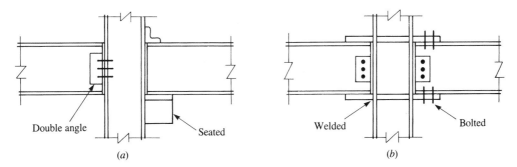

Fig. 11.5   Beam-to-column connections: (*a*) simple (shear) connections; (*b*) moment connections

In connections combining bolts with welds, only high-strength bolts designed as slip-critical can share the load with the welds. Otherwise, the welds alone must resist all connection forces.

Groups of welds or bolts that transmit axial force into a member should preferably be proportioned so that the center of gravity of the group coincides with the centroidal axis of the member. Likewise, when three or more axially loaded members meet at a joint, their centroidal axes should preferably intersect at one point. Where eccentricities are unavoidable, the additional moments they cause must be included in the design of the members and the connections.

BEARING ON STEEL AND CONCRETE

The design bearing strength for steel bearing on steel is ϕR_n, where $\phi = 0.75$

$$R_n = 2.0 F_y A_{pb} \qquad (J8\text{-}1)$$

and A_{pb} = the projected bearing area, in^2.

For steel bearing on concrete (e.g., column base plates bearing on footings), the design bearing strength is $\phi_c P_p$, where $\phi_c = 0.60$

$$P_p = \begin{cases} 0.85 f'_c A_1 & \text{(for bearing on the full area of concrete)} & [11.5] \\ 0.85 f'_c A_1 \sqrt{\dfrac{A_2}{A_1}} & \text{(for bearing on less than the full area of concrete)} & [11.6] \end{cases}$$

where f'_c = specified compressive strength of the concrete, ksi

A_1 = area of steel bearing on a concrete support, in^2

A_2 = maximum area of supporting surface that is geometrically similar to and concentric with the loaded area, in^2

and $\sqrt{\dfrac{A_2}{A_1}} \leq 2$.

The design of a column base plate involves

(a) The determination of its length N and width B. By setting the design bearing strength $\phi_c P_p \geq P_u$ the required strength (or factored column load), an appropriate plate area A_1 can be determined. The bearing plate dimensions N and B are selected to make $N \times B \geq A_1$.

(b) The determination of its thickness t_p. The thickness of base plates is not covered in the AISC LRFD Specification. However, according to the Column Base Plates Design Procedure in Part 2 of the AISC LRFD Manual, base plate thickness t_p (in inches) is the largest value obtained from the following three formulas.

$$t_p = m\sqrt{\dfrac{2P_u}{0.9F_y BN}}, \qquad t_p = n\sqrt{\dfrac{2P_u}{0.9F_y BN}}, \qquad t_p = c\sqrt{\dfrac{2P_o}{0.9F_y A_H}} \qquad [11.7]$$

where N, B, d, b_f, m, and n (all in inches) are as defined in Fig. 11-6, and

$$P_o = \dfrac{P_u}{BN} b_f d \qquad [11.8]$$

$$A_H = \dfrac{P_o}{0.6(0.85\sqrt{A_2/b_f d f'_c})} \geq \dfrac{P_o}{0.6(1.7 f'_c)} \qquad [11.9]$$

$$c = \tfrac{1}{4}[(d + b_f - t_f) - \sqrt{(d + b_f - t_f)^2 - 4(A_H - t_f b_f)}] \qquad [11.10]$$

The design of bearing plates for beams is covered in the next chapter.

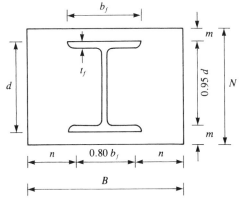

Fig. 11-6 Column base plate

Solved Problems

11.1. In Fig. 11-1(*a*) and (*b*), the plates are 3 in wide and $\frac{3}{4}$ in thick. The base material is A36 steel, for which the matching weld is E70 ($F_{EXX} = 70$ ksi). Determine the design tensile strengths (kips) for

(*a*) The complete penetration groove weld in Fig. 11-1(*a*).

(*b*) The minimum partial penetration groove weld, as in Fig. 11-1(*b*).

(*a*) For tension normal to a complete penetration groove weld (according to Table 11-1), the design strength

$$\phi F_{BM} = 0.90 F_y = 0.90 \times 36 \text{ ksi} = 32.4 \text{ ksi}$$

In kips

$$\phi P_n = \phi F_{BM} A_{BM} = 32.4 \frac{\text{kips}}{\text{in}^2} \times 3 \text{ in} \times 0.75 \text{ in}$$
$$= 72.9 \text{ kips}$$

(*Note*: As indicated in Table 11-1, matching E70 weld must be used with A36 steel in this case.)

(*b*) The minimum effect throat thickness of partial-penetration groove welds (as given in Table 11-2) is $\frac{1}{4}$ in for $\frac{3}{4}$-in plates.

According to Table 11-1, for tension normal to the effective area of a partial penetration groove weld, the design strength is the lower value of

$$\phi F_{BM} A_{BM} = \phi F_y A_{BM} = 0.90 \times 36 \text{ kips/in}^2 \times 3 \text{ in} \times \tfrac{3}{4} \text{ in} = 72.9 \text{ kips}$$
$$\phi F_w A_w = \phi(0.60 F_{EXX}) A_w = 0.80(0.60 \times 70 \text{ kips/in}^2) \times 3 \text{ in} \times \tfrac{1}{4} \text{ in}$$
$$= 25.2 \text{ kips}$$

if an E70 electrode is used. For an E70 electrode, the design tensile strength is 25.2 kips.

As indicated in Table 11-1, an E60 electrode (with strength $F_{EXX} = 60$ ksi, less than the matching E70 weld metal) may also be used. If the weld is E60, the design strength of the weld $\phi F_w A_w$ again controls: $\phi F_w A_w = 0.80(0.60\, F_{EXX}) \times 3 \text{ in} \times \tfrac{1}{4} \text{ in}$, where $F_{EXX} = 60$ ksi; $\phi F_w A_w = 21.6$ kips if an E60 electrode is used.

11.2. Repeat Prob. 11.1 for plates of unequal thickness: $\frac{3}{4}$ in and $\frac{3}{16}$ in.

The effective throat thickness for a complete-penetration groove weld is the thickness of the thinner plate joined, or $\frac{3}{16}$ in. For tension normal to the effective area of a complete penetration groove weld, a matching E70 electrode must be used. The design tensile strength is

$$\phi F_{BM} A_{BM} = \phi F_y A_{BM} = 0.90 \times 36 \text{ kips/in}^2 \times 3 \text{ in} \times \tfrac{3}{16} \text{ in}$$
$$= 18.2 \text{ kips}$$

11.3. A vertical complete-penetration groove weld is used to join the two halves of a W24×176 beam (A36 steel). Determine the design shear strength of the web splice.

According to Table 11-1, for shear on the effective area of a complete-penetration groove weld, the design strength is the lower value of

$$\phi F_{BM} = 0.90(0.60 F_y) = 0.9 \times 0.6 \times 36 \text{ ksi} = 19.4 \text{ ksi}$$
$$\phi F_w = 0.80(0.60 F_{EXX})$$
$$= \begin{cases} 0.8 \times 0.6 \times 70 \text{ ksi} = 33.6 \text{ ksi for E70} \\ 0.8 \times 0.6 \times 60 \text{ ksi} = 28.8 \text{ ksi for E60} \end{cases}$$

Regardless of whether an E60 or E70 electrode is used, the strength of the base material in the web of the W24×176 beam ($\phi F_{BM} = 19.4$ ksi) governs.

$$\phi V_n = 19.4 \text{ ksi} \times dt_w$$

$$= 19.4 \frac{\text{kips}}{\text{in}^2} \times 25.24 \text{ in} \times 0.750 \text{ in} = 368 \text{ kips}$$

The tabulated design shear strength of a W24×76 beam (on p. 3-31 of the AISC LRFD Manual) is, in fact, 368 kips.

11.4. Two vertical partial-penetration groove welds, each with an effective throat thickness of $\frac{1}{4}$ in, are used to join the two halves of a W24×176 beam. Determine the design shear strength of the web splice.

According to Table 11-1, for shear parallel to the axes of partial-penetration groove welds the following limit states should be considered:

Shear fracture of the base material [Eq. (J4-1)]

$$\phi R_n = 0.75(0.6 A_{ns} F_u)$$

$$= 0.75 \times 0.6(25.24 \text{ in} \times 0.750 \text{ in}) \times 58 \frac{\text{kips}}{\text{in}^2}$$

$$= 494 \text{ kips}$$

Shear yielding of the base material [Eq. (J5-3)]

$$\phi R_n = 0.90(0.6 A_{vg} F_y)$$

$$= 0.9 \times 0.6(25.24 \text{ in} \times 0.750 \text{ in}) \times 36 \frac{\text{kips}}{\text{in}^2}$$

$$= 368 \text{ kips} \qquad \text{as in Prob. 11.3.}$$

Shear yielding of the weld (Table 11-1)

$$\phi F_w = 0.75(0.60 F_{EXX})$$

$$= \begin{cases} 0.75 \times 0.6 \times 70 \text{ ksi} = 31.5 \text{ ksi for E70} \\ 0.75 \times 0.6 \times 60 \text{ ksi} = 27.0 \text{ ksi for E60} \end{cases}$$

The shear area for the two partial-penetration groove welds is $d \times 2 \times \frac{1}{4}$ in; i.e.

$$A_w = 25.24 \text{ in} \times 2 \times 0.25 \text{ in} = 12.62 \text{ in}^2$$

$$\phi R_n = \phi F_w A_w$$

$$= \begin{cases} 31.5 \frac{\text{kips}}{\text{in}^2} \times 12.62 \text{ in}^2 = 398 \text{ kips for E70} \\ \\ 27.0 \frac{\text{kips}}{\text{in}^2} \times 12.62 \text{ in}^2 = 341 \text{ kips for E60} \end{cases}$$

In conclusion, the design shear strength at the splice is

368 kips (based on the limit state of shear yielding of the base material) for E70 electrodes

341 kips (based on the limit state of shear yielding of the weld material) for E60 electrodes

11.5. In Fig. 11-1(c), the plates are 3 in and 4 in wide and $\frac{3}{4}$ in thick. The base material is A36 steel. The two fillet welds are each 3 in long. Determine the design tensile strength of the splice for the minimum size fillet weld: (a) E70, (b) E60.

According to Table 11-3, $\frac{1}{4}$ in is the minimum size fillet weld for $\frac{3}{4}$-in plates. The effective area of weld equals its length times the effective throat thickness. As shown in Fig. 11-7, a fillet weld is approximated

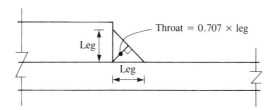

Fig. 11-7

as an equal-leg right triangle. The throat thickness (which is the minimum distance from the root of the joint to the face of the fillet weld) is calculated as 0.707 times the leg dimension. In this case, for a leg dimension of $\frac{1}{4}$ in

$$\text{Throat} = 0.707 \times 0.25 \text{ in} = 0.18 \text{ in}$$

The total effective area of weld

$$A_w = 2 \times 3 \text{ in} \times 0.18 \text{ in} = 1.06 \text{ in}^2$$

According to Table 11-1, the design strength for fillet welds is

$$\phi F_w = 0.75(0.60 F_{EXX}) = 0.45 F_{EXX}$$

(*a*) For E70 electrodes

$$\phi F_w = 0.45 \times 70 \frac{\text{kips}}{\text{in}^2} = 31.5 \frac{\text{kips}}{\text{in}^2}$$

In kips, the design strength

$$\phi F_w A_w = 31.5 \frac{\text{kips}}{\text{in}^2} \times 1.06 \text{ in}^2 = 33.4 \text{ kips}$$

(*b*) For E60 electrodes

$$\phi F_w = 0.45 \times 60 \frac{\text{kips}}{\text{in}^2} = 27.0 \frac{\text{kips}}{\text{in}^2}$$

In kips, the design strength

$$\phi F_w A_w = 27.0 \frac{\text{kips}}{\text{in}^2} \times 1.06 \text{ in}^2 = 28.6 \text{ kips}$$

As indicated in Table 11-1, for tension parallel to the axis of the weld, the design tensile strength of the plates should also be checked, as follows.

$$\phi F_{BM} = 0.90 F_y = 0.90 \times 36 \frac{\text{kips}}{\text{in}^2} = 32.4 \frac{\text{kips}}{\text{in}^2}$$

$$\phi P_n = \phi F_{BM} A_{BM}$$

where A_{BM} is the cross-sectional area of each plate. For the narrower plate, $A_{BM} = 3 \text{ in} \times \frac{3}{4} \text{ in} = 2.25 \text{ in}^2$.

$$\phi P_n = 32.4 \frac{\text{kips}}{\text{in}^2} \times 2.25 \text{ in}^2 = 72.9 \text{ kips}$$

Since $(\phi P_n = \phi F_{BM} A_{BM}) > F_w A$, the design tensile strengths of the plates are not critical in this case.

11.6. In Prob. 11.5, determine the design tensile strength for the maximum size of fillet weld: (*a*) E70, (*b*) E60.

According to Sec. J2.2(*b*) of the AISC LRFD Specification, the maximum size of fillet welds

Equals plate thickness, if $< \frac{1}{4}$ in

Equals plate thickness $- \frac{1}{16}$ in, if plate thickness $\geq \frac{1}{4}$ in

In this case, for a $\frac{3}{4}$-in plate, the maximum fillet weld $= (\frac{3}{4} - \frac{1}{16})$in $= 0.75$ in $- 0.06$ in $= 0.69$ in. For a leg dimension of 0.69 in, throat $= 0.707 \times 0.69$ in $= 0.49$ in. The total effective area of weld $A_w = 2 \times 3$ in $\times 0.49$ in $= 2.92$ in^2

(a) For E70 electrodes, $\phi F_w = 31.5$ ksi, as determined in Prob. 11.5. In kips, the design strength $\phi F_w A_w = 31.5$ ksi $\times 2.92$ in$^2 = 91.9$ kips. However, since the design tensile strength of the narrower (3-in) plate is less, it governs. As determined for Prob. 11.5, $\phi P_n = 72.9$ kips, based on the limit state of yielding of the plate.

(b) For E60 electrodes, $\phi F_w = 27.0$ ksi, as determined in Prob. 11.5. In kips, the design strength

$$\phi F_w A_w = 27.0 \frac{\text{kips}}{\text{in}^2} \times 2.92 \text{ in}^2 = 78.8 \text{ kips}$$

Again, the design tensile strength of the plate governs: $\phi P_n = 72.9$ kips.

11.7. Determine the design tensile strength of a $\frac{7}{8}$-in-diameter bolt if it is (a) A325, (b) A490, (c) A307.

The nominal cross-sectional area of a $\frac{7}{8}$-in-diameter bolt is

$$A = \pi \left(\frac{D}{2}\right)^2 = \pi \left(\frac{\frac{7}{8} \text{ in}}{2}\right)^2 = 0.60 \text{ in}^2$$

The design tensile strength of a bolt

$$\phi P_n = \phi F_m A$$

where $\phi = 0.75$ and F_m is as listed in Table 11.5.

(a) For a $\frac{7}{8}$-in-diameter A325 bolt, the design tensile strength

$$\phi P_n = 0.75 \times 90 \frac{\text{kips}}{\text{in}^2} \times 0.60 \text{ in}^2 = 40.6 \text{ kips}$$

(b) For a $\frac{7}{8}$-in-diameter A490 bolt, the design tensile strength

$$\phi P_n = 0.75 \times 112.5 \frac{\text{kips}}{\text{in}^2} \times 0.60 \text{ in}^2 = 50.7 \text{ kips}$$

(c) For a $\frac{7}{8}$-in-diameter A307 bolt, the design tensile strength

$$\phi P_n = 0.75 \times 45.0 \frac{\text{kips}}{\text{in}^2} \times 0.60 \text{ in}^2 = 20.3 \text{ kips}$$

11.8. Determine the design shear strength of a $\frac{7}{8}$-in-diameter bolt if it is (a) A325-N, (b) A325-X, (c) A490-N, (d) A490-X, (e) A307.

Bolts may be utilized in *single shear* or *double shear*. As shown in Fig. 11-8, the terms *single* and *double shear* refer to the number of planes across which shear is transferred through the bolts. The shear strength values in Table 11-5 are for single shear; for double shear, they may be doubled. Single shear is assumed in this exercise.

Single shear   Double shear

Fig. 11-8

The suffixes N and X refer to a bearing-type (i.e., non-slip-critical) connection, where

N designates threads *included* in the shear plane.

X designates threads *excluded* from the shear plane.

The design shear strength of a bolt

$$\phi V_n = \phi F_{vn} A$$

where ϕ and F_{vn} are as listed in Table 11-5.

The nominal cross-sectional area of a $\frac{7}{8}$-in-diameter bolt is $A = 0.60$ in² (as calculated in Prob. 11.7).

(a) For a $\frac{7}{8}$-in-diameter A325-N bolt, the design shear strength

$$\phi V_n = 0.65 \times 54.0 \frac{\text{kips}}{\text{in}^2} \times 0.60 \, \text{in}^2 = 21.1 \, \text{kips}$$

(b) For a $\frac{7}{8}$-in-diameter A325-X bolt, the design shear strength

$$\phi V_n = 0.65 \times 72.0 \frac{\text{kips}}{\text{in}^2} \times 0.60 \, \text{in}^2 = 28.1 \, \text{kips}$$

(c) For a $\frac{7}{8}$-in-diameter A490-N bolt, the design shear strength

$$\phi V_n = 0.65 \times 67.5 \frac{\text{kips}}{\text{in}^2} \times 0.60 \, \text{in}^2 = 26.4 \, \text{kips}$$

(d) For a $\frac{7}{8}$-in-diameter A490-X bolt, the design shear strength

$$\phi V_n = 0.65 \times 90.0 \frac{\text{kips}}{\text{in}^2} \times 0.60 \, \text{in}^2 = 35.2 \, \text{kips}$$

(e) For a $\frac{7}{8}$-in-diameter A307 bolt, the design shear strength

$$\phi V_n = 0.60 \times 27.0 \frac{\text{kips}}{\text{in}^2} \times 0.60 \, \text{in}^2 = 9.7 \, \text{kips}$$

11.9. A $\frac{7}{8}$-in-diameter A325 bolt is subjected to combined shear and tension. Determine the design tensile force assuming the required shear force is 10 kips.

The nominal cross-sectional area of a $\frac{7}{8}$-in-diameter bolt is 0.60 in².

The shear stress $f_v = 10 \, \text{kips}/0.60 \, \text{in}^2 = 16.6 \, \text{kips/in}^2$

(a) According to Table 11-6, for A325-N bolts (threads included in the shear plane), the design tensile stress

$$F_t = (85 - 1.8 f_v \leq 68) \, \text{ksi}$$
$$= (85 - 1.8 \times 16.6 \leq 68) \, \text{ksi}$$
$$= 55.1 \, \text{ksi}$$

The design tensile force

$$F_t A = 55.1 \frac{\text{kips}}{\text{in}^2} \times 0.60 \, \text{in}^2 = 33.0 \, \text{kips}$$

(b) For A325-X bolts (threads excluded from the shear plane), the design tensile stress

$$F_t = (85 - 1.4 f_v \leq 68) \, \text{ksi}$$
$$= (85 - 1.4 \times 16.6 \leq 68) \, \text{ksi}$$
$$= 61.7 \, \text{ksi}$$

The design tensile force

$$F_t A = 61.7 \frac{\text{kips}}{\text{in}^2} \times 0.60 \text{ in}^2 = 37.1 \text{ kips}$$

11.10. Determine the shear strength of a $\frac{7}{8}$-in-diameter A325 bolt in a slip-critical connection.

(*Please note*: The strengths of slip-critical connections are expressed as unfactored forces in Table 11-7.) Assuming standard-size holes, $f_v = 17$ ksi for A325 bolts. Shear strength

$$f_v A = 17 \frac{\text{kips}}{\text{in}^2} \times 0.60 \text{ in}^2 = 10.2 \text{ kips}$$

Maximum service load shear on the bolt is 10.2 kips. As noted in Table 11-7, $f_v = 17$ ksi and the other shear strengths tabulated therein are for class A surfaces (with slip coefficient 0.33). Higher shear strengths for high-strength bolts in slip-critical connections are available for class B (slip coefficient 0.50) and class C (slip coefficient 0.40) surfaces. The higher values are given in the *Specification for Structural Joints Using ASTM A325 or A490 Bolts*, which appears in Part 6 of the AISC LRFD Manual.

11.11. Repeat Problem 11.10 for a service tensile force of 20 kips acting in combination with the shear.

If tension is present, the shear values in Table 11-7 are to be multiplied by $(1 - T/T_b)$, where T is the service tensile force and T_b is the minimum pretension load for the bolt in Table 11-4.

$$10.2 \text{ kips} \times \left(1 - \frac{T}{T_b}\right) = 10.2 \text{ kips} \times \left(1 - \frac{20 \text{ kips}}{39 \text{ kips}}\right) = 5.0 \text{ kips maximum service load shear}$$

11.12. Check the bearing strengths of the $\frac{7}{8}$-in-diameter bolts in Probs. 11.8 and 11.10. Assume two or more bolts in the line of force connecting two $\frac{3}{8}$-in plates of A36 steel; standard holes; center-to-center distance of 3 in; and edge distance of $1\frac{1}{2}$ in.

Edge distance $(L = 1.5 \text{ in}) \geq (1.5d = 1.5 \times \frac{7}{8} \text{ in} = 1.31 \text{ in})$. Spacing $(C = 3.0 \text{ in}) \geq (3.0d = 3.0 \times \frac{7}{8} \text{ in} = 2.63 \text{ in})$. Equation (*J3-1a*) is applicable and the design bearing strength is ϕR_n, where $\phi = 0.75$ and $R_n = 2.4 \, dt \, F_u$.

$$\phi R_n = 0.75 \times 2.4 \times \tfrac{7}{8} \times \tfrac{3}{8} \text{ in} \times 58 \text{ kips/in}^2$$
$$= 34.3 \text{ kips per bolt}$$

In Prob. 11.8, the only bolt governed by bearing strength is the A490-X in part (*d*), for which $(\phi R_n = 34.3 \text{ kips}) < (\phi V_n = 35.2 \text{ kips})$. All the other bolts are governed by shear strength, because $\phi V_n < (\phi R_n = 34.3 \text{ kips})$.

Regarding Prob. 11.10, where the bolt is in a slip-critical connection, the limiting service load shear of 10.2 kips obviously governs over the limiting factored load bearing value of 34.3 kips.

11.13. The end of a W12×87 beam (A36 steel) has been prepared as shown in Fig. 11-9 for connection to a supporting member. The three holes are $\frac{15}{16}$ in diameter for $\frac{7}{8}$-in-diameter bolts. Determine the design shear strength of the beam web.

The applicable limit states are shear yielding, shear fracture, and block shear rupture. For shear yielding

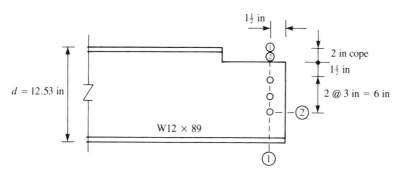

Fig. 11-9

[of gross section (1) in Fig. 11-9]

$$\phi R_n = 0.90 \times 0.6 A_{vg} F_y \qquad\qquad (J5\text{-}3)$$

$$A_{vg} = (d\text{-cope})t = (12.53 \text{ in} - 2 \text{ in}) \times 0.515 \text{ in} = 5.42 \text{ in}^2$$

$$\phi R_n = 0.9 \times 0.6 \times 5.42 \text{ in}^2 \times 36 \text{ ksi} = 105 \text{ kips}$$

For shear fracture [of net section (1) in Fig. 11-9]

$$\phi R_n = 0.75 \times 0.6 A_{ns} F_u \qquad\qquad (J4\text{-}1)$$

$$A_{ns} = (d\text{-cope-}3d_h)t = (12.53 \text{ in} - 2 \text{ in} - 3 \times \tfrac{15}{16} \text{ in}) \times 0.515 \text{ in} = 3.97 \text{ in}^2$$

$$\phi R_n = 0.75 \times 0.6 \times 3.97 \text{ in}^2 \times 58 \text{ ksi} = 104 \text{ kips}$$

For block shear rupture [of section (2) in Fig. 11-9] $\phi = 0.75$ and R_n = the greater value of

$$0.6 A_{vg} F_y + A_n F_u \qquad\qquad (C\text{-}J4\text{-}1)$$

$$0.6 A_{ns} F_u + A_g F_y \qquad\qquad (C\text{-}J4\text{-}2)$$

where A_{vg} = gross area of the vertical part of (2)

A_{ns} = net area of the vertical part of (2)

A_g = gross area of the horizontal part of (2)

A_n = net area of the horizontal part of (2)

$$A_{vg} = (1\tfrac{1}{2} \text{ in} + 2 \times 3 \text{ in}) \times 0.515 \text{ in} = 3.86 \text{ in}^2$$

$$A_{ns} = (1\tfrac{1}{2} \text{ in} + 2 \times 3 \text{ in} - 2\tfrac{1}{2} \times \tfrac{15}{16}) \times 0.515 \text{ in} = 2.66 \text{ in}^2$$

$$A_g = 1\tfrac{1}{2} \text{ in} \times 0.515 \text{ in} = 0.77 \text{ in}^2$$

$$A_n = (1\tfrac{1}{2} \text{ in} - \tfrac{1}{2} \times \tfrac{15}{16} \text{ in}) \times 0.515 \text{ in} = 0.53 \text{ in}^2$$

R_n is the greater of

$$0.6 \times 3.86 \text{ in}^2 \times 36 \frac{\text{kips}}{\text{in}^2} + 0.53 \text{ in}^2 \times 58 \frac{\text{kips}}{\text{in}^2} = 114 \text{ kips}$$

$$0.6 \times 2.66 \text{ in}^2 \times 58 \frac{\text{kips}}{\text{in}^2} + 0.77 \text{ in}^2 \times 36 \frac{\text{kips}}{\text{in}^2} = 120 \text{ kips}$$

$$R_n = 120 \text{ kips}$$

$$\phi R_n = 0.75 \times 120 \text{ kips} = 90 \text{ kips}$$

The design shear strength is 90 kips, based on the governing limit state of block shear rupture.

11.14. Design a base plate for a W14×90 column with a factored axial load of 700 kips. All steel is A36. The base plate is on a footing 2 ft 0 in × 2 ft 0 in; $f'_c = 4$ ksi.

The design bearing strength for steel bearing on concrete is determined from Eq. (11.5) or (11.6); the former for bearing on the full area of concrete, and the latter for bearing on less than the full area. The dimensions of the W14×90 column d b_f = 14.02 in × 14.52 in. Try a 16 in × 16 in base plate and use Eq. (11.7).

$$A_2 = 24\text{ in} \times 24\text{ in} = 576\text{ in}^2 \qquad A_1 = 16\text{ in} \times 16\text{ in} = 256\text{ in}^2$$

$$f_c' = 4\frac{\text{kips}}{\text{in}^2} \qquad \phi = 0.60$$

The design bearing strength

$$\phi_c P_p = 0.85 f_c' A_1 \sqrt{\frac{A_2}{A_1}}$$

$$= 0.85 \times 4\frac{\text{kips}}{\text{in}^2} \times 256\text{ in}^2 \times \sqrt{\frac{576\text{ in}^2}{256\text{ in}^2}}$$

$$= 1306\text{ kips} > 700\text{ kips required} \qquad \text{o.k.}$$

Referring to Fig. 11-6

$$N = 16.0\text{ in}, \qquad d = 14.0\text{ in} \qquad m = 0.5(N - 0.95\,d)$$
$$= 0.5(16\text{ in} - 0.95 \times 14\text{ in}) = 1.35\text{ in}$$

$$B = 16.0\text{ in}, \qquad b_f = 14.52\text{ in} \qquad n = 0.5(B - 0.80 b_f)$$
$$= 0.5(16\text{ in} - 0.80 \times 14.52\text{ in}) = 2.19\text{ in}$$

To determine c, solve Eqs. [11.8] to [11.10]

$$P_o = \frac{P_u}{BN} b_f d = \frac{700\text{ kips}}{16\text{ in} \times 16\text{ in}} \times 14.02\text{ in} \times 14.52\text{ in}$$

$$= 556\text{ kips}$$

$$A_H = \frac{P_o}{0.6(0.85\sqrt{A_2/b_f d f_c'})} \geq \frac{P_o}{0.6(1.7 f_c')}$$

$$= \frac{556\text{ kips}}{0.6(0.85\sqrt{576\text{ in}^2/(14.52\text{ in} \times 14.0\text{ in})}\,4\text{ kips/in}^2)}$$

$$\geq \frac{556\text{ kips}}{0.6 \times (1.7 \times 4\text{ kips/in}^2)}$$

$$= 162\text{ in}^2 \geq 136\text{ in}^2$$

$$= 162\text{ in}^2$$

$$c = \tfrac{1}{4}[(d + b_f - t_f) - \sqrt{(d + b_f - t_f)^2 - 4(A_H - t_f b_f)}]$$

$$(d + b_f - t_f) = (14.02 + 14.52 - 0.71)\text{ in} = 27.83\text{ in}$$

$$c = \tfrac{1}{4}[27.83\text{ in} - \sqrt{(27.83\text{ in})^2 - 4(162\text{ in}^2 - 0.71\text{ in} \times 14.52\text{ in})}]$$

$$c = 4.26\text{ in}$$

Referring to Eq. [11.8]

$$m = 1.35\text{ in}, \qquad n = 2.19\text{ in} \qquad c = 4.26\text{ in}$$

$$\sqrt{\frac{2P_u}{0.9 F_y BN}} = \sqrt{\frac{2 \times 700\text{ kips}}{0.9 \times 36\text{ kips/in}^2 \times 16\text{ in} \times 16\text{ in}}} = 0.41$$

$$\sqrt{\frac{2P_o}{0.9 F_y A_H}} = \sqrt{\frac{2 \times 556\text{ kips}}{0.9 \times 36\text{ kips/in}^2 \times 162\text{ in}^2}} = 0.46$$

Base plate thickness t_p is the largest of $(1.35 \text{ in} \times 0.41 = 0.55 \text{ in})$, $(2.19 \text{ in} \times 0.41 = 0.90 \text{ in})$, and $(4.26 \text{ in} \times 0.46 = 1.96 \text{ in})$. Use a base plate 16 in $\times$ 2 in $\times$ 16 in.

Supplementary Problems

11.15. Complete penetration groove welds are used to join the flanges of the two halves of the W24×176 beam (A36 steel) in Prob. 11.3. Determine (a) the design flexural strength at the splice and (b) the appropriate electrode.

Ans. (a) $\phi_b M_x = 1115$ kip-ft, (b) matching E70.

11.16. The flanges of the two halves of the same W24×176 beam are joined by $\frac{1}{2}$-in partial-penetration groove welds. Determine (a) the design flexural strength at the splice and (b) the appropriate electrode.

Ans. $\phi_b M_x = 446$ kip-ft for E70; $\phi_b M_x = 383$ kip-ft for E60.

11.17. In Fig. 11-1(d), the plates are 3 in wide and $\frac{3}{4}$ in thick. the base material is A36 steel. Determine the design tensile strength of the splice for the minimum size fillet weld: (a) E70, (b) E60.

Ans. (a) 33.4 kips, (b) 28.6 kips.

11.18. In Prob. 11.17, determine the design tensile strength for the maximum size fillet weld: (a) E70, (b) E60.

Ans. (a) 72.9 kips, (b) 72.9 kips.

11.19. Repeat Prob. 11.8 for a $\frac{3}{4}$-in-diameter bolt.

Ans. (a) 15.5 kips, (b) 20.7 kips, (c) 19.4 kips, (d) 25.8 kips, (e) 7.2 kips.

11.20. Repeat Prob. 11.9 for a $\frac{3}{4}$-in-diameter bolt.

Ans. (a) 19.6 kips, (b) 23.6 kips.

11.21. Repeat Probs. 11.10 and 11.11 for $\frac{3}{4}$-in-diameter bolts.

Ans. 7.5 kips, 2.1 kips.

11.22. Determine the bearing strength of $\frac{3}{4}$-in-diameter bolts connecting $\frac{1}{4}$-in plates of A36 steel; standard holes; center-to-center distance of $2\frac{1}{2}$ in; and edge distance of $1\frac{1}{4}$ in.

Ans. 19.6 kips.

11.23. Determine the design shear strength of the web of the W21×44 beam (A36 steel) in Fig. 11-10. The five holes are $1\frac{1}{16}$-in-diameter for 1-in-diameter bolts.

Ans. 121 kips.

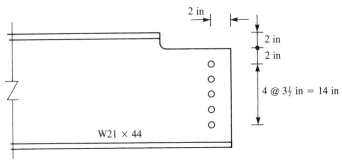

Fig. 11-10

11.24. Design a base plate for a W8×67 column with a factored axial load of 450 kips. All steel is A36. The base plate will occupy the full area of concrete support; $f'_c = 3.5$ ksi.

Ans.   Base plate 14 in × $1\frac{1}{2}$ in × 14 in.

Chapter 12

Other Design Considerations

NOTATION

b_f = flange width, in

d = depth of the member, in

d_c = web depth clear of fillets, in = $d - 2k$

F_y = specified minimum yield stress

K = effective length factor for columns

k = distance from outer face of the flange to web toe of the fillet, in

l = stiffener height, in

N = length of bearing, in

P_n = nominal axial compressive strength of the column, kips

P_u = required axial compressive strength of the column, kips

R_n = nominal strength, kips

R_u = required strength, kips

R_v = nominal shear strength, kips

t_f = flange thickness, in

t_w = web thickness, in

X = parameter in Eqs. (K1-6) and (K1-7)

Y = parameter in Eqs. (K1-6) and (K1-7)

ϕ = resistance factor

ϕR_n = design strength, kips

ϕR_v = design shear strength, kips

INTRODUCTION

Additional provisions for steel structures are given in the final three chapters of the AISC LRFD Specification, as follows:

Chap. K—Strength Design Considerations

Chap. L—Serviceability Design Considerations

Chap. M—Fabrication, Erection, and Quality Control

The strength and stability provisions relating to concentrated forces are discussed herein.

CONCENTRATED LOADS AND REACTIONS

A concentrated force acting on a member introduces high stresses in its vicinity. To prevent failure, the required (or factored) concentrated load or reaction R_u (kips) must be checked against the design strength ϕR_n (kips), as determined by the appropriate limit states. For each limit state, ϕ is the resistance factor and R_n is the nominal strength.

(1) Local Web Yielding. This limit state applies to all concentrated forces (tensile or compressive) in the plane of the web. The design strength of the web at the toe of the fillet

is ϕR_n, where $\phi = 1.0$ and R_n depends on whether the concentrated force is a load or a reaction.

a. For a concentrated *load* (acting along a member at a distance from either end greater than d, the depth of the member)

$$R_n = (5k + N)F_y t_w \qquad (K1\text{-}2)$$

b. For a concentrated *reaction* (acting at or near the end of the member)

$$R_n = (2.5k + N)F_y t_w \qquad (K1\text{-}3)$$

In the preceding equations

$k =$ distance from outer face of the flange to web toe of the fillet, in

$N =$ length of bearing, in

$F_y =$ specified minimum yield stress, ksi

$t_w =$ web thickness, in

If a pair of stiffeners is provided on opposite sides of the web at the concentrated force, covering at least half the member depth, this limit state need not be considered.

(2) Web Crippling. This limit state applies to all concentrated compressive forces in the plane of the web. The design compressive strength of the web is ϕR_n, where $\phi = 0.75$ and R_n depends on whether the concentrated force is a load or a reaction.

a. For a concentrated *load* (acting along a member at a distance from either end greater than $d/2$)

$$R_n = 135 t_w^2 \left[1 + 3\left(\frac{N}{d}\right)\left(\frac{t_w}{t_f}\right)^{1.5} \right] \sqrt{\frac{F_y t_f}{t_w}} \qquad (K1\text{-}4)$$

b. For a concentrated *reaction* (acting at or near the end of the member)

$$R_n = 68 t_w^2 \left[1 + 3\left(\frac{N}{d}\right)\left(\frac{t_w}{t_f}\right)^{1.5} \right] \sqrt{\frac{F_y t_f}{t_w}} \qquad (K1\text{-}5)$$

where d is the depth of the member, in, and t_f is flange thickness, in. If the concentrated force exceeds ϕR_n, a pair of stiffeners must be provided in accordance with the Stiffener Requirements section later in this chapter.

(3) Sidesway Web Buckling. This limit state relates to concentrated compressive force applied to one flange in the plane of the web, where no lateral bracing or (half-depth) stiffeners are provided. The design compressive strength is ϕR_n, where $\phi = 0.85$ and R_n depends on whether the loaded flange is restrained against rotation.

a. For the loaded flange restrained against rotation

If $Y < 2.3$: $R_n = X(1 + 0.4Y^3)$ $\qquad (K1\text{-}6)$

If $Y \geq 2.3$:   this limit state need not be checked

b. For the loaded flange not restrained against rotation

If $Y < 1.7$: $R_n = X(0.4Y^3)$ $\qquad (K1\text{-}7)$

If $Y \geq 1.7$:   this limit state need not be checked

In the preceding expressions

$X = \dfrac{12,000 t_w^3}{d_c}$;   however, if the web flexural stresses (due to the factored loads) $< F_y$ at the concentrated load, the value of X may be doubled.

$$Y = \frac{d_c b_f}{l t_w}$$

l = maximum laterally unbraced length along either flange at the point of load, in

b_f = flange width, in

d_c = web depth clear of fillets, in = $d - 2k$.

(4) Compression Buckling of the Web. This limit state relates to concentrated compressive forces applied to both flanges. The design compressive strength is ϕR_n, where $\phi = 0.90$ and

$$R_n = \frac{4100 t_w^3 \sqrt{F_y}}{d_c} \qquad (K1\text{-}8)$$

If the concentrated force exceeds ϕR_n, a pair of stiffeners must be provided in accordance with the Stiffener Requirements section later in this chapter.

(5) Local Flange Bending. This limit state applies to a concentrated tensile force acting on one flange. The design strength is ϕR_n, where

$$\phi = 0.90 \qquad \text{and} \qquad R_n = 6.25 t_f^2 F_y \qquad (K1\text{-}1)$$

If the length of loading perpendicular to the member web $< 0.15 b_f$ (the member flange width) or if a pair of (half-depth) web stiffeners is provided, this limit state need not be considered.

(6) Columns with Web Panels Subject to High Shear. This limit state applies to column webs at beam-to-column moment connections. The design shear strength of the column web is ϕR_v, where $\phi = 0.90$ and R_v, the nominal shear strength, depends on the (factored) column axial load P_u.

a. If

$$P_u \leq 0.75 P_n: \qquad R_v = 0.7 F_y d_c t_w \qquad (K1\text{-}9)$$

b. If

$$P_u > 0.75 P_n: \qquad R_v = 0.7 F_y d_c t_w \left[1.9 - 1.2 \left(\frac{P_u}{P_n} \right) \right] \qquad (K1\text{-}10)$$

where P_u is the required axial compressive strength of the column, kips, and P_n is the nominal axial compressive strength of the column, kips.

Column web shear can be determined as shown in Fig. 12.1. If it exceeds the design shear strength [calculated from Eqs. $(K1\text{-}9)$ or $(K1\text{-}10)$], the column web must be reinforced with diagonal stiffeners or web doubler plates.

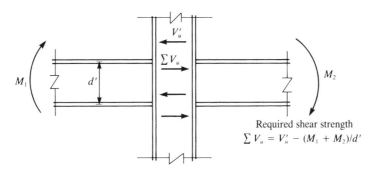

Fig. 12-1 Column web panel shear

STIFFENER REQUIREMENTS

When web stiffeners are required at a concentrated force because of (2) crippling of the web or (4) compression buckling of the web, they must satisfy the following additional provisions of the AISC LRFD Specification. They are to be designed as columns (i.e., as axially compressed members, as in Chap. 4) with an effective length $Kl = 0.75h$. As specified in Sec. K1.8 of the AISC LRFD Specification, part of the beam web can be considered as working with the pair of stiffeners.

For all web stiffeners provided at concentrated loads and reactions: If the concentrated force is tensile, the stiffeners must be welded to the loaded flange. If the force is compressive, the stiffeners can either bear on or be welded to the loaded flange.

Solved Problems

12.1. The unstiffened end of a W21×62 beam of A36 steel rests on a concrete support ($f'_c = 3$ ksi). Design a bearing plate for the beam and its (factored) end reaction of 100 kips. (See Fig. 12-2.) Assume the area of concrete support $A_2 = 6 \times A_1$ (the area of the bearing plate).

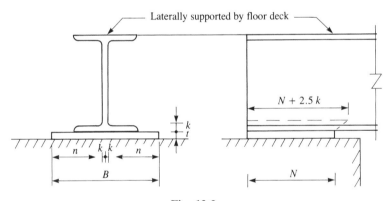

Fig. 12-2

For the concentrated compressive reaction of 100 kips acting on the bottom flange, the applicable limit states are (1) local web yielding and (2) web crippling. (It is assumed that the beam is welded to the base plate and both are anchor-bolted to the concrete support. This should provide adequate lateral bracing to prevent sidesway web buckling.)

Corresponding to the applicable limit states are Eqs. (K1-3) and (K1-5), each of which has N, the length of bearing, as a parameter.

Solving for N, we obtain

$$R_u \le \phi R_n = \phi(2.5k + N)F_y t_w$$

$$100 \text{ kips} \le 1.0(2.5 \times 1\tfrac{3}{8} \text{ in} + N) \times 36 \text{ kips/in}^2 \times 0.40 \text{ in} \qquad (K1\text{-}3)$$

$$N \ge 3.5 \text{ in}$$

$$R_u \le \phi R_n = \phi 68 t_w^2 \left[1 + 3\left(\frac{N}{d}\right)\left(\frac{t_w}{t_f}\right)^{1.5}\right]\sqrt{\frac{F_y t_f}{t_w}} \qquad (K1\text{-}5)$$

$$100 \text{ kips} \le 0.75 \times 68(0.40 \text{ in})^2 \left[1 + 3\left(\frac{N}{20.99 \text{ in}}\right)\left(\frac{0.40 \text{ in}}{0.0615 \text{ in}}\right)^{1.5}\right]\sqrt{36 \frac{\text{kips}}{\text{in}^2} \times \frac{0.615 \text{ in}}{0.40 \text{ in}}}$$

$$N \ge 8.6 \text{ in}$$

The minimum length of bearing is $N = 8.6$ in. Rounding up to the next full inch, let $N = 9$ in.

The area of the bearing plate is determined by the bearing strength of the concrete support. Using Eq. [11.6] from Chap. 11, the design bearing strength is

$$\phi_c P_p = \phi_c \times 0.85 f'_c A_1 \sqrt{\frac{A_2}{A_1}}$$

where $\sqrt{A_2/A_1} \leq 2$.

Substituting in Eq. [11.6], we obtain

$$100 \text{ kips} = 0.60 \times 0.85 \times 3 \frac{\text{kips}}{\text{in}^2} \times A_1 \times 2$$

The area of the bearing plate $A_1 = 32.7 \text{ in}^2$.

Because the bearing plate dimensions are

$$BN \geq A_1: \qquad B \geq \frac{A_1}{N} = \frac{32.7 \text{ in}^2}{9 \text{ in}} = 3.6 \text{ in}$$

However, B cannot be less than the flange width of the W21×62 beam, $b_f = 8.24$. Rounding up, let $B = 9$ in. A formula for bearing plate thickness is given on page 3-50 of the AISC LRFD Manual:

$$t = \sqrt{\frac{2.22 R n^2}{A_1 F_y}}$$

where $R = 100$ kips

$$n = \frac{B - 2k}{2} = \frac{9 \text{ in} - 2 \times 1\frac{3}{8} \text{ in}}{2} = 3.13 \text{ in}$$

$$A_1 = BN = 9 \text{ in} \times 9 \text{ in} = 81 \text{ in}^2$$

$$F_y = 36 \text{ ksi}$$

$$t = \sqrt{\frac{2.22 \times 100 \text{ kips} \times (3.13 \text{ in})^2}{81 \text{ in}^2 \times 36 \text{ ksi}}} = 0.86 \text{ in}$$

Use a bearing plate 1 in × 9 in × 9 in.

12.2. In Prob. 12.1, can the bearing plate be eliminated?

For the W21×62 beam to bear directly on the concrete support, its bottom flange must be sufficiently thick to act as a bearing plate.

Let

$$t = \sqrt{\frac{2.22 R n^2}{A_1 F_y}} = 0.615 \text{ in}$$

the flange thickness of the W21×62 beam. Because $B = b_f = 8.24$ in

$$n = \frac{B - 2k}{2} = \frac{8.24 \text{ in} - 2 \times 1\frac{3}{8} \text{ in}}{2} = 2.75 \text{ in}$$

$$t = \sqrt{\frac{2.22 \times 100 \text{ kips} \times (2.75 \text{ in})^2}{A_1 \times 36 \text{ kips/in}^2}} = 0.615 \text{ in}$$

$$A_1 = 123 \text{ in}^2 \ (>32.7 \text{ in}^2 \text{ required for bearing on concrete})$$

$$N = \frac{A_1}{B} = \frac{A_1}{b_f} = \frac{123 \text{ in}^2}{8.24 \text{ in}} = 15.0 \text{ in}$$

By increasing the length of bearing of the beam on the concrete to 15 in, the bearing plate can be eliminated.

12.3. A column with a 12-in-long base plate rests on the top flange of a W18×50 beam (A36 steel), 20 ft long. Determine the maximum column load if the beam is (a) not stiffened or braced along its entire span and (b) not stiffened but braced at the load point.

(a) For a concentrated compressive force acting on the top flange of a beam, the applicable limit states are (1) local web yielding, (2) web crippling, and (3) sidesway web buckling. The corresponding equations are (K1-2), (K1-4), and (K1-7) (assuming no restraint against rotation).

$$P_u \le \phi R_n = 1.0(5k + N)F_y t_w = 1.0(5 \times 1.25 \text{ in} + 12 \text{ in}) 36 \frac{\text{kips}}{\text{in}^2} \times 0.355 \text{ in} \qquad (K1\text{-}2)$$

$$P_u \le 233 \text{ kips}$$

$$P_u \le \phi R_n = 0.75 \times 135 t_w^2 \left[1 + 3\left(\frac{N}{d}\right)\left(\frac{t_w}{t_f}\right)^{1.5} \right] \sqrt{\frac{F_y t_f}{t_w}} \qquad (K1\text{-}4)$$

$$= 0.75 \times 135 (0.355 \text{ in})^2$$

$$\left[1 + 3\left(\frac{12 \text{ in}}{17.99 \text{ in}}\right)\left(\frac{0.355 \text{ in}}{0.570 \text{ in}}\right)^{1.5} \right] \sqrt{36 \text{ ksi} \times \frac{0.570 \text{ in}}{0.355 \text{ in}}}$$

$$P_u \le 192 \text{ kips}$$

$$P_u \le \phi R_n = 0.85 \times X(0.4Y^3)$$

$$Y = \frac{d_c b_f}{l t_w} \cdot d_c = d - 2k = (17.99 \text{ in} - 2 \times 1.25 \text{ in}) = 15.49 \text{ in}$$

$$= \frac{15.49 \text{ in} \times 7.495 \text{ in}}{\left(20 \text{ ft} \times 12 \frac{\text{in}}{\text{ft}}\right) 0.355 \text{ in}} = 1.36 < 1.7 \qquad (K1\text{-}7)$$

Since $Y < 1.7$ and the loaded flange is not stiffened, braced, or restrained against rotation, Eq. (K1-7) must be checked.

$$X = \frac{12,000 t_w^3}{d_c} = \frac{12,000(0.355 \text{ in})^3}{15.49 \text{ in}} = 35$$

$$P_u \le 0.85 \times 35 \times 0.4(1.36)^3$$

$$\le 30 \text{ kips}$$

The maximum (factored) column load is 30 kips based on the governing limit state of sidesway web buckling [Eq. (K1-7)].

(b) If the top flange is braced at the load point, the limit state of sidesway web buckling does not apply. The governing limit state is web crippling [Eq. (K1-4)], with a design strength of 192 kips. The shear strength of the web of the beam should always be checked. For a W18×50.

$$\phi_v V_n = 0.90 \times 0.6 F_y d t_w$$

$$= 0.90 \times 0.6 \times 36 \frac{\text{kips}}{\text{in}^2} \times 17.99 \text{ in} \times 0.355 \text{ in}$$

$\phi_v V_n = 124$ kips. If, for example, the concentrated column load $P_u = 192$ kips acts at midspan and is the only load on the beam except for its own weight, the required shear strength

$$V_u = \frac{192 \text{ kips}}{2} + \frac{0.050 \text{ kips/ft} \times 20 \text{ ft}}{2}$$

$$(V_u = 96.5 \text{ kips}) < (\phi_v V_n = 124 \text{ kips}) \qquad \text{o.k.}$$

12.4. Determine the maximum load that can be hung from a plate (12 in long × 7 in wide) welded to the bottom flange of a W18×50 beam. All steel is A36.

For a concentrated tensile force acting on the bottom flange of a beam, the applicable limit states are (1) local web yielding and (5) local flange bending. The corresponding equations are $(K1\text{-}2)$ and $(K1\text{-}1)$. In solving Eq. $(K1\text{-}2)$ for a W18×50 with a 12-in load bearing (in Prob. 12.3) it was determined that $P_u \leq 233$ kips.

Because the width of plate = 7 in > $0.15b_f$ ($= 0.15 \times 7.495$ in $= 1.12$ in), Eq. $(K1\text{-}1)$ must be checked:

$$P_u \leq \phi R_n = 0.90 \times 6.25 t_f^2 F_y$$

$$= 0.90 \times 6.25(0.570 \text{ in})^2 \times 36 \text{ ksi}$$

$$P_u \leq 66 \text{ kips}$$

The maximum (factored) hanging load is 66 kips, based on the limit state of local flange bending. If stiffeners are provided or if the hanging load is confined to the central $0.15b_f$ ($= 1.12$ in) of the beam flange, 233 kips can be hung.

12.5. Two W27×84 beams are rigidly connected to a W14×145 column (all of A36 steel). The forces due to the various loadings are shown in Fig. 12-3. Determine whether column web stiffeners are required.

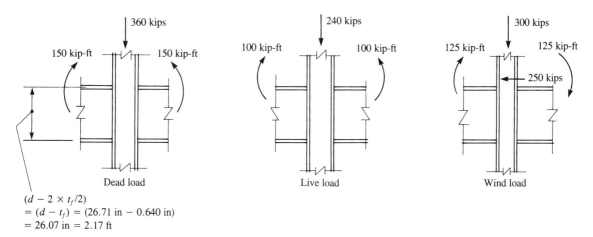

$(d - 2 \times t_f/2)$
$= (d - t_f) = (26.71 \text{ in} - 0.640 \text{ in})$
$= 26.07 \text{ in} = 2.17 \text{ ft}$

Fig. 12-3

In determining whether column web stiffeners are required, the significant parameters are F, the beam flange forces (tension and compression); V, the column shear; and P, the column axial load.

Under *dead load*

$$F = \frac{150 \text{ kip-ft}}{2.17 \text{ ft}} = 69 \text{ kips}$$

$$V = 0$$

$$P = 360 \text{ kips}$$

Under *live load*

$$F = \frac{100 \text{ kip-ft}}{2.17 \text{ ft}} = 46 \text{ kips}$$

$$V = 0$$

$$P = 240 \text{ kips}$$

Under *wind load*

$$F = \frac{125 \text{ kip-ft}}{2.17 \text{ ft}} = 58 \text{ kips}$$

$$V = 250 \text{ kips} - 2 \times 58 \text{ kips} = 134 \text{ kips}$$

$$P = 300 \text{ kips}$$

The relevant load combinations from Chap. 2 are

$$\underline{1.4D} \tag{A4-1}$$

$$F_u = 1.4 \times 69 \text{ kips} = 97 \text{ kips}$$

$$V_u = 0$$

$$P_u = 1.4 \times 360 \text{ kips} = 504 \text{ kips}$$

$$\underline{1.2D + 1.6L} \tag{A4-2}$$

$$F_u = 1.2 \times 69 \text{ kips} + 1.6 \times 46 \text{ kips} = 156 \text{ kips}$$

$$V_u = 0$$

$$P_u = 1.2 \times 360 \text{ kips} + 1.6 \times 240 \text{ kips} = 816 \text{ kips}$$

$$\underline{1.2D + 1.3W + 0.5L} \tag{A4-4}$$

$$F_u = 1.2 \times 69 \text{ kips} + 1.3 \times 58 \text{ kips} + 0.5 \times 46 \text{ kips} = 181 \text{ kips}$$

$$V_u = 1.3 \times 134 \text{ kips} = 174 \text{ kips}$$

$$P_u = 1.2 \times 360 \text{ kips} + 1.3 \times 300 \text{ kips} + 0.5 \times 240 \text{ kips} = 942 \text{ kips}$$

$$\underline{0.90D - 1.3W} \tag{A4-6}$$

$$F_u = 0.9 \times 69 \text{ kips} - 1.3 \times 58 \text{ kips} = -13 \text{ kips}$$

$$V_u = -1.3 \times 134 \text{ kips} = -174 \text{ kips}$$

$$P_u = 0.9 \times 360 \text{ kips} - 1.3 \times 300 \text{ kips} = -66 \text{ kips}$$

Regarding stiffening the web of the W14×145 column, all the significant required strengths (F_u, V_u, and P_u) are maximum under load combination ($A4$-4): $1.2D + 1.3W + 0.5L$. They are as follows: $F_u = 181$ kips, $V_u = 174$ kips, and $P_u = 942$ kips.

The applicable limit states are

(1) local web yielding, (2) web crippling, (4) compression buckling of the web, (5) local flange bending, and (6) columns with web panels subject to high shear.

The corresponding equations are Eqs. ($K1$-2), ($K1$-4), ($K1$-8), and ($K1$-1).

$$\phi R_n = 1.0(5k + N)F_y t_w \tag{K1-2}$$

For the W14×145 column, $k = 1.75$ in, $t_w = 0.680$ in. Let the length of bearing $N = 0.640$ in, the flange thickness of the W27×84 beam

$$\phi R_n = 1.0(5 \times 1.75 \text{ in} + 0.640 \text{ in}) \times 36 \frac{\text{kips}}{\text{in}^2} \times 0.680 \text{ in}$$

$$= 230 \text{ kips}$$

$$\phi R_n = 0.75 \times 135 t_w^2 \left[1 + 3\left(\frac{N}{d}\right)\left(\frac{t_w}{t_f}\right)^{1.5} \right] \sqrt{\frac{F_y t_f}{t_w}} \tag{K1-4}$$

$$= 0.75 \times 135 \times (0.680 \text{ in})^2 \left[1 + 3\left(\frac{0.640 \text{ in}}{14.78 \text{ in}}\right)\left(\frac{0.680 \text{ in}}{1.090 \text{ in}}\right)^{1.5} \right] \sqrt{36 \frac{\text{kips}}{\text{in}^2} \times \frac{1.090 \text{ in}}{0.680 \text{ in}}}$$

$$= 378 \text{ kips}$$

$$\phi R_n = 0.90 \times \frac{4100 t_w^3 \sqrt{F_y}}{d_c} \tag{K1-8}$$

where $d_c = d - 2k$. For the W14×145 column, $d_c = 14.78$ in $- 2 \times 1.75$ in $= 11.28$ in.

$$\phi R_n = 0.90 \times \frac{4100(0.680\ \text{in})^3 \sqrt{36\ \text{ksi}}}{11.28\ \text{in}}$$

$$= 617\ \text{kips}$$

$$\phi R_n = 0.90 \times 6.25 t_f^2 F_y \qquad\qquad (K1\text{-}1)$$

$$= 0.90 \times 6.25 \times (1.090\ \text{in})^2 \times 36\ \text{ksi}$$

$$= 241\ \text{kips}$$

Because $(F_u = 181\ \text{kips}) < \phi R_n$ for all the preceding limit states, horizontal stiffeners for the column web, between beam flanges, are not required.

Regarding the last limit state cited, column web panels subject to high shear, Eq. $(K1\text{-}9)$ or $(K1\text{-}10)$ may apply, depending on P_u and P_n. Assuming the column is laterally supported by beams in both perpendicular directions at the connection level (i.e., the unbraced length $l = 0$), $P_n = A_g F_y$ [from Chap. 4, Eqs. $(E2\text{-}1)$ to $(E2\text{-}4)$]. For the W14×145 column

$$P_n = 42.7\ \text{in}^2 \times 36\ \text{ksi} = 1537\ \text{kips}$$

Since $(P_u = 942\ \text{kip}) < (0.75 P_n = 0.75 \times 1537\ \text{kips} = 1153\ \text{kips})$, Eq. $(K1\text{-}9)$ governs

$$\phi R_v = 0.90 \times 0.7 F_y d_c t_w$$

$$= 0.90 \times 0.7 \times 36\ \frac{\text{kips}}{\text{in}^2} \times 11.28\ \text{in} \times 0.680\ \text{in}$$

$$= 174\ \text{kips}$$

Because $V_u = \phi R_v = 174$ kips, the shear capacity of the web panel is sufficient; it need not be reinforced.

If $V_u > \phi R_v$, the column web panel would require reinforcement by either (a) a vertical plate welded to the column web, to increase t_w in the panel to that required to make $\phi R_v \geq V_u$, or (b) diagonal stiffeners in the column web panel to resist the portion of the shear beyond the capacity of the column web.

Regarding horizontal stiffeners in column webs between beam flanges for moment connections, a stiffener design procedure and additional design aids are provided on pp. 2-12 to 2-14 of the AISC LRFD Manual.

Supplementary Problems

12.6. The unstiffened end of a W16×50 beam of A36 steel rests on a concrete support $(f_c' = 4\ \text{ksi})$. The beam end reaction is 100 kips. Assume the area of concrete support equals the area of the bearing plate.

(a) Design a bearing plate for the beam.

(b) Can the bearing plate be eliminated?

Ans. (a) Beam bearing plate 1 in × 7 in × 7 in.

(b) Yes, if the length of bearing is increased from 7 in to 11 in.

12.7. A W14×82 column rests directly on the top flange of a W27×146 beam, 30 ft long. If the beam has no stiffeners, but is braced at the load point, determine the maximum column load.

Ans. $P_u = 495$ kips.

12.8.   In Fig. 12-3, assume there is a W27×84 beam on the left side only. The forces on the W27 beam and the W14×145 column are as shown. If column web stiffeners are required, design them.

Ans.   Stiffeners not required.

12.9.   In Fig. 12-3, assume the column web panel has a required shear strength of 300 kips. Determine the thickness of the web plate to be welded to the panel.

Ans. $t = \frac{1}{2}$ in.

Index

SCHAUM'S INTERACTIVE OUTLINE SERIES

Schaum's Outlines and Mathcad™ Combined. . .
The Ultimate Solution.

NOW AVAILABLE! Electronic, interactive versions of engineering titles from the Schaum's Outline Series:

- *Electric Circuits*
- *Electromagnetics*
- *Feedback and Control Systems*
- *Thermodynamics For Engineers*
- *Fluid Mechanics and Hydraulics*

McGraw-Hill has joined with MathSoft, Inc., makers of Mathcad, the world's leading technical calculation software, to offer you interactive versions of popular engineering titles from the Schaum's Outline Series. Designed for students, educators, and technical professionals, the *Interactive Outlines* provide comprehensive on-screen access to theory and approximately 100 representative solved problems. Hyperlinked cross-references and an electronic search feature make it easy to find related topics. In each electronic outline, you will find all related text, diagrams and equations for a particular solved problem together on your computer screen. Every number, formula and graph is interactive, allowing you to easily experiment with the problem parameters, or adapt a problem to solve related problems. The *Interactive Outline* does all the calculating, graphing and unit analysis for you.

These "live" *Interactive Outlines* are designed to help you learn the subject matter and gain a more complete, more intuitive understanding of the concepts underlying the problems. They make your problem solving easier, with powe to quickly do a wide range of technical calculations. All the formulas needed to solve the problem appear in real math notation, and use Mathcad's wide range of built in functions, units, and graphing features. This interactive format should make learning the subject matter easier, more effective and even fun.

For more information about *Schaum's Interactive Outlines* listed above and other titles in the series, please contact:

Schaum Division
McGraw-Hill, Inc.
1221 Avenue of the Americas
New York, New York 10020
Phone: 1-800-338-3987

To place an order, please mail the coupon below to the above address or call the 800 number.

------------------------------------✂--

Schaum's Interactive Outline Series
using Mathcad®

(Software requires 80386/80486 PC or compatibles, with Windows 3.1 or higher, 4 MB of RAM, 4 MB of hard disk space, and 3 1/2" disk drive.)

AUTHOR/TITLE	Interactive Software Only ($29.95 ea) ISBN	Quantity Ordered	Software and Printed Outline ($38.95 ea) ISBN	Quantity Ordered
MathSoft, Inc./DiStefano: Feedback & Control Systems	07-842708-8	_____	07-842709-6	_____
MathSoft, Inc./Edminister: Electric Circuits	07-842710-x	_____	07-842711-8	_____
MathSoft, Inc./Edminister: Electromagnetics	07-842712-6	_____	07-842713-4	_____
MathSoft, Inc./Giles: Fluid Mechanics & Hydraulics	07-842714-2	_____	07-842715-0	_____
MathSoft, Inc./Potter: Thermodynamics For Engineers	07-842716-9	_____	07-842717-7	_____

NAME_____   ADDRESS_____

CITY _____   STATE_____   ZIP_____

ENCLOSED IS   ❏ A CHECK   ❏ MASTERCARD   ❏ VISA   ❏ AMEX   (✓ ONE)

ACCOUNT #_____   EXP. DATE _____

SIGNATURE_____